MISSIONS IN SOUTH INDIA

MISSIONS IN SOUTH INDIA

VISITED AND DESCRIBED

JOSEPH MULLENS

GYAN

Published by

Gyan Publishing House
5, Ansari Road
Daryaganj, New Delhi-110002
Phone: 011-47034999, 9811692060
E-mail: books@gyanbooks.com

Distribution Network
gyanbooks.com
India, USA, Canada, UK, Australia, France

ISBN : 978-81-212-9512-3 (PB)
First Published, 1854

2nd Impression 2023

Printed at: Gyan Press, Delhi.

MISSIONS IN SOUTH INDIA
Author: JOSEPH MULLENS

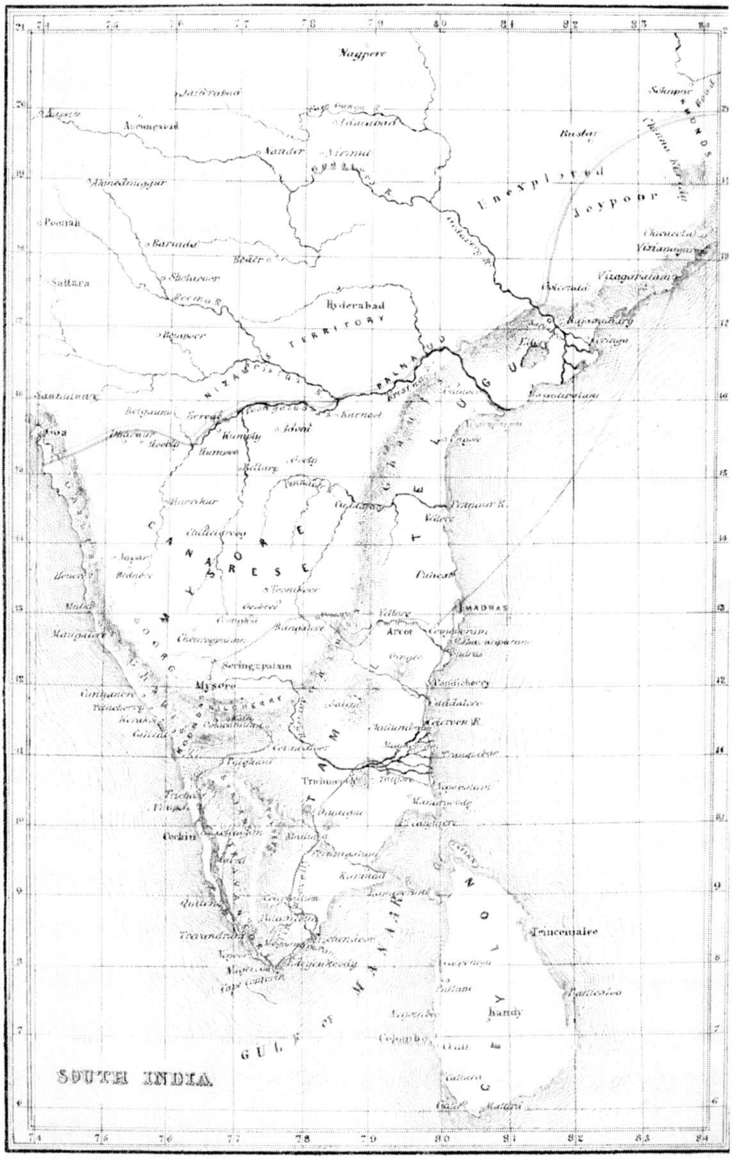

Constructed by the Revd. J. Mullens.

T. Black, lithr. Asiatic lith. Press Calcutta Sept. 1854.

MISSIONS IN SOUTH INDIA

VISITED AND DESCRIBED

BY

JOSEPH MULLENS,

MISSIONARY OF THE LONDON MISSIONARY SOCIETY IN CALCUTTA.

1854.

PREFACE.

Having, during my residence in India, made numerous enquiries into the Missionary Statistics of different parts of the country; and having read much concerning the progress of the gospel in Tanjore, Tinnevelly and Travancore, I left Calcutta at the close of 1852, in order personally to visit these localities, whose names have become so well known to the christian church at large. My tour through the Presidency of Madras occupied the first three months of 1853. The farther I travelled and the more I saw of the Missions conducted by members of different Societies; the more deeply did I feel impressed with the extent, the variety and the influence of the labours, which are carried on in South India for the conversion of its idolatrous population. The farther I travelled, on the other hand, the more deeply did I feel the immeasurable extent of the ignorance and idolatry which yet exist. On my return to Calcutta I delivered a short course of Lectures, on the history, condition, and prospects of these various Missions. In publishing these lectures, I desire earnestly to encourage the Church of Christ, from a sight of attained success, to pray and labour more earnestly for that which yet remains. Even writers who have lived in India endeavour to depreciate the work and the fruits of Christian Missions. Would that such men would first ponder the facts which those Missions present for their consideration. To furnish such facts is one chief object of this little sketch.

CONTENTS.

Page

THE TAMIL MISSIONS FROM MADRAS TO MADURA.

MISSIONS AMONG THE SHANARS IN TINNEVELLY AND SOUTH TRAVANCORE.

THE SYRIAN CHRISTIANS.

THE JESUIT MISSIONS IN SOUTH INDIA.

GOVERNMENT EFFORTS AMONG THE KHONDS.

THE RELIGIOUS CLAIMS OF THE MADRAS PRESIDENCY.

LECTURE FIRST.

ON THE TELUGU AND CANARESE MISSIONS.

INTRODUCTION.

THE missionary spirit of the present age has turned with peculiar interest towards HINDUSTAN. The savages of Tahiti, New Zealand, and the Sandwich Islands; the slaves of Guiana and Jamaica; the Hottentots, Kaffres and Bechuanas of South Africa; the Negro tribes of Lagos and Badagry; uncivilized and barbarous all, have asked in their ignorance for the instructions of Christ's servants and been taught the way of everlasting life. The Jews in Hungary, Poland and Tunis; the Armenian Christians of Constantinople and Beyrout; the Copts of Cairo; and the Nestorians of Oorumiah; have been called upon to awake from their spiritual sloth and receive the heart of the gospel as well as its external forms. Twelve hundred missionaries, the messengers of the churches, now preach the gospel in various countries of the globe; and few places that have ever given them admittance remain entirely unoccupied. But of these valued teachers, BRITISH INDIA has secured by far the largest share. That security of property, that order and stability in the Government, which in India have attracted the indigo and sugar planter, the cotton speculator and the merchant, have, added to the free enjoyment of religion, drawn thither the feet of those who seek not the goods of India, but the people themselves. Thus it happens that more than one-third of the missionaries scattered through the world have been located within its ample territories; of whom as many as one hundred and thirty have entered it from America, Germany and Switzerland.

Many considerations shew the importance of the Missionary AGENCY how at work in India, and the value of the RESULTS which have already been attained. Two years ago, the writer of these pages published a few such facts for the information of those by whom Indian Missions are carried on, and proved beyond all question that the position they occupy, is one of the most promising and hopeful kind. A later and more complete enquiry, undertaken for the purpose of correcting any error that might have arisen in the former instance, confirmed the previous account in almost every particular, and shewed that on most points, the results had even been understated: whilst every year is found to add to the agency, and realises increased fruit from the labours both of past and present days.

During the present year, the number of European and American MISSIONARIES labouring only amongst the native population in India and Ceylon amounts to *four hundred;* together with *forty-eight* ordained NATIVE MISSIONARIES, and *seven hundred* NATIVE CATECHISTS. These agents are employed in the public preaching of the gospel in the vernacular tongues; in courteous public discussions upon the errors of the Hindu and Mahomedan religions; in the instruction of the young; in the pastoral care of native churches; in the composition of Christian works in the native languages, and in the translation of the Word of God. The Native Christian CHURCHES are now *three hundred* and *thirty-one* in number, and contain *eighteen thousand five hundred* COMMUNICANTS. Connected with them, and with them enjoying the regular instruction and discipline of the gospel is a body of individuals, termed NATIVE CHRISTIANS, entirely separated from the Hindu and Musalmán communities. The entire Native Christian population now includes *one hundred and twelve thousand* persons, young and old. The VERNACULAR DAY-SCHOOLS maintained in Indian Missions, *thirteen hundred and fifty* in number, contain *forty-seven thousand, five hundred* boys. *Ninety-three* BOARDING Schools for boys contain *two thousand four hundred* scholars: and a *hundred and two* BOARDING schools for GIRLS, contain *two thousand eight hundred* girls. There are maintained *one hundred and twenty-six* ENGLISH day-schools giving a superior education to more than *fourteen thousand* SCHOLARS and STUDENTS. Female education is carried on in *three hundred and fifty* DAY-SCHOOLS, with about *twelve thousand* GIRLS, both Christian and heathen; in addition to the boarding schools mentioned, whose superior advantages are confined almost exclusively to Christian children. Efforts are still continued to improve the *ten* TRANSLATIONS of the WHOLE BIBLE, and the *five* other versions of the NEW TESTAMENT, which have already been completed: as well as to increase the valuable stock of vernacular Christian works, suitable both for heathens and Christians, now available in all the chief Indian languages. Christian TRACTS and the FOUR GOSPELS are widely scattered beyond the immediate boundaries of Missionary stations; and *twenty-five* PRINTING PRESSES are engaged in supplying them. Upon this agency, vast in itself, but small compared with the sphere in which it is maintained and with the aims which it seeks to accomplish, the liberality of *twenty-two* MISSIONARY SOCIETIES spends nearly *two hundred thousand* pounds a year.

The number of actual converts in India is frequently spoken of as small, and none will deny the fact, in view of the millions upon millions who remain heathen still. But he, who considers actual converts as the sole fruit of missionary labour, takes but a partial view of the subject, and submits it to but an imperfect test. Missionary instruction, while aiming to secure such converts on the largest scale, has intermediately obtained results of another kind, which indirectly remove obstacles to its progress and are a guarantee of perfect ULTIMATE SUCCESS. Acting with influences derived from the Government, from commerce and from general intercourse with a foreign people, it has done much to break down the exclusiveness, in which Hindu Society was shrouded, and especially to diminish the high esteem in which the brahminical priesthood was once held. It has in various ways met the powerful difficulties which prevent the conversion of the Hindus, and has encountered them successfully. The bonds of caste, reverence for the sacred books, veneration for a long-established priesthood, and a blind attachment to their idolatries, constitute the chief obstacle to their reception of an enlightened and reasonable religion. But missionary teaching has assailed these obstacles, diminished their influence, and produced on an extensive scale, a state of mind admirably preparative of great religious changes in future days. Where this teaching has been most effective, many signs have been manifested of a decay in the strength of Hinduism. The decrease in the number of those who frequent the native seats of learning and study the ancient and authoritative Shastras: the diminished regard paid by the better-educated class to their Hindu spiritual teachers; the repudiation by that class of the scientific portions of the Vedas and Purâns; the decay and ruin of the ancient temples; the small number of new ones erected in their stead; the great decrease in many parts of the country in the number of people gathered to celebrate the annual feasts and draw the huge idol cars; the increase of the new sects under new leaders, holding as prominent doctrines the folly of idolatry and the necessity of a holy life: the discussion by Hindus of various castes, of questions like female education and the re-marriage of widows, which were supposed to belong to pundits only and to have been settled by the Shastras ages ago: the extensive acknowledgment by the common people of the folly of idolatry, and of the wicked character ascribed to their gods; a more correct appreciation of the real character of moral evil, and the awakening of a conscience long dimmed by ignorance and vice—ALL attest the spread of purer knowledge and a loosening of the bonds which bind the people to their wretched ancestral faith. On the other hand, the diminution of angry discussions with missionaries, and a greater readiness to listen to what they preach; the willing reception of portions of the Bible and of religious tracts; the large number of copies which are beyond all doubt privately read and pondered; the respect with which the name of Christ is in many places received; and the very strenuousness of the opposition offered to Christianity where it is best known, are signs that its power is felt both by friend and foe, and that many regard it as the religion which shall ultimately prevail. To the decrease of Hinduism, many influences contribute. Intercourse with Europeans, whether connected with the Government or with trade; the introduction of European notions of justice into legislation; European ideas of science and morality, as well as religious instruction, tend to exhibit by contrast the weakness, and expose the errors of the religion of their Hindu ancestors; but it must be allowed that Missionary teaching on the subject has been the most direct, the most widely spread; has continued for the longest time and been applied in the most systematic way. The spread of Christian light by the direct preaching of the gospel is of course its peculiar province.

PRESIDENCY OF MADRAS.

Amongst the different territories of Hindustan which have enjoyed the benefit of missionary labours, and have exhibited many of their fruits, the Presidency of MADRAS naturally first attracts the Christian's eye. Though not the largest of the Presidencies, nor the most important, either in relation to government, commerce, or political events, it has had the largest share of missionary effort, and exhibits the largest amount of palpable results. This Presidency was the first into which missionaries entered, and has therefore been cultivated the longest time. Nearly one hundred and fifty years ago the first Danish missionaries took up their residence in Tranquebar; and steadily maintained a course of instruction for the enlightenment of the pagan mind. During the whole of last century, one and another continued to arrive to occupy the places of those who died, and to extend the labours of the mission to new districts.

Thus it happened that while nearly all the heathen world lay in dense darkness, the Gospel was preached successfully in Southern India. While the cannibals of New Zealand destroyed each other without hinderance; while the idolatry and vice of Tahiti remained unknown; while the Negro race were being subjected to the darkest horrors of the slave-trade; while the Hottentots in South Africa were shot unmercifully by their Dutch Masters; while China, (its infanticide and idolatry unknown,) was reckoned by some European infidels as the abode of piety and peace; —the province of Tanjore and the town of Madras were benefiting by the same system of gospel-instruction which has since elevated these degraded people. During all last century, in these two localities the Word of God was preached and read in the Tamil language, Christian books were circulated in small numbers, and a steady witness offered for Christ, amid the native heathenism and European irreligion, which then so extensively prevailed. The history and progress of these Missions, and the position which they have at present attained must on this account alone, be matters of deep interest to all Christian minds: while that interest is deepened and lastingly secured by the internal character of many of the missions themselves. The following is the number of Missionaries and converts which the whole Presidency now contains.

Missionaries,	182
including Ordained Natives,	18
Catechists,	405
Churches,	128
Communicants,	10,662
Native Christians,	76,591
Vernacular-school boys,	24,500
English-school boys,	4,286
Day-school girls,	6,639
Boarding-school girls,	1,470

GEOGRAPHICAL DIVISIONS OF THE PRESIDENCY.

A few words premised on the Geography of South India, will help our readers to understand clearly the progress of its Christian Missions: especially as the country is divided so simply and naturally that its details can be easily remembered. The great continent of Hindustan, after projecting into the sea, slopes off to a point towards the south, and that extreme point is termed *Cape Comorin.* Almost all the projected part with those sloping sides, is included in the PRESIDENCY of MADRAS. On the eastern slope lies the Bay of Bengal; on the western, the broad Indian Ocean: and on the north of the Presidency are situated Orissa, Hydrabad, and the Presidency of Bombay. The Presidency naturally divides itself into three great districts. On each side there is a narrow slip of plain close to the sea, varying generally from ten to eighty miles in breadth; in the centre is a broad and undulating plateau, three thousand feet high; this includes the Provinces of *Mysore, Coorg* and the *Ceded Districts.* Ranges of hills, called *Ghauts,* run along the country on both sides, between the low plain near the sea, and the higher land of Central India: they are called the *Eastern* and *Western Ghauts* respectively. These natural physical divisions of the country are accompanied by somewhat similar divisions of the people and of their languages. The Eastern sea-coast and plain are inhabited by two different nations; the *Telugus,* who occupy the district from Orissa to Pulicat: and the *Tamils* who possess that which extends from Pulicat to Cape Comorin. The high central province contains the pure *Canarese* population: the Western strip of sea-coast is possessed by the *Canarese* people in the north, whence the province is called Canara; and by the *Máleális** in the south. The *Máleális* occupy the province of Malabar, with the districts of *Tellicherry* and *Calicut;* also the little kingdom of *Cochin,* and the chief portion of *Travancore.* Thus *Telugu* is found in the north-east; *Tamil* in the south-east; *Canarese* in the centre and north-west; and *Máleálim* in the south-west. The *Tamil and Máleálim* of course meet near Cape Comorin.

The MISSIONS of the Presidency may be also divided on the same principles: being much separated from each other by the difference of tongue. Beginning along the Bay of Bengal, after passing Orissa and the town of Puri, we find Missions among the Telugus at Vizagapatam, Masulipatam, Guntoor, Rajmundry, Nellore and Cuddapah. Passing through their country, we come to the Tamil Missions at Madras; at Tranquebar; Tanjore and Trichinopoly. Farther south, they are flourishing in the districts of Dindigul and Madura: and next in Tinnevelly, and at Cape Comorin. In the centre of the Presidency, Bangalore is the head of the Canarese Missions which have been also established at Bel-

* This word is usually written in the form *Malayalim;* a form which both suggests a wrong pronunciation, and some connection with the Malay people; with whom however it has nothing to do. Each *a* is accented and pronounced as *a* in *hard.* The name is connected with *Mala-bar.*

lary, Goobee and Mysore. On the West coast the Basle Society has Canarese Missions at Dharwar, Honore, Mangalore and Cannanore: and chief stations in the Máleálim country at Tellicherry and Calicut. The Jews at Cochin speak Máleálim: so also do the Syrian Christians of North Travancore, to whom the Church Missionary Society has for many years preached the gospel. Each of these groups of Missions I propose to notice in the course of these lectures, adopting the following order:

The *Telugu, Canarese* and *Tulu* Missions.
The *Tamil* Missions in Madras, Tanjore and Madura.
The *Shánár Missions* in Tinnevelly and South Travancore.
The *Syrian Christians* in North Travancore.
I also add Lectures on subjects of a similar kind, and of great interest;
The *Romish Missions* in South India:
The *Government Mission* among the Khonds:
The CLAIMS of the Madras Presidency for more missionaries.

THE WRITER'S JOURNEY.

To describe in full the numerous incidents of the writer's journey through so large a portion of the Madras Presidency, is not the purpose of these lectures: but, in order to shew the authority upon which many statements are made, and many descriptions offered, it may be useful to give a mere outline of the course which that journey took, and the places which I visited.

In going down the Bay of Bengal towards Madras, the ship stayed a week at *Vizagapatam.* I thus had the opportunity of examining the oldest Telugu Mission in the country, and of recciving from Mr. Gordon the oldest missionary, and from his brethren, much information concerning the progress of other missions since established. After a short stay in Madras, during which I saw almost all the missionaries of that city, I set out on my journey into the interior. In order to make the best use of my limited time and to prevent the necessity of going over the same ground twice in certain places, I proceeded in the first place straight westward into the very heart of the Presidency, to *Bangalore:* visiting on the way the town of Arcot and the celebrated temples at *Conjeveram.* At Bangalore I met all the missionaries both of the Wesleyan and London Societies, and visited their chapels, press and schools. Thence I went south to *Mysore,* where there is a Wesleyan Mission; went over the palaces of Hyder and Tippu at *Seringapatam:* saw the gateway where Tippu was killed, and visited their celebrated tombs. Crossing "the valley of death," a jungle twenty-five miles deep, resembling the pestilential Terai at the base of the Himálaya, I entered the *Nilgherry Hills* on the north side, and spent two days at *Ootacamund.* Four miles from Ootacamund at *Kaity,* the residence of the late Mr. Casamajor, I saw the German Mission which he established and the villages of Badagas for whom it was specially designed. Descending the Nilgherry Hills on the east side by the splendid Pass of Konoor, I came down into the eastern plains to the London Mission at *Coimbatoor,* being the first missionary from Bengal that had ever visited those parts. I then passed through the great gap in the Ghauts, at Palgaut, to the West coast of India, and reached *Trichoor* the most northerly station of the Church Missionary Society among the Syrian Christians of Travancore. Thence I sailed down 'the Backwater' to *Cochin,* passing on the way numerous Roman Catholic Churches, in the island of Verapoli and its neighbourhood. In Cochin I visited the Jewish synagogue with Mr. Laseron its missionary and also his Jewish school. Thence I proceeded to *Cottayam,* the head-quarters of the Syrian Mission, and saw its handsome Gothic Churches, its excellent schools and useful press. I visited also *Mávelikári,* one of the most flourishing stations, and thence proceeded to *Quilon.* In these parts, I travelled close to the western coast, often along the sea beach itself, looking over the broad waters of the Indian Ocean which stretch away without interruption to the coast of eastern Africa. Leaving *Quilon* which has been for thirty years a station of the London Missionary Society in Travancore, I proceeded to *Trevandrum,* another station, the residence of the Raja of Travancore, who sent the ivory throne to the Great Exhibition: thence I went to *Pareychaley,* a third station of the London Mission, and concluded the first portion of my journey by arriving finally at *Nagercoil,* the head-quarters of the mission, a few miles from Cape Comorin. I spent a fortnight among these interesting missions, visiting all their chief stations in turn; and greatly enjoying the society of the missionaries in whose charge they lie. After a visit to Cape Comorin I set out on my return to Madras by coming up the *east coast,* and through the *Tamil* country. I first spent twelve days among the many stations in *Tinnevelly;* and then went on to *Madura, Dindigul* and other stations of the American Mission. Thence I proceeded to *Trichinopoly* where Swartz lived and Heber died; and to *Tanjore,* where Swartz is buried. I next visited *Negapatam* and saw both the Wesleyan Mission and Jesuit College: and thence continued my journey to the oldest Mission in India, that at *Tranquebar*. Passing the temples of *Chillumbrum;* the old Mission at *Cuddalore,* founded by Mr. Kiernander; the Jesuit College in *Pondicherry;* and the *Seven Pagodas* at *Mávalipuram,* I proceeded to Madras, which I reached after an absence of twelve weeks. In this journey I travelled thirteen hundred and sixty miles; including Madras, I saw altogether FIFTY Missionary STATIONS and *ninety* MISSIONARIES. [As an illustration of the extent to which Missions are now carried on in Hindustan, I may state that I have myself seen and spoken to no less than *one hundred and ninety-four* living Indian Missionaries: in addition to *twenty-seven* others, who have died or left the country.]

I cannot conclude this short sketch of my interesting and delightful journey without gratefully recording the kind and hospitable manner in which I was everywhere received. The missionary brethren of all Societies welcomed me with the utmost cordiality, and in many cases, though personally a stranger, seemed to regard me as an old friend. This kind reception arose probably from the correspondence I had previously had with them when compiling my missionary statistics in previous years. They entered readily into my enquiries and gave me much information concerning the history, condition and prospects of their different spheres of labour. We were able to compare notes on the character and difficulties of missionary work in different parts of Hindustan: and to derive therefrom mutual instruction and mutual encouragement. I was also greatly pleased to hear the cordial manner in which they spoke of each other's labours. Though belonging to many Societies they know each other personally, join in common labours and make use of each other's works. This cordial union is nothing new in India, but I mention it as a patent fact which struck me both as excellent in itself, and as a token of the future success of their common labours. The pleasure of my visits to so many of the labourers in the Lord's vineyard, and the impressions which they made upon my heart will, I trust, abide with me as long as life lasts.

THE TELUGU MISSIONS.

THE country entirely occupied by the TELUGU nation is the narrow strip of sea-coast on the Bay of Bengal, which stretches from Ganjam to Pulicat. It is about six hundred miles long, and varies in breadth from ten to eighty miles. It is bounded on the western side by a broad chain of Ghauts, the undulating country above which is also inhabited by the Telugu people far back into Hydrabad. Near *Ganjam* these Ghauts come down close to the sea, and continue to throw off spurs towards the coast as far as Coringa. It was a great treat to those of us who had lived for some time in the flat plains of Bengal, as we sailed along the Telugu coast, to see these hills following one another in quick succession, clothed with jungle to their very summits. In the highest of all, the hills of GOOMSUR, we remembered that once the Meriah sacrifice so widely prevailed among the Khoonds; though that cruel rite has now, through the efforts of Government, been almost entirely extinguished. The level country is fertile and from it the peasants raise abundant crops of corn. Indigo, sugar and cotton also are found among its productions. It is well watered by numerous smaller streams, but numbers also the Kistna and Godavery among its rivers. The population is large; though in some of its districts, especially in Masulipatam and Guntoor, immense numbers, reckoned by hundreds of thousands, were swept away in the great famine of 1833. Owing to the abundant population we find throughout the country flourishing towns and villages. *Vizagapatam,* the head-quarters of the Military Division in the Northern Circars, contains now 50,000 people; having increased from 20,000 in about forty years. *Vizianagram* the residence of a Raja, numbers 28,000. *Masulipatam,* a pretty town nearly two miles square, built in the usual Indian style and containing about twenty pagodas, has 90,000. *Rajamundry, Guntoor, Nellore* and *Ongole* are also large and important places. To these must be added the town and district of *Cuddapah.*

The first effort to extend the gospel to the *Telugu people* was made by Dr. Schultz, one of the early Tranquebar missionaries, who founded a mission in Madras. Finding among the Madras population a large number of Telugus, (then called Gentoos) he began to translate the Bible into their tongue; and established, and maintained for years, Telugu classes in his schools. There is reason to believe that his Telugu Munshi died a true Christian, the first fruits to Christ of that great nation. Dr. Schultz completed his translation of the Bible; but having no means of printing it, took it to Halle on his return to Europe; and it has never since been heard of.

The first settled Mission to the people in their own country was established by Messrs. CRAN and DESGRANGES of the London Missionary Society, who proceeded to *Vizagapatam* in 1805. Like others of their day, they began their ministerial work with religious services among

Europeans and the neglected children of the English regiments: but they also applied themselves diligently to the Telugu language, and soon became known among the natives as religious teachers for them. They admitted native boys into their school, conversed frequently with their neighbours, and itinerated among the surrounding villages. They compiled tracts, consisting of scripture passages on particular subjects, which were printed at Madras; and began to prepare a complete translation of the Gospels and Acts. They were much encouraged at the outset by the aid furnished by a Telugu bráhman who had been baptized first by the Roman Catholics and afterwards received at Tranquebar. In the mysterious Providence of God these two brethren who had entered on their work so well, were cut off in the beginning of their usefulness. Mr. Cran died in 1809 and Mr. Desgranges in 1810. Two new missionaries however arrived, Messrs. Gordon and Lee; they again were soon joined by Mr. Pritchett, who had been to Rangoon, and had been compelled to retire from his mission there. Mr. Lee left in 1815, but Mr. Dawson arrived the same year and occupied his place. The three brethren, Gordon, Dawson and Pritchett, continued their preaching and school instructions uninterruptedly for some years; during which they endeavoured to enlarge the mission by founding a branch at Ganjam. They found that the people had begun to understand the gospel, and at Chicacole some who had never seen any thing but their tracts, had declared they would become Christians. The translation of the New Testament was completed before Mr. Pritchett's death, and put, I believe, into circulation. That of the Old Testament was far advanced and was completed by Mr. Gordon. It is now being printed for the first time by the Madras Bible Society: only small portions, like the Psalms, having been circulated hitherto. Mr. Pritchett died in 1820, after eight years' labour; the brethren Gordon and Dawson remained alive; the former till 1828; the latter till 1832. They were not privileged to see many converts drawn from the district; but they had extensively spread the knowledge of the gospel among the villages and towns in their neighbourhood, and proved a great blessing to the poorer European population, who would otherwise have lived destitute of religious instruction. The houses where they resided, the garden they planted, and the chapel they erected still exist: and their sons are now carrying on the labours from which they ceased only with life.

A second Mission among the Telugus was founded at *Cuddapah,* in the Ceded Districts below the Ghauts, in 1822. Its first Christians were

Tamils from Chittoor; and the extreme inconsistency, weakness and irreligion which prevailed among them for many years, proved a strong barrier to the spread of Christianity among the people, for whose good the mission had been commenced. The administration of a sound and faithful discipline at length purified the church of these evils, although its numbers were reduced. From that time an eminent blessing rested on it from above, and Christianity began to take firm root in the Telugu villages by which Cuddapah is surrounded.

These two stations, *Vizagapatam* and *Cuddapah,* under the London Missionary Society, continued to be the only Missions among the Telugus till the year 1836, now seventeen years ago. The famine of 1833 drew marked attention to this interesting people, and efforts were specially made to spread the gospel where it had not been hitherto declared. The first additional station was established at *Narsapore* by Messrs. Bowden and Beer in 1836. These labourers for Christ were two young tradesmen from Barnstaple, who had come to India anxious to carry on missionary work while supporting themselves by their trades. The latter part of the scheme failed, as it has done elsewhere; but friends took up their cause and sent them money, and have continued to support them to the present time. Both learned the language well; and have been exceedingly useful. Mr. Bowden is said to speak Telugu like a native, and it is remarkable that he has been especially successful among the *chuklas,* or shoe-makers, to whom in a manner he himself once belonged. He was for sometime engaged by Col. Cotton to preach to the natives engaged in the construction of the great *Anicut* or dam across the River Godavery near which they live. Another station was established in 1839 at *Cicacole* by the London Mission, as an offshoot from Vizagapatam from which it is a few miles distant. In 1841, the Church Missionary Society took up *Masulipatam,* incited thereto by an offer made to Bishop Corrie by some gentlemen of the station, to provide a considerable portion of two missionaries' salaries. It was this offer which brought out to India one of the most spiritual and gentle, yet energetic missionaries of modern days, the Rev. Henry Fox. His career was short but striking, more useful perhaps to his countrymen, as an example of self-devotion, than distinguished by success among the heathen. Since its establishment in 1841, the mission has been well supplied with agents, has been well managed, and is one of the most efficient missions in the Telugu land. *Nellore* was taken up by the American Baptists in 1840: *Rajmundry* and *Guntoor,* in 1845 by the Society of North Germany. The

Free Church also opened schools at Nellore. Thus has provision been made for a more extensive proclamation of the gospel among this long-neglected people.

It will readily be supposed that missionaries pursue in the Telugu country, plans very similar to those adopted in other parts of India: particularly in the mofussil districts. They act as pastors and teachers of the churches which they have gathered: have near them boarding schools for christian children and orphans; superintend and instruct vernacular schools, where only elementary knowledge can be communicated: and in the best towns have established English schools besides. They also frequently undertake extensive itinerancies into country districts: their opportunities for such labour, as in *all* the Madras Presidency, not being nearly so limited as in Bengal: the sun and weather being more favourable.

The general knowledge and religious condition of the people at large seem to be much the same as they are in villages in Bengal. They have their periodical festivals and melas: with this peculiarity, that at certain places they worship particular *Avatárs* or incarnations of Vishnu. At one place near Vizagapatam, a crowd of 25,000 people assembles annually to worship the Boar-incarnation: in another, to worship the *Norsingh* or incarnation of the man-lion. If the small-pox or cholera rages badly, they all bring their sacrifices to the *Ammávaru*, each caste having its own priests; who slaughter buffaloes, sheep and fowls in her honour: in her name the swinging feasts are held. Snakes, Hanuman and the brahmin-kites are extensively honoured and even worshipped. The brahmins of course are superior to all. Fakeers are accounted peculiarly holy. The same shastras, the same legends prevail there as in Upper India. The same rules of caste are obeyed. The same vices too abound. Lying is especially common. "How could the world," say they, "go on without lying." The doctrines of Pantheism and Transmigration are continually advocated, and bring forth the same apathy and indifference among them, as they produce elsewhere.

But the work of the Lord is steadily making progress. Here and there an individual conversion takes place in the upper classes, rending families asunder and causing the thoughts of many hearts to be revealed. Every year witnesses additions to the infant churches. Although the majority of the Telugu missions have been in operation only about twelve years, yet the religious impressions produced upon the people in general are plainly discernible. A great amount of Bible knowledge has been widely spread; in some heathen families it has been found that the Bible is daily read and prayer daily offered. Wherever new temples are built or old ones repaired, it is usually observed that the obscene figures which once formed their chief ornament are removed; a fact owing doubtless to the light which from the gospel is now breaking upon the darkness of ages. It is manifest that the leaven of the Word of God is working. In many places the people acknowledge that Christianity will prevail; that their gods are weak; that idolatry is foolish. In proof of this the singular fact is exhibited, that they have begun to give up many of the inferior deities, and to appeal especially to RAM believing him to be Almighty. Processions are constantly formed of persons carrying lights and singing hymns in praise of RAM. I saw one such when in Vizagapatam.

Missionaries frequently meet with facts like these during their extensive itinerancies; it is in their journeys that they come into closest contact with purely native life, and gain a thorough insight into native notions especially in the country villages. For instance; at Narsampett, several years ago, Mr. Edward Porter was preaching to a congregation of upwards of a hundred persons, and found it heart-cheering to see the regard which these poor people paid to the word of life. One old woman about eighty years of age, listened with marked attention for some time; Mr. Porter was much struck with her appearance, and having finished his address turned aside to converse with her. He asked if she worshipped idols: "No;" she replied, "I have left them off." "How long have you left them off?" "Ever since the great famine:" (very likely the year 1833). "Whom then do you worship?" She pointed to the heavens and said: "That God, he only is God and no one else. These people," she continued, "have a thousand opinions and a thousand religions, therefore God does not dwell with them: you speak of one God and one true way, therefore God dwells with you." It was delightful to hear such a testimony from a poor decrepit old woman, surrounded as she was with all the abominations of idolatry.

In the village of Dhoosee, in 1845, Mr. Dawson had little less than the whole population to hear his preaching; men, women and children thronging around him from morning till night. Many from their looks and expressions seemed convinced of the truth, but felt the difficulties in their way to be very great. A little company of ten persons returned to his tent in the dark, after others had gone home, and calling to the servants asked; "What is the name of that Saviour, that Master has been telling us of; we try to recollect it, but cannot." The servants, thinking it perhaps too bad of them to trouble the missionary again at night, after being with him all the day, replied, "Master is just gone and laid himself down; don't trouble him again." Mr. Dawson however called to them: and asking them to come in, one of their number, rather an old man, entered the tent, and sitting down, said; "Sir, we have been hearing all that has been said, and we have felt persuaded that the truth is on your side. A few of us have therefore consulted together that it is not right for us to disregard your message, and your disinterested concern for our welfare; and we have thought that we would henceforth, though we cannot do all that you have told us, give up the worship of idols and false gods and think of and pray to THIS SAVIOUR alone, but we could not recollect his name. Is it *this?*" he said, pronouncing it rather incorrectly. Mr. D. repeated the name of Jesus to them several times, and after speaking to them a little more of its being the only name under heaven given among men whereby we must be saved, proposed to them, to send a man to stay with them continually and teach them the worship of the true Saviour, of whom they were so anxious to hear.

Pleasing as these indications are of an improved state of things, too much importance should not be attributed to them: the very circumstances of the case forbid it. At Peddapur, a blacksmith several times visited Mr. Gordon, declaring his dissatisfaction with Hinduism, and his desire to become more acquainted with the claims and doctrines of christianity, with the narratives of which he seemed to be much interested. "But how," was his sensible question, "are we to become acquainted with it? You are here to-day and away to-morrow, and we have no means of obtaining the instructions we want?"

A native baptized by Mr. Dawson at Chicacole, was in the first instance led to think of the interests of his soul, through the instrumentality of a Telugu tract. He had been contemplating a visit to Jagannáth, and was on the eve of preparation, when a copy of the tract on the worship of Jagannáth was accidentally discovered by him in his box. He read it, relinquished the project of his pilgrimage; became a stated attendant at Mr. Dawson's chapel; and a steady adherent to the truth.

At both the Church Missionary English School in *Masulipatam,* and that of the London Mission at *Vizagapatam,* young men have been led (as in Calcutta and Madras), to give up Hinduism and profess the religion of Christ. The same uproar has followed there as here. The same violence; the same stern trial of the best affections; the same attempts to deceive by lavish promises; the same appeal to the magistrate, and the same stand made by the convert—that he wished to be a Christian because the Bible is true—have occurred with them as they do in Bengal or Bombay; proving that the work of the Lord is one, and that opposition to its progress springs every where from the same cause.

In 1849, considerable religious enquiry took place among the villagers of the *Palnaud*, a district to the west of Guntoor, among the Ghauts. They were under the instruction of Mr. Heyer, of the American Lutheran Mission, who had shortly before taken up a permanent residence in their midst. Of these people, thirty-nine were baptized in 1849; and one hundred and twenty-five the following year. Whether ultimately a sincere and well-based church of Christ has been formed among them I know not: but one important guarantee for their sincerity, exists in the fact that they are well off in the world. They are both farm-labourers and weavers: land-owners must employ them in the former capacity: while in the latter also they can earn enough for their support: they are thus rather independent. Mr. Heyer also has taught them, that he who would eat must work. The people were baptized perhaps rather hastily: but there was reason to believe them sincere.

During the last eight years the gospel has made special progress in the neighbourhood of *Cuddapah*. Of the four out-stations attached to the central mission, that of Cherlopilly seemed first to awake to a sense of the evils of idolatry. In 1845, owing to the instructions of the catechists and the influence of the Reddy or headman, himself almost a Christian, all public idolatrous festivals entirely ceased in the village; a chapel was erected and a small congregation regularly met to be instructed in the Word of God. In 1849, the son of the chief Reddy wished to be baptized, and strangely enough received the full consent of his parents to this public profession of his Christianity. Other villages have since exhibited a similar spirit; and the native catechists, who frequently itinerate among them, have borne the most pleasing testimony to the impression which the gospel has produced on the people's minds. It would be easy to multiply the most interesting examples; but the following may serve as a specimen.

One says: "On the thirty-first of October, 1850, I arrived at *Door*. About thirty persons assembled to hear the word. After I had spoken to them, *Unkunnah* received me kindly into his house and wished me to stay to instruct him and his friends. Accordingly I staid with him all that day, explained the Christian religion, and at night ten other persons joined us to whom I preached the word of life. I read and explained the fifteenth and sixteenth chapters of Luke and the third chapter of John. We then knelt down and prayed to God. Though Hindus they all knelt down with us and prayed, and appeared much interested in what was said to them. One man of the assembly called Parvah said;—Sir, I am very desirous to embrace the Christian religion, because I have searched many Hindu books, but have not found such precious words as these. He said also; Sir, since you visited us eight months ago, I have not had any comfort in my heart on account of my heathen ways, and though I have often intended to come and see you, yet I have been hindered on account of my family, but now you are come I am very glad." He and some others are desirous of embracing the Christian religion, and to have their children instructed in this good way. This inquirer followed the catechists to Cuddapah and staid ten days, receiving instruction. Unkunnah, his host, and three others from the village were baptized the following year. At *Pedalah,* also in the neighbourhood of Door, fifteen families gave up idolatry and presented their idol to the missionary; several individuals have been since baptized as Christians.

Another catechist preached in a large village, at a feast in honor of Vishnoo. When they brought out the idol on a large car, he went near and spoke to the people: Why are you all looking at that idol, if you speak to it will it speak to you, and if you set fire to it will it not be burned? He then declared the glory, power and goodness of the great God, and of the salvation which he had wrought out by Jesus Christ for poor sinners. The people replied: What you say, Sir, is very good: our idols are vain and can do us no good. You must come, Sir, from time to time and declare to us these good words. When asked by the catechist why they came to the feast if they did not believe in the idol, they said, '*We only come to look at the sight and laugh, but we have no faith in the idol.* We believe in one God; we have read your books and like the wisdom they contain.' At Yeypuralu a man came to the same catechist and embracing him with great affection said: Are you a disciple of our Lord Jesus? He then took him to his house, lodged him for two days and heard the word of God with great attention. He said that he had heard about this true religion some time ago at Cuddapah, and that ever since that time he had left off the worship of idols and was in the habit of praying to God. He also begged the catechist to stay and instruct his children.

Among the converts baptized in 1850, there was one who had been led to profess himself a christian by the reading of tracts and the regular hearing of the word. He came to Mr. Porter one morning and with much feeling delivered up his brass idols, the former objects of his worship. Throwing them on the ground, he said: Enough of these, I have done with them and wish to have no more to do with them. I have read much and learnt much in my heathen books; but I have found no rest. In Christ alone is rest. After Mr. Porter had conversed with him for some time on the delightful change that had taken place in his views and feelings, his soul seemed to gather fresh strength, and taking from his neck a silver chain bearing the name of his god, he cast it on the ground saying: Enough, nothing but sin has cleaved to me all the time I have kept this close to me. Let it go, I have done with idols; please, Sir, take it: I now know of something better. The love of Jesus! O how different to all this. I know I must be persecuted by my friends and relations, but I must not mind that. After being under further instruction for three months, he was baptized at Muddunpilly the out-station, in the month of May; since which time he has continued steadfast in his attachment to the Christian religion. Through his influence and instructions his aged father, who was once the chief guru or priest in the village, has renounced idolatry, and is now a regular attendant at the Mission Chapel.

During last year the fruits of missionary labour in Cuddapah and the villages which surround it, were manifested in a still more striking manner. The congregation at Cuddapah increased to two hundred; and ten members were added to the Church. Mr. Porter baptized no less than *fifty-one* adults, chiefly at the out-stations: and many others for the first time renounced idolatry, and placed themselves under christian instruction. Of this large number thirty-two reside at *Ubdalapuram,* sixty miles from Cuddapah. On making their profession they delivered up their idol to the missionary and set apart the temple as a christian school-room. Surely none can read of facts like these without saying concerning degraded India: "Lift up your heads; the day of redemption draweth nigh."

Thus the fruits of missionary labour appear. Knowledge of the gospel is spread amongst old and young, by public preaching; in itinerancies; by the gift of gospels and tracts; by schools both English and vernacular. A few are added to the churches: in many more doubts and fears are excited respecting the idolatry they now profess: and some believe the truth they fear to confess. At the present time there exist among the Telugus, eleven missionary stations, with twenty missionaries. The Churches contain 210 members, in a community of 720 christians. The 23 vernacular schools contain 600 boys and 30 girls: the boarding schools number 43 boys and 110 girls: six English schools contain 340 boys. The New Testament has just been revised: and the Old Testament is nearly completed: a small stock of tracts and books has been prepared. A mission-press at Vizagapatam is wholly devoted to Telugu literature. But sixteen years ago, few of these agencies were in operation in only two localities: under God's blessing they have all increased and are being employed efficiently. May they be speedily rendered fruitful in the conversion of souls!

THE GHAUTS.

The Telugu country is separated from the high land of central India, by a rugged belt of mountains called the Ghauts. Whoever therefore wishes to go from the plains of the Carnatic into the Mysore, must pass through the mountain chain. These Ghauts are in most places immense conical hills varying from six hundred to eleven hundred feet in height: they run generally in a direction from North East to South West. In some parts they stand close together; the few ravines are abrupt; and the rugged fronts of these rocky hills present an almost perpendicular wall to the traveller. In other places the ravines are wider, and allow opportunities for constructing carriage roads. A few of the passes are easy of ascent, but the majority are very difficult. The belt of Ghauts, varies from three to ten miles in depth: and in passing through this district or along its face, the traveller sees near and around him nothing but these majestic hills. Sometimes they seem to be following each other like mighty waves over the land: sometimes they form a solid barrier to all advance. Their individual appearance greatly varies. Some are covered with jungle to the very summit: others are more bare, and from the loose masses of bleached rock lying upon their surface, seem at a distance covered with well-built towns. Some have only broken fragments of rock scattered over their grassy slopes: but others are adorned with mighty boulders, that assume the most singular forms. Of these boulders some resemble huge heads, or solid cottages, or hulls of ships: all are of granite, blackened and weather-worn by the storms of thousands of years. Whose hand scattered them there in such profusion? From the day when the first aborigines that took possession of the land, walked in their midst, all changes in Indian Society have passed before their eyes. The Brahmin and the Khetriya passed through them to conquer the first owners of the soil. Before them the Mogul seized the Brahmin's patrimony. Through them the Mahrattas on their swift horses carried off the plunder of the plains: and Hyder and Tippu fought battles at their feet. They have seen injustice, oppression and war, and before God are witnesses. Man has passed away; generation has followed generation: but the hills abide there still. Their very stability is to us an element of comfort. Solid and long enduring as they have been "the mountains shall depart and the hills be removed; but the Word of the Lord endureth for ever." That word has said that the *knowledge of the Lord* SHALL *cover the earth.* "*All nations shall serve* HIM."

THE CANARESE MISSIONS IN THE MYSORE.

The high table-land to which the Ghaut-passes lead, and which lies three thousand feet above the Carnatic plains, is a noble sphere for missionary labour. It stretches away five hundred miles from north to south, from Belgaum in the Mahratta country to the Nilgherry hills: and contains nearly five millions of inhabitants. It contains the Principality of Coorg, the districts of Bellary and Kurnool, and the great province of MYSORE. It presents to the eye a broad undulating plain, pierced here and there by hills; some of which like Nundydroog and Severndroog, from their precipitous character, furnish natural fortresses for the defence of the territory. Grey granite every where abounds; and its fine slabs furnish the natives with their doorsteps and the front of their shops. Of these several districts the MYSORE is best known and in the best condition. Its Government is efficient; the administration of justice is prompt; the roads are in the finest order: the climate is salubrious, heat rising only to 88° in the hot weather, and falling to 61° in the colder season. Trade is prosperous: the soil is fertile: property is secure. Every thing invites the missionary to come forth and exhibit to perishing idolaters the life-giving gospel of Christ. The town of *Bangalore,* in the centre of the province, is its chief city. It contains more than 100,000 inhabitants. Of these the real native Canarese population reside in the Pettah or native town, but the larger number are Tamils attached to the cantonment. The military force consists of no less than three native Regiments; a Regiment of English Foot, one of European cavalry: the usual detail of artillery and the staff. The town is also the seat of the Government, the

Mysore Commission. It lies opposite the best passes between Madras and the west coast, and from it branch out roads to Bellary on the north, to Mangalore on the India ocean, as well as to all parts of the province of Mysore itself. Immense trade too is carried through it, thus completing the other elements by which its importance is determined. But there are other large towns in the province. *Chittledroog*, the head of a Subdivision, has 14,000 people. *Goobee* with 6000; *Coonghul* with 10,000 and *Toomkoor* are all purely native towns. *Mysore*, the residence of the deposed Raja, is also a most important spot; as well as the decayed town of *Seringapatam*. The people which occupy this immense territory are the Canarese. They are an interesting race; thoroughly Hindu; and have been little affected by the Musalmán conquest of India which fell on them from Bijnagar. Their simple village habits, government, hospitality, and gentleness still continue; Europeans even having had but little intercourse with them.

They have been almost entirely neglected by missionary societies. The first attempt at missionary labour among them was made by Mr. Hands and Mr. Reeve of the London Missionary Society at *Bellary*, at the very north of the Canarese territory, in 1810. Mr. Hands by whom the station was opened had great disadvantages to contend with in native work. He had neither Grammar, Dictionary, nor Vocabulary: he had to form all for himself: but met his difficulties with a patient spirit and soon began to conquer them. Meanwhile he made friends among the Europeans, for whose good he maintained regular services: and opened a free school for the destitute children of the soldiery. He thus sought to be useful to his countrymen, while yet unable to speak the Canarese tongue. In 1813, he established an English school for the natives, selecting the best scholars in the Telugu and Canarese schools. He began also to translate the Bible and was aided in this work by his colleague Mr. Reeve. Subsequently a native church was founded, boarding schools were opened: and a mission press established. A second Canarese mission was begun in 1820 at *Bangalore*, a more central station than Bellary, by two missionaries of the same Society. At first much attention was paid to the large English population in the Cantonment: and to the Tamil people connected with them. As the town of Bangalore was under the Government of the Mysore Raja, the missionaries could not venture to preach in its bazars and streets to the Canarese population. They endeavoured however to get their native teachers placed in the surrounding towns: and on one occasion resorted to an ingenious device to secure their object which may be noticed. There is a custom among Hindus, when one native wishes to obtain a gift from another, which is at first refused, that he should sit pertinaciously at his door, day after day, until his request is granted. As any evil which may happen to him is superstitiously believed to revert to the person who refuses, such a proceeding is much dreaded. It is called sitting in *dherna.* When Mr. Campbell wished to get ground for his catechist's house in a town near Bangalore, and had obtained the Raja's order, the *Foujdar* who was hostile, purposely delayed executing it. Mr. Campbell then said to one of his catechists; "Now, Jacob, you must go every day to the cutchery and sit in dherna on the Foujdar, while we pray for success." For six weeks he went, each day reminding the Foujdar that he waited for his final orders: and at length they were issued. Things went on unsatisfactorily for ten years, till 1830; when the system of government was changed, the province was taken under the charge of the Hon. East India Company and the way for preaching the gospel every where was opened in the fullest degree. A very interesting fact occurred in connection with this change of government which made a deep impression on the people and is worth mentioning. In order to see it well carried out, Lord William Bentinck, then Governor-General, went up to the Mysore: but he travelled without escort of any kind. The country people were astounded when they saw him riding alone in his palankeen, and conceived from the circumstance the highest idea both of his character and of English greatness. "Why! say they to this day, if only a little Polygar goes to the next village, he must have his guards and attendants with their swords, and so on: but here the man that rules from the Himálaya to Rameswaram, comes as if he were *nobody*. *Abáh!* what a wonderful people you are!"

The *Wesleyans* established a mission in Bangalore in 1821: but it was long confined to English and Tamil services, the former of which were exceedingly useful among the soldiery. The Canarese mission was commenced in 1836 by Mr. Garrett: when an English school was established and a press put up. Both these establishments are now very efficiently conducted;—in fact almost more so than any of their kind that I saw out of Madras. The English school receives from the government a monthly allowance of three hundred and fifty rupees, and is admirably provided with materials for instruction. Both the missions at Bangalore are prosperous. Their services for the heathen; their Christian chapels in both native languages: their boarding, vernacular and English schools are all maintained by a good staff of missionaries. There is one unfortunate circumstance about their location which may be noticed. The two missions, with their mission houses and land, stand side by side just out of the native town. This is not however their fault. The Wesleyans were there first; and when the London Missionaries were wishing to build their Canarese mission houses quite clear of the Cantonment, they chose a spot just away from the native town, but on the side opposite to that of their Wesleyan brethren. They then applied through the proper officer, to the head of the Mysore Commission for a grant of the land: but he replied: "What! do these missionary gentlemen want to SPREAD *their webs* like spiders, to catch the natives. No, no; put them down alongside of the others." And there unfortunately they are. The greatest harmony however has always prevailed between the brethren of the two bodies: they travel together, preach together, and are intimate personal friends. I had the pleasure of meeting the whole of them at one time during my short visit to Bangalore.

In the limited compass of these Lectures it is impossible to detail at length the history of these useful Missions: or to describe, as they deserve, the interesting events which have taken place during the growth of their prosperity. We might contemplate with pleasure the gradual progress of *Canarese christian literature;* the translation of the BIBLE; the compilation of the Dictionary; the preparation of the Grammars both in English and Canarese: the increase of christian tracts and school-books: and other useful labours of the presses at Bellary and Bangalore. We might shew the great benefits which have resulted from the Christian *Boarding Schools,* especially that at Bellary, under Mr. Reid: record the usefulness of the Theological Class at Bangalore; or detail the progress of the *Native Churches.* Most worthy too of special mention are the life, character and history of SAMUEL FLAVEL, the Native Pastor of the Bellary Church, whose steady consistency, fidelity and zeal for the Lord's work, present an excellent model for the imitation of his countrymen the native preachers. But all these things we must pass by, in order rather to describe the progress of the gospel among the people generally.

Instances might readily be multiplied of individual conversions that have occurred in connection with these various missions: all illustrating the silent but sure progress of the gospel, the difficulties in the way of its profession, and the all-powerful grace of the Saviour by which those difficulties are triumphantly overcome. One convert, in his heathen days the priest of a temple, said on his baptism at Goobee;—"I have travelled day by day to gather flowers; I have talked and put on temple garments; I have made offerings to the idols. Yet no idol, either in dreams or when awake, has said to me, 'Thy sins are forgiven; thou receivest salvation; thy sins are washed away.' I have fasted and prayed; but it has never said to me: 'Thou shalt escape hell and enjoy heaven.' The idol is a lie, I forsake it and embrace Jesus Christ as my Saviour and God." How many have borne similar testimony: and for the same reasons have passed over from the domains of Hinduism, into the kingdom and church of Christ.

At the present time in the purely Canarese country, the Mysore and Balaghat (of which Bellary is the capital), there are *seven* missionary stations, with *sixteen* missionaries and *fifteen* catechists. The church members are 284 in number, and the Christian community consists of 736 individuals. The only boarding schools are in the London Missions at Bellary and Bangalore: they contain *forty-three* boys and *sixty* girls. These schools have been found extensively useful, and from them have come forth several useful labourers in the mission; both school teachers and native preachers. Twenty vernacular boys' schools are maintained in and around the principal stations, with 560 scholars; and five girls' day-schools with 130 girls. Five hundred boys are studying in the English schools.

It will be seen from this statement that a great deal more might be done for the MYSORE, than what is doing at the present time. Only Bangalore and Bellary are well maintained stations. Yet the whole country, salubrious and healthy, with a simple and intelligent people, is open to missions which, judging from the recent growth of the older stations, might soon be prosperous.

The state of public feeling with respect to Christianity is no longer what it was. Indifference in former days was added to ignorance. But the extensive itinerancies of the Missionaries, and the wide spread of tracts and portions of the Bible which are both read and talked over by the people, have enlightened them greatly as to the truths of the Bible, have excited a universal expectation of their ultimate triumph, and produced in many individual minds, the secret conviction that to be a Christian is both right and good. Mr. Hardey of Bangalore, the Wesleyan Missionary, in one of his recent Reports has furnished some remarkable illustrations of this fact, which are best given in his own words.

In 1850, Messrs. Hardey and Sanderson took a tour of more than six hundred miles, from Mysore to Bangalore, and thence northward through an immense number of villages and towns. They preached to thousands of people, many of whom had never heard the gospel before, and distributed a large number of scriptures and tracts. Their hearers listened with marked attention. In places where Christian truth was somewhat known, there was opposition and fierce argument: and in one village, the sight of a converted brahmin excited a tremendous outburst of rage. In the large towns of Davanagerry and Chittledroog, the interest aroused by their visit was intense, and visibly increased during their stay. Congregations of all classes amounting sometimes to five hundred persons, heard their addresses with solemn stillness. Missionaries had never been there before. "In journeying through the country," says Mr. Morris of Coonghul, "one sees temples left to decay, the worship of idols rejected and ceremonies abolished. We want an increase of human instrumentality, under Divine Providence and grace. Had we more labourers much might be done." In Bidnagairy for eight years the people have forsaken their temple, declaring that as the idol could not protect himself, he is no God. They assert also that they are Christians: but like hundreds in Bengal, they have never had the courage and grace needed to profess the gospel. The same thing happened at Singonhully near Goobee. A missionary one day going near the temple of *Runga* found that it wore a very desolate appearance. Might he go in?—he asked of the people. Oh yes, he was at perfect liberty. With his shoes and hat? Yes: it did not matter. He went in and found the whole going to ruin. He asked the reason and was told the following story. "You one day told us that *Runga* could not be God, because he could do nothing for himself; much less could he do good to us who worshipped. We thought this was a wise speech, and agreed to leave the god alone and try. We soon found that his light went out; and that his garlands of flowers became dry and shrivelled. Moreover just at that time, the roof fell in over his head, exposing him to the heat and rain. We saw that he was helpless and there we left him." Who will say after such a fact that missionary labours are useless? The people of that village have not however embraced the gospel. One man was most reluctant to hold intercourse with the missionaries, apparently dreading its results. That man was the first to come out, and he and his family, now grown up, have proved most zealous and consistent christians.

In 1851, Mr. Hardey who was stationed at Bangalore thus spoke of his general preaching labours. "This year has been decidedly the most interesting I have known amongst the Natives. Our congregations have uniformly been large, and in general deeply attentive. We have always commenced our street services by singing a Canarese hymn, which never fails to secure a good congregation. When I came to Bangalore, three years ago, it was next to impossible to speak for five minutes without interruption from a low class who were not satisfied with interrupting merely, but abused us before the whole assembly, which was not to be endured if we wished to stand our ground and be respected in the streets. I determined to put a stop to this in the beginning, and very soon an opportunity offered. One evening whilst we were preaching, standing on an elevation, which I always aim at doing, a profligate-looking man, mounted the elevation, on the opposite side of the street; and pulling out a book from under his cloth, he marched backward and forward, and imitating our intonations of voice, made use of much abusive language, and called me such foul names, that it was with difficulty I could restrain my Catechist. Several brahmins entreated me to go away, saying, it was not proper for a European gentleman to stand and hear himself thus abused. I continued, however, to address the people. By this time at least two hundred persons had assembled; and when I was leaving, the man evidently became alarmed at having used so much abusive language, and began walking quickly down the street. I went over to the Choultry opposite, and pointing out the man, desired the policeman to seize him. He ran and quickly turned the man's face towards the multitude, who were now all anxiety to see what was to be done. As soon as he was brought to the Choultry, I said to the standers by: 'So long as I was preaching I bore with this man's abuse, but now I will shew you that I am not to be insulted in the street by any man. I will now see whether the authorities will protect me against any man who feels himself at liberty to abuse me at pleasure.' The people were all excitement, and I said; 'Bring him at once to the Amildar, and we will see if he persists in this conduct towards me, who have done nothing to provoke his anger.' At once the man was led away towards the main street, followed by the entire mass, who were now greatly excited to know what would become of the matter. We had not gone very far when a respectable man, a friend of ours, came out of breath and entreated me to spare his relation who was a bad fellow, and had done very wrong in using abusive language to an English gentleman. I said, 'If before all these people,'—who had increased to at least five hundred, 'he will confess that he has done wrong, and will never again speak to me in the streets, I will forgive him.' But no, his proud spirit could not submit to this, though his increasing fear was every moment becoming more apparent. I said to the policeman, 'Bring him to the Amildar,' and having proceeded a little further, the man's friend again entreated me not to take him before the authorities. I replied, 'If he will ask forgiveness, and confess he has done wrong, I will forgive him: but if not, I will not allow him to escape, till I have known the mind of the Amildar.' Seeing me determined in my purpose, and feeling that we were drawing near to the cutcherry, and that the people were staring upon him in every direction, he became greatly excited and alarmed. Before the multitude I then catechized him to the following effect:—'Have you done me an injury in abusing me in the public street, and in interrupting me in the discharge of my duty?' 'Sir, I have.' 'Will you promise me never to speak to me again in the street, or interrupt me when preaching?' 'I will promise.' 'Now then, before all these witnesses I forgive you, and never wish to see your face again, but as a friend.' I then dismissed him, and was thankful enough that I had gained a victory before five or six hundred people, without having appeared before the authorities.—The effect of this proceeding was almost magical! The news of it flew all over the Pettah, and from that time to this, our congregations have been better, more attentive, more interesting; and in scarcely a single instance, since that time, have these characters interrupted us in the streets."

The circulation of scriptures and tracts is adopted among the Canarese as well as in Bengal, and meets with the same result. All over India, especially in village districts, an intense desire is exhibited to get books. Mr. Arthur, on this subject tells the following story. He was one day in the town of Biddiri. He had preached and distributed a number of tracts, when he saw a tall boy trying to elbow his way through the crowd with great earnestness. He could not succeed and called out; Sir, you must keep one for me: you *must* keep one for me. Mr. A. amused at his earnestness, said: Why for you above all others. He replied, 'Oh, Sir, we want it for our school?' It then came out that once before a boy belonging to a heathen school a few miles off had obtained some books: and pleased with their wonderful sense, the master and scholars had discarded their old books in order to study *them*. Hearing that the missionary was expected at Biddiri, they had despatched the boy on an expedition to get as many more for the school as he could.

Mr. Hardey also gives most pleasing testimony to the same effect. "Were we to give books to all who ask for them in the streets, or to all who come to our houses, the supply could not be furnished. We are compelled to use much discretion, and to refuse many who appear very urgent, but who we have reason to believe would not make a good use of them. Yet we are bound to give to all those whom we know sufficiently, and who can assign a reason why they wish to possess the books of the Christian Religion. It has been very gratifying to us during the year to find so many persons who know the names of the different tracts and portions of Scripture, and who ask for them by name. This convinces us that the books are not only known and read, but talked about. We have always made it a practice to promise a second book, if an account of the contents of the first book taken, can be given. In many instances the first book given has been brought back, that an examination might be made as to its contents. In one instance a man copied the entire tract entitled, "In whom shall we trust?" which he had copied as nearly like the printed work as possible. He sent to us by post saying we had given it to him at Cuddoor, which is 130 miles from this; and to shew us that he had read it carefully he had sent us a copy of the book. He earnestly requested more, which we sent by post. It is quite true that many of our books are destroyed, not maliciously, but principally for kites. There was one Brahmin in the cutcherry who employed persons to collect tracts from us, and then tore them up for the amusement of the by-standers. It would betray a singular apathy on the part of the people, if they received all we gave them and destroyed nothing. Their tearing up our books is rather a good than a bad sign. It shews they fear them, and are conscious that they are powerful though silent messengers.

A most interesting circumstance occurred last year in connection with the *Musalmans* of Bangalore. It is thus detailed by the same writer.

"In the early part of the year, the Musalmans were much excited against us. One who had read in Mr. Rice's School, challenged me to prove that Christ is the "Son of God." I said, I was not in the habit of discussing with every man in the streets who thought himself qualified to speak on religion; but if he would call his Kajee, or priest, I would discuss the matter with him. Being near to the mosque, he quickly brought his Kajee, and we at once entered upon the subject in hand. But knowing the slippery character of these men, and their fearful propensity for lying, I determined to have everything upon paper, that there might be no escape until the matter was brought to a close. I then called two or three respectable witnesses, and in their presence, Ibrahim Sahib, Kajee, engaged to prove from the Christian Scriptures, or as he called it, the "Holy Bible," and from the Koran, that Jesus Christ is not the "Son of God." I engaged to prove from the Christian Scriptures that Jesus Christ is the "Son of God," and therefore God. At the Musalman's particular request it was added; "If the Missionary be overcome he shall become a Musalman. If the Musalman be overcome, he shall become a Christian." I allowed this insertion the more readily, knowing their great anxiety to make proselytes, and that to secure a missionary they would put forth their utmost strength. We each put his signature to the paper, and the witnesses did the same. The next morning we met to conclude all preliminaries. A Hindoo Jury consisting of two Brahmins, one Rajpoot, one Modaliar, and one Chetty, were named, and their signatures obtained as such. Into their hands I gave my five Canarese volumes, and my English Bible, stating that the one was the Holy Bible in Canarese, the other in English. In each volume the Jury put their distinctive mark, that the same books might always be consulted. But a difficulty arose about the Koran, for the Jury insisted upon its being produced. After much delay, discussion, and anger, amongst the Musalmans, it was brought carefully folded in a handkerchief, and a chair provided for its reception. Besides the Koran beautifully written in Arabic, and as beautifully interlined with Hindoostanee, two other books, as beautifully written, were produced. These contained several great discussions which had been held between the Musalmans and the missionaries in the North; as the Jury could not deface these books, or even touch them, they were carefully folded up in the handkerchief, and the mark was put upon the knot, so that it could not be opened, but by the consent of the Jury. The preliminaries thus arranged, and it being agreed that two chairmen should be nominated, one by me and the other by my opponent, who should preside alternately; we parted to meet again the next morning.

At six o'clock, on the morning of the 4th of April, 1851, we met at the gate of the Mosque, and as a suitable place had not yet been provided, I walked into the yard of the Mosque, all the people following. I went straight to the large shed, in which several of their things for the yearly feast were kept. An oily chair was brought for me and another for my opponent. As I did not on that morning succeed in obtaining a Christian Chairman, Shankrappa, an elderly Brahmin, occupied the Chair. He opened the proceedings in the presence of many Brahmins, Musalmans, and others, by addressing me to the following effect:—"Why have you come to this place?" "To prove that Jesus Christ is the Son of God, I am come." "How will you establish this?" "From these five Canarese Books, marked by the Jury, and called the Holy Bible, will I establish this truth." Then turning to the Musalman, the Chairman asked:—"Why have you come to this place?" "To prove that Jesus Christ is not the Son of God, I am come here." "How will you establish this?" "From the Christian Scriptures, and from the Koran will I establish this." Then addressing us both, the Chairman required that we should not interrupt each other, and should submit to the Chair.—As this was altogether a heathen assembly, and I was anxious to give the Musalman a fair chance to make good his cause, I commenced the discussion by quoting passages of Scripture, shewing that Jesus Christ is the "Son of God." But having only half an hour each, being determind to keep as near to the English custom as possible, that the people ever hereafter might understand our method of public disputation, I only produced fourteen passages of Scripture with explanations, remarking, that I had more than ninety passages to produce upon a future occasion.—The Chairman then called upon the Musalman to reply, but he asked for eight days to prepare, which was conceded.

"The difficulty now was to obtain a large and neutral place of meeting. Though there were several, the owners were alarmed at the idea of being connected with a dispute between the missionary and the Musalmans. I engaged if possible, to obtain the loan of Mr. Rice's large school room in the neighbourhood. This was readily and kindly granted. On the 11th of April, we assembled to hear the Musalman's reply. A Musalman gentleman took the Chair on their side, and the Rev. Colin Campbell on my side.—The reply consisted of twenty passages of Scripture, in which Jesus Christ is called the "Son of Man." These passages were torn from their connexion; and apparently selected at random. In my reply I took occasion to reproduce each passage in its connexion, and shew that in the connection in which it stood, Jesus Christ was also called the "Son of God." The divine and human natures of Christ had not yet entered into his understanding; but the subject being of vital importance to both the Musalman and myself, it could not fail to be interesting and exciting to the various classes present. On this occasion there must have been four or five thousand Musalmans inside and outside the building; and with all Mr. Campbell's self-possession and tact, he could not controul the Musalman multitude. They had produced twenty passages, I had produced only fourteen. Twenty was six more than fourteen, and in this consisted their victory. Nothing would satisfy the Musalmans, but a declaration on the part of the Jury that twenty was a larger number than fourteen, and that twenty had overcome fourteen. The Jury protested, saying that, until I acknowledged I had no more to say, the matter could not be concluded. Sometime before the close of the meeting, as soon as the Musalman tumult commenced, the Brahmins had managed to convey themselves out of the place, being alarmed at nothing so much as Musalman fury.

"On the 18th of April, I again appeared to reply to the Musalman. My opponent was not forthcoming, though I had waited half an hour in his mosque, and in reply to the messengers of the Jury he said, he was coming. After waiting some time, my reply was read, and as my opponent was not present, the Jury gave him other eight days for consideration; at the same time handing over my reply.—At the expiration of the eight days, the Jury again sat to hear the Musalman's reply to my second paper, but he not making his appearance, they declared the discussion at an end.

"On the morning of the 18th instead of being in his place, Ibrahim Sahib collected all the Musalmans at the corners of the different streets, and haranguing them, declared the missionary was beaten; the Musalman had conquered, and now the missionary must become a Musalman. This occurred at the very time when the Jury were sending messengers after him. The discussion being over, the difficulty now was to obtain the decision in writing from the Jury, as until that could be obtained, the Musalmans must enjoy their street triumph. Besides, the intelligence of the discussion was spread all over the Mysore country, in less than a week from its commencement, and it was of great importance to myself to have the matter cleared up. In every street I was asked what the Jury had decided in the matter. Had I allowed the matter to slip through, I should have been hooted through the streets, perhaps as long as I remained in the town. It cost me two months hard work to get the entire matter settled. Several of the Jury being Government servants, felt their honour at stake, but two of their number were greatly afraid of the future conduct of the Musalmans towards them; and it required every exertion of the remaining three to screw up their courage to put their signature to the documents. At the close of two months the Jury furnished me with a most lawyer-like statement of the whole affair, not omitting a single matter. It occupied seventeen pages of foolscap paper, and besides those there were other seventeen foolscap sheets which came before them, but which, my opponent not being present to hear, are not included in this document. During the two months which intervened, between the close of the discussion and delivery of the decision of the Jury,

I was hooted by the Musalmans in every street in which I preached. One morning, one of them in his rage cursed me, by saying, I should become ashes, if I took the name of the Koran into my lips. Another said, suiting his action to the words, he would cut me to pieces if I did not let the Koran alone. Another said, that before they began to discuss with me they ought to have given me a thorough beating. Their anger was much increased, because the discussion had lead me to read very carefully, the entire of Sale's edition of the Koran, with Savary's notes. I referred them to chapter and verse, and told them many things before the Hindoos, of which the latter had never heard, and which were very unpalatable. This, I believe, was the great reason why the discussion so soon closed, for I promised them I would make known all the matters of the Koran before I had done with them.

"As soon as the papers from the Jury were sent to me, I published their account of the discussion, and their decision thereon, with their signatures. This I distributed through the Pettah. The effect of this has been very remarkable. From the first day on which I circulated the tract up to this time, not a single Musalman has opened his mouth to me in the way of opposition. They listen to our preaching in greater numbers than formerly, but it is always in silence. If I had dropped the matter, at any point short of publishing the tract, I saw clearly that the Musalmans would have the advantage over me in the streets, as they could lie ad-infinitum. But when there was once the decision of the Jury to which to appeal, I should have no occasion to fear the face of any man.

"For two years past there has been a remarkable demand for the four Gospels in Hindoostanee by the Musalmans. Up to this time, we are quite at a loss to know what is done with all the books we have given amongst them. Matthew appears to be the favourite gospel with them. Nothing is clearer than that many of them read the gospels, for they talk about their contents. But there is a fatal blindness resting upon their minds. They cannot perceive in Christ, "God manifest in the flesh." Their principal aim appears to be, to collect passages in which Christ is called the "Son of man;" and we have been surprised many times at their total rejection of the divinity of our Saviour.—Some of them say, the Paraclete promised by Christ to come after Him, is Mohammed. But in this case they shew their blindess, for they leave the entire connexion, and entertain two ideas only, the Paraclete is to come;—the Paraclete is Mahommed.—Thus, they fully believe that Mahommed being promised, and having come as a prophet, is superior to Christ."

During the last few years, the people in the neighbourhood of *Bellary*, the oldest station in the Canarese country, have seemed to be drawing nearer to the kingdom of God. For a long period the missionaries have preached in the town, and wandered through the villages; have visited, revisited and visited again the great festival at Humpee, proclaiming the love of Christ to a sinful world; yet almost in despair of penetrating the dense mass of ignorance and irreligion in which they were engulphed. But signs appear that their labours have not been in vain, and that if carried on still, with faithfulness and zeal, they will soon result in widespread and substantial fruits. In the towns near Bellary a considerable acquaintance with the facts and principles of Christianity is found to prevail. In parts where the gospel has been longer and more fully preached than in others, the people evince a deeper interest in it: although in some minds there is exhibited a steady and bitter dislike. The missionaries are no longer regarded as strangers. Their character and errand are well known, and many are most anxious to hear their message.

Not long since Mr. Shrieves set out on a preaching tour through the district, and met with the most striking illustrations of the progress which the gospel has made in the people's minds. On his arrival at Kosgee, the people crowded round, and being encouraged by the presence of several hundreds, he preached to them upwards of three hours. They did not like to go away as long as he was able to speak. On telling them that he intended to stay with them for eight days, they were pleased and came in great numbers daily. He was obliged to make two companies of the people who came, to enable the teacher and himself to speak to them audibly.

Again he proceeded to Kumply, a large town where there are many weavers. On beginning to preach in the Pettah, the people came in crowds to hear him. He invited them all to visit his tent at any time they wished: they consequently came every day in increasing numbers: those who came were mostly weavers, but there were some of other castes also. He always had a large and attentive congregation from five to nine o'clock in the evening. Seeing the people were so anxious for instruction, he felt it necessary to stay longer with them than he had intended. On learning this fact they were much pleased. Many of the people called him into their houses, when many gathered together to hear and to ask questions. Some acknowledged that Christianity was true, saying; we see that this is the only way by which we can be saved. Others said; we are ready to embrace Christianity. A remarkable spirit of enquiry was prevalent among them. He distributed nearly three cooly loads of Scriptures and tracts. After staying with them twenty-four days, he told them that he was going away: *they asked him to remain another week still.*

The native catechists meet with a similar reception, and are often hospitably entertained by enquirers, as we saw in the neighbourhood of Cuddapah. The catechist, *John Reid,* in one of his journeys visited *Kumply, Errode* and other places, in all of which he preached the gospel and had conversations with the people. Many heard the message, and most listened with attention. Some assented fully to the excellence of Christianity, and said they were hindered from embracing it by *caste.* At Errode, which is in the Nizam's country, after he had preached, the people brought rice and milk, and said if any thing else were required, they would readily furnish it, and refused money when offered to them. A man who had seen him before, said he remembered with pleasure what he had heard about Christ. The tracts offered were taken with great eagerness. At *Kundakul* the people expressed much pleasure in hearing the gospel. They took a light away from a neighbouring temple, saying it was of no use there and would do for him to read by. They urged him to remain another day, promising to supply him with all he required.

When Mr. Stanger was recently returning to Bellary from a tour, he found two men who had come from a distant village, and said they were going to Bellary. On being asked why they were going thither, they said; We want to hear of the true God and to be instructed in the Christian religion. Mr. Stanger asked; Why are you so anxious about this. They replied; We have often heard that the padres at Bellary say that an idol is nothing, and that all who worship idols will go to hell; we have given up the worship of idols for the last year, and wish to serve the true God. They accordingly came to Bellary. One of them after a short time left, and the missionaries have not seen him since; the other seemed much in earnest; he made very gratifying progress in the knowledge of the truth, and gave them every reason to believe that he loved it too. Accordingly he was baptized in the Mission Chapel.

The annual festival at Humpee has long been celebrated for the enthusiasm with which its rites were celebrated. But even there, the gospel is winning its way. Even there, where the Hindu kings once reigned in splendor, and where they rendered Hindu idolatry powerful, the gospel is beginning to enlighten the understanding and to change the heart. It is evident from the meagre attendances at the festivals, that although the self-interested and crafty supporters of idolatry, strain every nerve in decorating the cars, in order to dazzle the eyes and impress the minds of the multitude with superstitious fears, thereby to maintain their hold in their hearts, yet the people seem to invest them with less importance than they once did. They are being impressed with the fact that Hinduism is on the wane; and that Christianity is gaining ground, and will eventually be the only religion of mankind. The attendance at Humpee last year was smaller than it has ever been in years gone by. Tradition reports that formerly the yellow silk flag used in the idol's procession, was bought, in the days of his prosperity, for *thirty thousand* rupees, *i. e.* £3000. Last year a wealthy merchant bought it and placed it on the temple for *three hundred and fifty rupees or* £35! Is not the power of idolatry waning fast?

A step beyond the mere general assent to the truth of Christianity is the hard one of publicly professing it. Though many hold back, and endeavour to persuade others that they are Christians without that profession, yet some are found willing to make it, and brave all the difficulties by which such a step is beset. Others again are ready to make the profession without feeling the conviction, and thus put a difficulty on the missionary's side. These things are thus stated by Mr. Hardey.

"About June last, a Rajput, began to visit me, and brought with him a volume of the Old Testament in Canarese, which had been given to him many years ago in Bellary. He appeared very desirous to understand our Scriptures, and was particularly fond of the Book of Psalms. I engaged to read with him once a week. This continued for some time, when he invited me to his house. He had a large number of females and children, all of whom, in the Hindu fashion, he gave to me. He afterwards wished to be baptized and all his house. He said he would work in the garden, but I must provide for the women and children. But this providing for new converts always has been, and will, for a long time to come, be a great difficulty in the way of baptizing these people. Until there are many more Christians, most of those who now become such will be great sufferers, if not cared for by the Mission. One day I said to this man: If you become a Christian, you must renounce all caste. He at once replied, "I will forsake it, and I will give you a proof if you wish it, that I forsake it." I at once called a servant who was a heathen pariah, to bring the bread. I cut a piece of the bread and gave it to him, and he ate it in the presence of Mrs. Hardey, the servant and myself. I could have baptized these people, but then the burden of a large family was the difficulty, and I let the opportunity pass. This perhaps was wrong, but I was powerless as to supporting them. I am bold to say that, were I a Jesuit, or had I a Jesuit's means, I could baptize a hundred persons in the year. Nay, if I could secure a bare livelihood, in the shape of situations, I could baptize many. Not more than two months ago a man came fifty miles to be baptized, but I had no reason to believe that he had any thing in view beyond a livelihood, and I sent him away. In Goobbee, a brahmin, once came to me on the Saturday night, and urged me to baptize him at the public service next morning, saying, I must not delay. He offered me his sacred thread to convince me that he was in earnest.—I enquired if he had any debts, and he confessed that his creditors were pressing him. I suppose he thought he should throw his debts upon me by becoming a Christian. I knew him well, and knew his character was not good, and refused to take his sacred thread, or to baptize him. Another brahmin, of whose sincerity I had no doubt, actually took off his sacred thread, in a private room, and gave it into my hands, to convince me that he was sincere. These things shew that Hinduism is fast loosing its hold upon even the brahmins; and I attribute it all to Missions, and the distribution of the word of God.

"About four months ago, another Rajput came to my house, and in the midst of a conversation upon religion, he repeated page after page of Mr. William Campbell's Sermons. I was for some time at a loss to know what he was repeating, for he spoke very rapidly, and what he said was evidently well committed to memory. He told me he constantly read these Sermons and our Scriptures, and prayed to God morning and night through Jesus Christ. His statement is authenticated by one who is now a Christian, and lived several years in his house. Missionaries have not laboured in vain. The seed sown by our predecessors has been and will yet be found by us. The seed we are scattering will be found by our successors. 'Brethren, pray for us, that the Word of the Lord may have free course and be glorified, even as it is amongst you.'"

The last point illustrative of the growth of knowledge and increase of liberal ideas among the Hindus is seen in the change of their opinions respecting practices in their own system.

The subject of the Second Marriage of Hindu Widows is beginning to excite strong attention amongst the Brahmins of Bangalore. Some time ago a very valuable tract about it was written in Sanskrit by a learned Pandit in the North. Mr. Wilkinson, a civilian, who knew this Brahmin only from his learning, was so much struck with its reasoning, and its bold exposure of the horrid system of perpetual widowhood, that he wrote a long and valuable Essay in English to accompany the Sanskrit tract. This was sent to the Commissioner of the Mysore, together with the Tract, which he handed over to the Divan who has had it translated into Canarese. The Commissioner has sanctioned the printing of 1000 copies at the Government Press.—This translation was brought to Mr. H. early in the year, and after reading it carefully he began to talk about it amongst the brahmins. They almost all approve of the Second Marriage of Widows, but cannot see how it can be brought about.—So much interest is the subject exciting, that two brahmins have visited him several times urging him to assist in bringing about so desirable a result. They said, we have each a daughter, a widow: one twenty years old, the other fifteen; and we don't know how to save them from ruin. He was much gratified to find only one old Pandit who opposed the Second Marriage of Hindu Widows. He became very angry with the other brahmins, and said they were all going over to the Missionary, were bringing disgrace upon their own religion, and were giving the Missionary an insight into all their secret matters.—Another brahmin came and said, he would obtain the signatures of almost every brahmin in Bangalore in its favour, if Mr. H. wished. The Tract first spoken of is nearly printed, and when once circulated, it will doubtless produce great excitement. But this tract has had a narrow escape. The brahmin who had the original translation of the book wrote to Mr. H. in great perplexity saying, the Commissioner had sanctioned the printing of the book, but he could nowhere find the Manuscript. It had created much bad feeling on the part of the more rigid brahmins, and the manuscript had probably been destroyed by some of them. Fortunately, he had had the whole carefully copied, and the book is actually being printed from that manuscript. It may be perceived from these things that there is a friendship springing up between the more liberal brahmins and the missionaries which, in a few years, we trust, may lead to great results.

Infanticide, is perhaps the most glaring evil connected with the perpetual widowhood of the Hindu females. Thousands of young girls who have lost their husbands have their heads shaven and are doomed to perpetual degradation. The consequences of their ill-treatment are, they become prostitutes, and numbers of infants, the fruits of illicit intercourse, never see the light of day. Infanticide, though strictly forbidden by the law, is in this way carried to a very fearful extent. Several brahmins have asserted that *no less than thirty infants* are in this way destroyed *every month* in the year, *in the one town of Bangalore alone*.

THE GERMAN EVANGELICAL MISSION.

The west coast of the Madras Presidency from Honore to Calicut, including the provinces of CANARA and MALABAR, has been taken as a missionary sphere by the EVANGELICAL SOCIETY of BASEL. The country is but a narrow slip of land, between the western ghauts and the sea; it is hilly but fertile; and contains several large seaport towns, amongst which Mangalore and Cannanore are best known. The languages spoken are the Canarese, the Tulu and the Máleálim. All these tongues are ancient; and two of them contain an extensive native literature. It was the opening of Hindustan to foreign as well as English missionaries by the Company's Charter of 1833, that first led the Basel missionaries to settle in the country. The western coast of India, except Bombay and Travancore, had never been entered by other than Jesuit missionaries, and finding it still unoccupied, the Basel Committee anxious not to interfere in any way with the efforts of other Societies, but rather to preach to those that were left in ignorance, under the advice of friends in Bombay, adopted it as their sphere of labour. Three missionaries were therefore sent to *Mangalore* in 1834; and there established the first station of the mission. Four others followed in 1836, when *Dharwar* above the ghauts, in the very north of the Canarese country, was occupied. In 1838 a third mission was commenced to the south of Mangalore at *Tellicherry* among the Máleális; and on the arrival of five new brethren in the same year, a fourth station was fixed near Dharwar at *New Hoobly*. Putting forth its strength with earnestness and vigour, the Society despatched five more missionaries in 1840, and yet five others in 1842: upon which important missions were commenced at *Cannanore* upon the sea coast, at *Bettigherry* and also at *Calicut*. The climax of its European strength was reached by the mission about 1845: at which time twenty-six missionaries were engaged in the service of the Society. Since that year it has done little more than efficiently maintain the stations previously established, and allow for the absence of the usual proportion of invalids.

The mission, which thus sprang into maturity in less than twenty years, has been carried on with the vigour and energy which first led to its formation. The numerous introductory labours required every where at the outset of such undertakings have long been completed. Every station has its mission-houses, its school-buildings and its church; to which in the two principal stations have been added printing-offices and industrial schools. The missionaries have therefore long since been able to devote an undivided attention to the spiritual objects of their toil. In order to secure that end, they have pursued, to a great extent, the same plans as have been adopted by other Societies in other localities throughout Hindustan. They have preached the gospel in the vernacular tongues at their immediate stations, and by continued and extensive itinerancies, have carried it to the distant villages and towns, among whom their lot has been cast. Where a demand existed for English education they have established christian English schools; and have elsewhere offered a christian education in the native tongues alone. For the benefit of their native christians, they have maintained christian boarding schools and an industrial school to improve their means of livelihood. For the enlightenment of all, christian and heathen, they have engaged in the translation and circulation of the scriptures, and have kept two printing presses constantly employed. All these varieties of agency employed in faith, and sanctified by prayer, have received a blessing from on high: and the fruits of success which they are able already to exhibit, must be regarded by all interested in that agency with astonishment and thankfulness.

Nor should it be forgotten that in their labours, the missionaries of the Basle Society, in adopting plans similar to those of other missionaries in other parts of India, have met with a similar experience. They have found the same dense ignorance of the first principles of religion in Canara and Malabar, which have been met in north and eastern India. The same opposition to truth, the same love of idolatry in the Hindu, the same bigotry in the Musalman Moplah, have resisted them as have depressed others. Some converts have deceived them, who came for gain: others have backslidden, who were weak. Boys have run away from their boarding schools, and orphan girls proved incorrigibly wicked. Young people have been pressed forward into the church too soon; church-members have refused to give up caste; day-schools that promised well have been given up; and new converts have been forcibly carried back into hopeless heathenism. Thus they have fallen into the same mistakes of inexperience, as have been committed by others and have met with similar difficulties. But their work has been well based and though yet in "the day of small things" has made solid progress.

At the present time, when the oldest station has not been established twenty years, the Basel Society possesses in western India, thirteen principal stations, and twenty out-stations. At these localities the more direct missionary work is carried on by twenty-eight missionaries, of whom seventeen are married; and by sixty-three catechists. At each of the chief stations there is a christian congregation gathered from the natives of the place and of its neighbourhood; the church-members or communicants amounting to 750, and the christian community including 1578 individuals. The chief schools are vernacular boys' schools: of which nearly fifty are maintained, instructing sixteen hundred scholars. The boys' boarding schools, three in number, contain sixty-three boys: and the girls' boarding schools, one hundred and fifty-one girls. All these schools have christian masters. Ninety-six boys are studying English in two English schools. Industrial schools are maintained at Tellicherry and Mangalore, for the instruction of christian lads in agriculture, weaving and other employments suitable to their station in life. In the school at Mangalore are also taught watch and clock making, the construction of musical boxes, electro-plating, the weaving of shawls and handkerchiefs, book-binding and printing. Two printing-presses have for many years been maintained at Mangalore and Tellicherry: the former for the Canarese and Tulu books: the latter for Málcáli. The former press was a lithographic press, but has recently exchanged the lithograph for types. Last but not least, there is a Theological class at Mangalore for training christian teachers and preachers for the service of the mission. From this institution, nine young men were sent forth into the mission in January, 1852. A seminary for the training of school-masters is to be added when circumstances allow. Such is the amount of agency zealously applied by the missionaries of the Society for the spread of Christianity in the provinces which they occupy; and such are some of the results with which their labours have been followed.

For the sake of greater distinctness, a few words may be added concerning the differences observable in the labours of particular localities. The Basle missions are carried on in three separate districts and are therefore divided into three distinct groupes: viz. the purely Canarese mission in the DHARWAR district: the mixed Canarese and Tulu mission in north Canara, the head-quarters of which are at MANGALORE: and the Máleálim mission in Malabar, at CANNANORE, Tellicherry and Calicut. The station among the Nilgiri hills must be reckoned separately: it being not only the Sanatarium of the Society, but a distinct mission for the local hill tribes.

1. FIRST GROUP. MISSIONS AROUND DHARWAR.

The most northerly of these missions form a group by themselves in the country above the ghauts. They lie on the table-land stretching from the Mysore north and north-west into the Mahratta country, and are situated in the district of Dharwar, formerly a portion of the Beejapore province, and subject to the Peishwa of Poonah. Though called the Mahratta country, the language spoken is pure Canarese, but immediately to the north, in the district of Belgaum, the boundary between the two tongues is passed and the Mahratta begins. The first mission was established at the town of DHARWAR in 1837; a second was fixed in 1839 at Hoobly, a town with 50,000 people. Two years after, two additional stations were commenced at Bettigherry and Malasamudra. The last and fifth station was established at Guledgudda in 1851. All these missions have been steadily maintained from the first and continue to the present time. The native population amongst whom they are planted resemble the Canarese of the Mysore, and have a similar hold upon the Hindu religion and the laws of caste. It was long therefore before the gospel began to tell upon them, and draw its converts from the very localities in which it was proclaimed. For several years the only Christians in the church at DHARWAR were Tamils, connected with the native army: who by their weakness, and love of caste, gave their missionary the same trouble and grief, which the numerous christians of their nation have given to others elsewhere. The missionaries however established numerous schools and travelled extensively through their district, as well as among the towns and villages of Bellary and Belgaum. The effects of their instruction gradually appeared in the respect paid to the gospel, the frequent acknowledgments of its excellence and truth, and in the people's growing distrust of the idols which they had hitherto worshipped. During the last three years, in numerous cases converts of some standing in the community have openly embraced Christianity. Individuals from the goldsmiths' and coppersmiths' castes, with others of similar position and intelligence, have been baptized at Dharwar, Hoobly and Guledgudda: and the hope is confidently indulged that these churches will now grow in strength, receiving annually large additions from the heathen community around them.

THE LINGAITS.

Throughout the southern Mahratta country there is extensively spread a flourishing sect of Hindus, termed Lingaits. They belong chiefly to the trading and manufacturing classes of the community, who are by far the most intelligent and independent of the people, and have learned in some measure to think and act for themselves. The Lingaits, like other sects of the kind in other parts of India, have given up their reverence for the common idolatry of the country, and secretly adhere to a higher system of religion, which teaches among its prime doctrines the unity of God, and that all men are of one caste. Numerous verses are current among them to the effect that: He who worships wood and stone as God, shall fall into the lowest hell. On this ground in their own assemblies they eat together, though belonging in public to different castes that are forbidden to do so. The whole body are under the dominion of four high priests, whose insolence and avarice do not differ greatly from those of the brahmins, whose system they have in a measure supplanted. They are instructed also by a large number of priests or gúrús, who profess to expound their doctrines from the Linga shastras. They do not however all think alike. Whether from conviction or the love of power, individuals among the priests occasionally form separate schools amongst the adherents of the doctrine. The most important of these schools is termed the Nudi sect, and its followers are distinguished as Nudi Lingaits. Their system is laid down in a collection of books which are called Guru-Nudi. This guru, who was probably acquainted not only with the literature of the Lingaits, but also with Vedantism and the Koran, seems to have founded his school about three hundred years ago. He is said to have written his works under a large overhanging rock, called the umbrella rock, on the frontier of the Nizam's dominions, near which he lived for one and twenty years. His system contains a mixture of brahminical, Lingait, Vedantic and Mahomedan doctrine, and is distinguished by a belief in the resurrection of the body. These sects greatly resemble the Kortta Bhojas of Bengal, and the sect which was founded by Sundara Das in Orissa.

Belonging to the most intelligent classes of the community, accustomed to varieties in religious belief, and separated in a measure from the debasing superstitions of the ancient idolatry, it is evident that the adherents of sects like these are much more open to the gospel, and are naturally much better prepared to appreciate its ennobling doctrines, than the idolaters who never think at all. Accordingly it is among them, especially among the Nudi Lingaits, that the German Missionaries in Dharwar and the London Missionaries at Belgaum find that Christianity is making the most rapid progress. They have travelled constantly among them;

have scattered widely their christian books and portions of the Bible: have met with great numbers of sincere enquirers, and latterly have received several converts. Their intercourse with this interesting class of Hindus has sometimes exhibited features almost bordering on romance. On one occasion, a Lingait priest, with two hundred of his followers came to visit Mr. Albrecht at Dharwar. The visit occurred on a Sunday morning, and the whole company attended public worship, behaving in the most proper and orderly manner. They brought with them a number of Christian books which they had previously received, and assured the missionary not only that they constantly studied them, but were convinced that they were true, while their own books were false. They even asserted also their full belief in the Lord Jesus and called themselves his disciples. A year or two after, Mr. Würth of Hoobly, travelling through the country, came upon. another band of these disciples with their guru. They had never seen a missionary but had received a large number of Canarese tracts, one or two theological treatises, and a Canarese New Testament. These also professed their faith in the Lord's divinity and quoted passages to prove it. It was from just such a band of free thinking disciples of the old guru Sundara Dás, that the first converts were gathered into the christian church in Orissa. It may be remembered too by those acquainted with modern missionary history, that when the guru saw that his disciples were leaving him for the missionaries he gave himself out as an incarnation of Christ. Singularly enough one of these Lingait gurus fell into the same error. He had got the idea that he was an incarnation of the Lord Jesus, ordained to bring these idolaters to the true God. Such pretensions however have been treated as they deserved. Many of the Lingaits continued to visit the missionaries; and at length in the year eighteen hundred and forty-eight, four were baptized. One of these was a priest and from the influence he possessed proved very zealous and useful in bringing his former disciples and companions to the missionary. In the same year, three young men, Lingaits, two of whom were priests, came in to Dharwar from a village a hundred miles distant. They had received some tracts at second-hand and were greatly struck with their contents. A young christian came into their village, read over the books with them, and induced them to go with him into a temple at some distance that they might worship God together in secret. By degrees as they continued to study these books, they obtained a clear knowledge of the gospel and seemed thoroughly to be converted men. They were soon after baptized. Similar baptisms of Lingaits have also taken place at Belgaum. It was in consequence of the decided progress of the mission by these baptisms that the Basle Society resolved to retain the station at Bettigherry, and found a new one at Guledgudda.

It must not be supposed that, from the facilities presented to the gospel by these sects, its progress will be unattended with trouble, or that the missionaries have only to receive new converts. Amongst those who are acquainted with its truths and are convinced of its excellence, thousands will be delayed in a public profession by the fear of man, their attachment to their family, the influence of the priest, and their love of the world. Not unfrequently have such men mourned in the hour of death, that they had not possessed the courage to proclaim themselves christians. In one case a Lingait priest died in great trouble, full of self-accusations, because he had not confessed the Saviour's name and been baptized. "Alas! that I have made delays! I have no faith in idols, yet I am no christian: and now I must die!" He then got up on his knees, repeated the Lord's prayer, sank down, and expired. Another guru on his death-bed declared his conviction that the gospel was true and desired his disciples to embrace it. Apart from the influences derived from family and home, there is in India one strong hinderance to the profession of the gospel by men who are convinced of its truth. There is throughout the Hindu mind a broad separation between belief and practice. This striking phenomenon has been witnessed in all parts of India: in ancient as well as in modern times. It affected the ancient schools of philosophy; it influences the progress of christianity. A Hindu can apparently without difficulty adopt a course of conduct, entirely opposed to the convictions of his judgment or the feelings of his heart. He has no desire to be a martyr. It cannot then be wondered at, that many who believe the gospel, keep their faith to themselves.

In other cases, however, the gospel meets with strong opposition. "Why do you always preach Christ?" the people will say. "Tell us that there is one God, and that idols are nothing, and we will agree with you." As in ancient times so now, the peculiar doctrine of salvation exclusively by grace, by gift not by merit, is a great stumbling block. The cross is an 'offence' now as it was then. It is singular too, say the missionaries, that sometimes when the Saviour's name is uttered, the most dreadful rage is exhibited by individuals, who with bitter animosity pour forth the most blasphemous speeches against his character and doctrine. Nor are all Lingaits disposed to hear the truth, or sincere in their enquiry after a true religion. Many oppose its progress and contest its arguments. One instance of ingenious malice, by which preaching was hindered in a silent but most efficient manner, we cannot forbear to mention. A bigotted Lingait priest, finding a missionary preaching in a village, caused the pepper in a shop close by to be stirred up, and was mightily pleased when the fits of coughing which followed, drove both the missionary and his congregation from the spot.

The deepest ignorance and most perverted views of morality present another obstacle to divine truth. One illustration will suffice. Mr. Müller once appealing to a man's conscience, with respect to the rewards of good and evil, was answered by the following story: A certain butcher bought a cow, tied her by a rope, and was about to bring her home, when on a sudden she broke loose and ran away. In running after her he met a man, who in his whole life time never told a lie, and on his asking him, whether he had seen his cow, he was told by him, that if he followed this road he was sure to get her. On went the butcher; not far off he met another man, who in his life time never told the truth, and putting the same question to him he was told, that he was quite in the wrong road, and that he must go to the left if he wished to find his cow. After this, both these men died, they were called before the judgment seat of God (Yumana) and the final sentence was that the latter, because he had saved the *life of the cow* by telling a lie, was rewarded with being born twenty times a king: while the other, who by telling the truth would have caused her destruction, was condemned for twenty life-times to be gnawed by worms. Confounded and perverted ideas like these are constantly met with, and though they are absurd enough to confute themselves, yet the poor people applaud and adopt them with superstitious fondness.

COLONY AT MALASAMUDRA.

In connection with the Canarese mission in the Dharwar collectorate the Basel Society tried an experiment of a peculiar kind with a view to smooth the way for the passage of enquiring Hindus into the christian church. Believing that persecution from their family and caste-mates is one of the greatest hinderances which enquirers meet, and that the formation of a village where such may for a time reside, would supply a new society and furnish new associations into which they might at once enter; in eighteen hundred and forty-one, the Dharwar missionaries founded a christian COLONY at Malasamudra. The original cause of the establishment of the colony was, their desire to turn to good account a temporary religious excitement among a class of people who call themselves Kálagnánis from believing in a prophetic Purána, termed Kálagnána or knowledge of the times. In this extraordinary book which may be about two hundred years old, great changes regarding the prevailing sects Brahmans and Lingaits are prophesied. Teachers of the true religion are described as coming from the west: and the fall of the great city of Seringapatam is announced as a sign that these prophecies are about to be fulfilled. Stirred up by these predictions, some of the leaders of the Kálagnána sect applied to the London Missionaries at Belgaum for counsel and assistance. Having failed in convincing them of their sincerity, they addressed themselves in 1839 to the Basle missionaries at Dharwar, and requested them to come and teach them the way of truth; assuring them that there were thousands of people of the same mind, who desired most earnestly to be instructed in the doctrines of the true religion. It was evident from the first, that the wishes of these people were not altogether free from worldly considerations; but the missionaries felt it their duty to take the matter up. Several visits were accordingly paid to the Kálagnánis; and the brethren at Dharwar and Hubli were now and then much encouraged by manifestations of an apparently sincere desire after truth on their part. At last, Mr. Frey who was stationed at Hubli, determined on going amongst them, and staid for several months at Bentur, one of their principal villages, instructing all who would come. Matters came to a decision in the latter part of the year 1840, when only twenty people appeared steadfast. These assured Mr. Frey that they would follow him to the asylum which he promised to establish for them; and measures were adopted to commence it.

Early in 1841, the Government granted the mission a piece of waste land, including sixteen acres of stony ground for building, and about a hundred for cultivation, on the same conditions on which Hindu cultivators receive such waste lands: and Mr. Frey, with the consent of the Home Committee, commenced building a mission house and a few native huts. When, however, the settlement was so far advanced that colonists could be admitted, Mr. Frey and his brethren were sadly disappointed by their inconstancy. All who had promised to come refused to give up caste and their former connections. The movement of the Kálagnáni gradually subsided, as they found themselves persecuted by their own people, and the whole plan, as far as they were concerned, fell to the ground. The experiment added another to the long list of proofs already existing that a broad line separates the christian community from the Hindus; that he who passes it, even as an enquirer, is a marked man; and that even the smallest approach towards christian convictions is resented publicly and privately as a breach of caste rules. It costs as much therefore to enquire as to decide. Nothing apparently will alter such a state of things but the entire abolition of the caste system. That consummation is hastened by every violent disruption of its bonds; and such must our converts for a time be content to bear, assured that their own sufferings make the way more easy for their successors. Failing in its special object, the Malasamudra colony has proved a useful location for the few christian converts which the mission has gathered in from the heathen. There is hope that it will share in the success which the other stations of the Dharwar Mission have recently begun to enjoy.

SECOND GROUP OF MISSIONS: MANGALORE.

The second distinct group of stations and converts in the Basle Evangelical mission is found in and around Mangalore. This town was the first location of the mission on its establishment in 1834; it has always possessed the largest staff of missionaries, and has in several respects been made the head-quarters of the mission. The labours of the brethren however are not all alike; the chief difference being the same as is found over all India between those of town and country stations. Mangalore has a large and important mission in the town itself: but there are two country stations in connection with it, at Mulki and Honore, on the sea coast, and distant, we believe, respectively fifteen and forty miles from that town. Of the latter stations we will speak first.

The narrow strip of land on the west coast of India in north Canara is inhabited by several varieties and castes of people. They are to a great extent Hindu, and the brahmins exercise the same sway over them as they do over the Tamils of Tanjore. Two castes are specially abundant, the Billavas and Bants; they are both low and poor, and amongst them the mission has obtained a large number of converts. The BILLAVAS are cultivators of the palmyra tree from which they make toddy: in name they resemble the Yiravas of Travancore; in habits and employment they are like the Shanars of Tinnevelly. The BANTS, called also Vokilme, are the farmer-caste, and live by cultivating the soil: they are a rude, boisterous people and rather difficult to manage. The fishermen also have given converts to the mission, but they are much addicted to drinking and less ready to hear the gospel. These people, with others like them, evidently constitute a portion of the aboriginal tribes of India: they speak not the pure Canarese language, but a separate tongue the TULU: and though subject to the brahmins, who are numerous in some spots, especially at Uddapi, their religious notions are in many respects distinguished from those of their priestly masters. Like the Shanars and Yiravas, these castes retain the aboriginal worship of Hindustan, the worship of demons: and like them, from a variety of causes, are peculiarly open to the instructions of the christian church. Of the peculiarities of demon-worship we shall now speak but briefly, as the subject will be fully discussed in the lecture on the Shanar missions.

The belief in demons is very deeply rooted in the hearts of the Tulu people, and many of them defend it with great warmth. They believe that there are a great many demons who, in by-gone times, were mighty men upon this earth but have left it as spirits and are now in the presence of God. They assert according to their ancient legends, that the demons asked God for food, and He advised them to get it from the Tulu people. If these give them food, which consists in the offerings of rice, fowls, pigs, toddy and water, according to the commandment of God, the demons pray for their worshippers, bless them in their house and business, heal their diseases, protect them from the influence of evil spirits and bad men, punish those who hurt them and can even be intreated to torment and kill their enemies. For this reason the demons which are supposed to have taken up their abode in a house, are called together every evening by the sound of a drum, as they may have left during the day the house committed to their care. But if these demons do not get their food, they are believed to visit men and cattle with disease and even death. When misfortune or illness occurs, it is ascribed to the demons. The priest is immediately consulted. He first looks at the stars, as the brahmins do; or according to their own fashion, puts a winnowing fan upon fresh boiled rice, pronouncing at the same time some magic formula, as the sticking on or not of the rice to the fan is considered ominous. He then names one of the demons or some deity as the cause of the evil. Upon this revelation, sacrifices are immediately brought to the offended deity, either in secret or in the presence of many others, and if a god is the cause of the misfortune, money and feasts for the brahmins are promised. In their public sacrifices, the priest and another worshipper of demons pretend to be possessed by the spirit, which is to be appeased by the offerings. There are demons who are supposed to be the guardian not only of houses and families, but of whole villages; for these a great feast is celebrated at least once a year, at which all the inhabitants of the village present their offerings; and people come from a distance to offer such gifts as they may have vowed to the demons, when in danger. Thus are they kept in constant fear and slavery.

Absurd as it may seem, the people hold to this worship with great tenacity. They offer a variety of reasons in its defence: and endeavour to shew that they have no ground for accepting the gospel in its stead. "We too worship God. Daily we invoke him, saying: Nárâyan our Lord, thou art our preserver, give us our daily food. We do whatsoever God puts into our mind. He causes us to do both good and evil." "God has sent these demons, therefore we are obliged to serve them, or they will kill us, or torment us in various ways. They are servants of the Great God, whom we must do our best to please, as we try to keep on good terms with the officers of the East India Company." "If the demons were nothing, how could they work miracles, kill men suddenly or heal their diseases in a moment." "We must serve both God and the demons. Our forefathers have done so and prospered. We should die if we forsook this worship." "The demons are kind masters; when we fall sick, we make or promise offerings to them, and they make us whole. When we wish to revenge ourselves, we may ask them to vex our enemies and they will fulfil our prayer." "What can *we* know of these things, we are blockheads. Who of us has seen heaven and hell, who knows what will happen to-morrow?" "As soon as God will appear to us in bodily form, we shall believe in him." "How can we meditate on such sublime subjects; we are wholly occupied with care for our food." These arguments appear weak, and easy to be answered; but they have acquired great strength among the people, and prove a strong obstacle to the acceptance of a better faith. The missionaries do not generally spend much time in refuting these errors, but rather try to effect an entrance into their hearts by appealing to their consciences, by convincing them of their sins and directing them to Christ. Coming as a religion of gentleness and mercy, as a religion suited to the poor and degraded, and finding less hinderance from caste prejudices among them than among the Hindus, the truth of the Bible has met with great success among these classes of the people. Including Mangalore, there are three principal mission stations among them: and the churches number two hundred and twenty communicants, in a community of five hundred and sixty individuals. Twenty years ago not one of these was a Christian. Mulki is the most important of the village stations. It was founded, and for several years managed, by Mr. Ammann, one of the most energetic and persevering missionaries in the Tulu district. It has two outstations attached, at Uchila and Gudde, and its missionary is in constant intercourse with the people at Cáp, Pertur, Uddapi and other places near, in which the Bant and Billava castes abound. The gospel has entered the door which Providence opened for it, and its preachers have now only to work steadily in this garden of the Lord, reaping the fruit of souls converted by his grace. It will readily be imagined that congregations newly gathered from the degradation of Hindu idolatry and of demon worship exhibit great weakness of moral principle, even where that principle does exist. Such "little ones" have been numbered among the churches in all ages, and the defects which prevail in their practice now, are precisely those which form the burden of the apostolic epistles when Christianity was new. The intellectual incapacity of the lower castes is also much against their rapid progress. They do improve and will improve still more, but at the outset it is found that they comprehend with difficulty the great truths of the gospel. Long and repeated instruction is necessary. When examined on what they have heard, they often say: We have it in our heart, but it will not come into our mouth. There is considerable truth in what a woman once said to one of the missionaries, who complained of her dulness in learning the word of God: 'If you pour water into a sieve it all runs out, *but still the sieve is made clean.*'

The mission in the town of Mangalore, like others similarly circumstanced, has to deal with both the upper and lower classes of the population. From the latter it has drawn a very large number of its members, including of course a few of the ubiquitous Tamils; but the higher classes have not been forgotten. Several years ago an English school was established, which was attended by many of the younger members of influential native families: while constant discussions have taken place with the mercantile and priestly castes, and the gospel been preached throughout the town. By these means several individuals both from among the brahmins and the trading classes have been drawn into the church. In December, 1843, three young men, who had long known the gospel and had nursed their convictions of it in secret, resolved to profess it openly. They were all brahmins. Two of them, Bhagavantráo Kamsika and Mukundráo Kamsika, were Concan brahmins, in poor circumstances, who after receiving an education in the English school had obtained employment in the printing office. The third, Anandaráo Kaundinya was a Sárasvata brahmin, and son-in-law of the Moonsiff, or native Judge in one of the law courts. On making their decision known, a great uproar took place. Instigated by their relatives, a mob broke into the mission house and tried to carry the converts away by force; but they were defeated and driven back. Perjury was liberally resorted to by the relatives of Ananda, who declared that his mind was deranged from severe illness. A pig was cut up and thrown into the tank of the Musalman mosque, in order to rouse the Mahommedans against the mission as well as the Hindus, but all was in vain. The magistrate of the district succeeded in preserving public order: though an appeal was sent to the Madras Government, the young men were allowed to choose for themselves; and were soon baptized as christians. The converts have consistently maintained the profession then made. The two Concan brahmins passed through the Theological class at Mangalore and have long been employed as catechists in the mission, where they are known as Christian and Jacob Kamsika. Ananda, who received at his baptism the name of Hermann, went to Europe with Mr. Moegling; received an education in the Basle Seminary, and recently returned to India as an ordained missionary, the Rev. Hermann Kaundinya. He is now engaged as one of the Tutors in the Catechist Seminary at Mangalore.

THIRD GROUP.—THE MA'LEA'LIM MISSIONS.

The missions planted by the Basle Society in the province of Malabar are in several respects the most prosperous. They are carried on in the important towns of Cannanore, Tellicherry and Calicut; and have out-stations at Anjerkándi, Chombala and Palgaut. The Moplahs abound in this district, and notwithstanding their fanaticism, which occasionally brings them even under the lash of the Government, christian truth is making its way, and sometimes obtains converts even from these bigoted Mahommedans. Throughout the district the population is much scattered: it is also very poor: the fishermen and slave castes are very low and ignorant. But "to the poor the gospel is preached," and while the proud brahmins reject its loving message, the lowly accept it and are saved. The village of Anjerkándi, one of the earliest stations of the mission, inhabited by a large number of the despised Puleyars, has been entirely christianized. The fishing villages of Tahy and Chirakal also contain many christian families. An entrance has recently been made into one of the strongholds of idolatry, the town of Táliparambu, and in spite of the influence of brahminism, a mission station is in full operation within its borders. The missionaries of the district are men of great experience, and have been assisted by a large number of able catechists. The native christian population of this province now includes nearly eight hundred individuals, of whom five hundred are communicants: yet the first station, Cannanore, was established only in 1841. The language of the people is Máleálim and differs entirely from both the Canarese and Tulu, which are employed in the other branches of the mission.

The experiment made in the Dharwar district to draw the heathen to the gospel, by establishing a colony for their residence, was in a measure repeated in Malabar. Near Calicut, are found persons of a very low caste, common through North Travancore: they are called *Náyadis* and in the general community, rank even below bought slaves. They live only in the jungle, like wild animals; sleep in the branches of trees, and at most make only the poorest hut for themselves. They are looked upon with the greatest contempt by other branches of the community. If a brahmin comes in their way, they must move off at least sixteen paces: and never must they dare to touch any one of a superior caste. Mr. Conolly, the Collector of Calicut, formed a plan for drawing some of this degraded class within the bounds of civilized humanity. He set apart some ground for them, built them houses, and gave them fields to cultivate. The government after a time relinquished this effort, and the missionaries, at Mr. Conolly's request and by the aid of his liberality, took it up. They visited the little colony: encouraged the people; endeavoured by kindness to draw them from beggary to habits of industry; gave them a schoolmaster for their resident adviser, and established a school for their children. They had much to try their patience: the idleness of their protegés was so inveterate. If they had a little store of food in hand, nothing would induce them to work, even when the ripe rice-harvest only required reaping. They thought however they discerned signs of improvement, and persevered. At length after some trial two or three were baptized. The Musalmans however three years ago, were observed very busy in their neighbourhood, and apparently had set their heart upon proselyting this little colony entire. Suddenly the whole of the people left, except the three baptized, and were received into the Moplah community. Processions, fireworks and feasts loudly proclaimed the joy and triumph of Islám. Such is another illustration of what has been called the hot-house system of missions.

A NATIVE CHRISTIAN LITURGY.

Till recently the Basle missionaries were allowed, in respect both to modes of worship and of church discipline, to act as each thought best; exhorted however by their committee to ADAPT the practice of their several European churches to the immediate circumstances of their native converts. In pursuing this admirable plan, the Society was guided by the conviction that it would be neither expedient nor just, to transfer, without alteration, the arrangements of the Evangelical Churches of Germany and Switzerland to the soil of India. Believing, however, from the great increase of converts, that the time had come when the practice of the mission might be rendered somewhat uniform, the Director of the mission, the Rev. Principal Josenhans, during his recent visit to Western India to examine the stations of the Society with his own eyes, directed a Commission, formed of the wisest and oldest missionaries, to compile a Liturgy and Code of Regulations, which should be as suitable to the circumstances of their churches, as their experience could suggest. This Commission has, we believe, completed its task, and submitted the result to the Committee at Basle for their approval.

The principles, upon which the Home Society acted in founding their Indian Mission, and have continued to act since its commencement, seem to us so good, and so worthy of imitation by others, that we quote entire the passage from their reports, in which those principles are detailed.

"The name of Evangelical Missionary Society is sufficiently expressive of the principles to which the Committee adheres, with regard to doctrinal and ecclesiastical differences. They have hitherto maintained against considerable obloquy, that the chief end of the Protestant Missionary ought to be this: to promulgate among the heathen, the pure doctrine of the gospel unalloyed by the peculiarities of the modern distinctions which have arisen between the Lutheran, Calvinistic, and other parties of Protestantism; that the differences in the creeds of our Protestant church are rather to be deplored as the fruit of human weakness, than to be boasted of, as infallible Shibboleths of divine truth; that our confessions of faith bear marks of their age and of human imperfection: but the Word of God alone abideth for ever.

"As to church government, the question whether a church ought to be ruled by bishops, or consistories, or synods, may appear of great importance among Europeans, not so among heathen converts of the present age. You may set up the appearance of the one or the other form of church polity, yet it will exist but in name. The personal influence of an active missionary will and must be every thing among his convert churches for a long time, and the future history of those churches, which are now in their infancy, will not exhibit the same features which are presented by the history of our European churches, but develop themselves under other circumstances in a different manner."

On this the missionaries add:

"These are the principles of our Committee, and we have hitherto found them as good in practice, as they are sound in theory. We do not all of us belong to the same church in Europe, but we rejoice heartily in the brotherly communion which, by the grace of God, we have with each other here *in partibus infidelium*. We have not been taught the same catechism, and have not learned the same version of the system of divine truth, but we find, that both among the heathen and among our converts and infant churches, all of us teach the same gospel, proclaiming the utter depravity and helplessness of fallen man, the holiness and love of God, the great salvation established by Jesus Christ."

GENERAL LABOURS OF THE MISSION.

Of the general labours of the mission, it is impossible to speak much in this brief review. It will suffice merely to point them out. The Basle missionaries, like their brethren in other parts of India, have paid considerable attention to SCHOOLS. Of these they have maintained three kinds. For the special benefit of the christian community, they have kept up *boarding-schools* both for boys and girls. Native Christian children, living in their neighbourhood, were admitted to their instructions. Formerly all such children were boarded at the expense of the Society: but of late, boys whose parents could support them, were returned to their homes, and only orphans retained upon the school books. The girls however are fed and clothed as before: female education not being sufficiently at a premium to allow the bribe of such support to be withdrawn from the motives by which it is sustained. The education given in these schools is but elementary; but it is accompanied throughout with christian associations and christian example, and as in other missions has been blessed to the increase of intelligent, moral and truly christian converts, especially the females, in the native churches. At present the three boys' schools contain sixty-three boarders: and the three girls' schools, one hundred and fifty-one girls. Another school at Dharwar has recently been given up. The *vernacular schools* for the heathen are also elementary: but they have been extensively employed in the several stations. There are now about forty such schools with twelve hundred scholars. They were formerly more numerous: but such schools always fluctuate. Many circumstances influence their usefulness: they are easily set going, and as easily given up. The *English schools* of the mission are only two in number; of these the school at Mangalore has been twice almost destroyed. On the first occasion, the missionaries resolved to admit low caste boys as well as brahmins and nairs. The second time, the Musalman boys left in a body, because they would not read the Bible there. The same battle has been fought in all parts of India, with the same result. The missionaries maintained their ground, and the scholars soon found that it was to their own interest to return and be content. Each school has about fifty scholars. Both at Tellicherry and Mangalore, there are *Industrial schools* attached to the boarding schools for boys. In both, the boarders spend part of their time in learning, partly in physical labour. They dig, sow and weave: they practise typography and book-binding. The school at Mangalore now enjoys the service of a watchmaker and typographic printer. The German weaver instructs many of the people in the weaving of shawls, turbans and handkerchiefs. The book-binding gives to the mission an annual profit of three hundred rupees. No mission can spread itself without the services of well trained native catechists: and the Basle missionaries with this conviction have for years maintained a *Catechist school* with a view to secure such labourers for their extensive mission. In order also to render the school efficient they have given to it some of their best and most experienced missionaries. In 1852 nine catechists went forth into the mission; and fourteen entered the new class established at that time. The course of instruction extends over five years, and in addition to the usual theological studies, includes a careful study of the Canarese language. Our readers may smile when they hear that from a natural partiality for their native tongue, the missionaries also teach their students German.

LITERARY LABOURS.

The mission has from the first devoted much attention to the press, and for several years two printing establishments have been in efficient operation. Both were originally lithographic: but two years ago a printer came from Basle with a fount of Canarese types for the press at

Mangalore: and changed the character of the establishment. The press at Mangalore has been occupied with the Tulu and Canarese books of the mission: the press at Tellicherry has been confined almost entirely to the Máleálim. Among the productions of the latter are a Máleálim grammar: Barth's Bible Stories; Church History; part of the Pilgrim's Progress; a Harmony of the Gospels; various Christian tracts and portions of the Bible. Among those of the former are tracts on Caste, on the Hindu gods; Canarese Proverbs; Henry and his Bearer; the Pilgrim's Progress; Barth's Bible Stories; a Canarese hymn book and the like.

Biblical translation owes much to the Basle Missionaries. Mr. Weigle for a considerable time gave his chief time to the revision of the Canarese Bible. This object he carried out for the Madras Bible Society, in connection with the missionaries at Bangalore and Bellary. By their joint labours the whole book has been completed and put into circulation. This labour was founded upon the translations of earlier years: in other cases they have originated translations of their own. The Tulu churches are entirely indebted to Mr. Ammann of Mulki for the translation of the New Testament into their language. This work was all printed at the Mangalore press. Dr. Gundert has devoted much attention to a revision of the Máleálim translation: and has already printed at Tellicherry the latter half of the New Testament. Lastly, Mr. Bühler has given to the mountaineers of the Nilgiri hills the first book in their own language, the Gospel of Luke. The 'Badaga Luke' was printed at Mangalore. Besides these christian publications, the missionaries have been printing for a considerable time numerous selections from the classical Canarese literature. The object of this little library, called 'Bibliotheca Carnataca,' is to furnish the missionaries, their catechists and scholars with complete materials for mastering the language, and for meeting idolatry on its own ground. The scheme has been carried on at the expense of one of the most liberal friends of missions in South India; and several works have already issued from the Mangalore press.

ITINERANCIES.

The missionaries of the Basle Society, in addition to other labours, have maintained an extensive system of itinerancies, throughout the districts in which they reside. Not confining their preaching to the immediate neighbourhood of their homes, they have endeavoured to spread gospel knowledge widely in the towns and villages near them. Each one of their annual reports contains interesting facts met with in their journeys: and pleasant is it indeed to follow them through the country villages, dealing with all classes of the community and discussing the great things which concern the salvation of souls. Thus the reader sees Mr. Albrecht gathering the Lingaits of Dharwar: while Mr. Ammann assails demon-worship among the lowlands near the sea. Thus Mr. Hebich is pelted with stones among the hills of the Coorgs, and Mr. Moerike makes his home in Badaga huts, that he may bring the Badagas to Christ. Among the fruits of such labour, imperfect in itself, but an important means of future usefulness, is the spread of Christian truth, the proclamation of the gospel as the one exclusive plan of salvation, among the population at large. The Basle missionaries accordingly report that the knowledge of the distinctive doctrines of that gospel is very extensively possessed by the people in their districts. Hence a conviction widely prevails that idolatry is foolish and must go down; the people attend the great festivals, more to see the crowd and to buy goods, than to worship heartily and in faith. In this way the *Yellama* jattra near Belgaum, and the Humpee festival near Bellary, are much reduced in numbers: and the cars cannot be drawn out and home. The moment a missionary stands up to preach, the people say "Ah, the padri is come, he will tell us that we are sinners, that we must repent and believe in the Saviour Jesus Christ." "Why do you always preach Jesus Christ, says another. Only say that God is one, and that idols are nothing and we agree."

On one occasion a missionary from Mangalore, travelling through the country to preach the gospel, was invited by the Rajah of Vittla to pay him a visit. He was most hospitably entertained for several days, and enjoyed many opportunities of conversing on religious questions with the Rajah himself, and with the numerous courtiers and attendants by whom he was surrounded. During one of these conversations the Rajah expressed particular anxiety on two things. He wished to know first, whether there was any medicine in the world to cure all diseases and prevent death: secondly, whether the art of changing metals into gold was known in Europe. On this text, the fear of death and the desire of wealth, the missionary preached unto him Jesus. All the Rajah's people, in his absence, expressed their conviction that idolatry and caste were the inventions of men: and declared at the same time their own intention to seek final freedom from trouble, not by works of merit, but by the attainment of spiritual 'wisdom.' Examples of such convictions can be readily multiplied from the Mission Reports. They shew the same results from public preaching as are being witnessed over all India wherever the same exertions have been made.

MISSIONARY EXPENDITURE.

There are one or two arrangements in the missionary economy of the Basle Society which differ from the practice of other Societies. For instance, it is a rule, made by the Home Committee, and re-affirmed by the missionaries themselves, that every missionary and mission family shall receive only a subsistence allowance, instead of a fixed salary. And in order to reduce expenditure as much as possible unmarried missionaries are expected to reside with others, receiving a very small pittance beyond the food which they eat. We believe also that they cannot marry without the consent of their committee being first obtained. In this way it happens that annually, twenty-five missionaries and sixteen missionaries' wives are maintained for the small sum of twenty-three thousand rupees. House-rent is not included in this calculation: their dwelling-houses belong to the Society, and the missionaries live rent-free. Building and repairs cost six thousand rupees more. The missionaries' journeys, moonshees, and postage are also all separately paid for. One result of this plan is; that the missionaries are able to save nothing. Those therefore who have children are left without means for sending their children to Europe; or for educating them either in Europe or in India. It was once thought that India was the best place for their children; but the most experienced of their number entertain a perfectly opposite opinion; an opinion entertained by all medical men; and confirmed by the practice of the whole European community, who from North India at least send their children to England by hundreds every year. The whole question has been remitted for final settlement to the Committee at Basel. They have received it in the kindest way, and are anxious to make such arrangements for the reception and education of the missionaries' families, as shall give perfect satisfaction to their brethren. For brethren, who have given up every thing but their daily support, the Committee can scarcely do less. In England and America, Societies exist for aiding the education of missionaries' children: and the Basel Society might benefit by some such Institution, either separate from, or as a branch of, itself.

A very large portion of the funds of this mission is obtained from christians in this country. The missionaries draw about forty-five thousand rupees from Germany; and receive from ten to twelve thousand rupees in India. One year they received as much as eighteen thousand rupees. This proof of the great liberality of the English christians in India to a German mission deserves special mention. It shows the great sympathy which is felt for their labours; and the hearty confidence with which the missionaries are regarded. The individual donations which their subscription lists exhibit are perfectly amazing. Subscriptions of *one hundred* rupees are quite common: but those of *two hundred, three hundred* and *five hundred* also occur. Such assistance has been eminently useful to the mission from its very commencement, and without it the operations of the Society in India would necessarily be greatly curtailed.

MISSION IN THE NILGIRI HILLS.

It only remains to give a brief account of the Basle Mission in the Nilgiri Hills. This beautiful cluster of hills lies on the southern border of Mysore, and forms a part of the great block of mountains in which the Ghaut ranges on the east and west coasts of India are fused into each other. The mighty convulsions by which they were produced, have left here the broadest and deepest marks. Several distinct ranges, of varied formation, have been thrown up within a small space; of these the Koondas on the west and the Nilgiris on the east are the most conspicuous. The Koondas are the most majestic: the Nilgiris the most beautiful. The pass of Konoor, by which the traveller descends the latter into the eastern plains, is one of the most lovely vallies in all South India. Upon its beetling crags and deep dense woods; on the light green jungle, and the gushing streams, amongst which the road winds for sixteen miles, the worn out dweller on the plains gazes his fill and turns away only to look again.

These hills are peopled by various sections of the aborigines of India, who in language, religion and habits differ entirely from the Hindus of the plains. They include 12,000 Badagas or Burgers: 400 Todawars; 500 Kotas, and 300 Irulas. The Irula tribe inhabit the feverish jungle which surrounds the base of the hills, and are in consequence a weak and sickly race. The Kotas occupy the eastern side of the Nilgiris, and from them the European sanatarium of Kotagherry is named. They have only seven villages. They cultivate the ground, have large herds of cattle, and are the blacksmiths, potters and musicians of the country. They are more energetic than other hill men, but are the most filthy and abject of all. The Badagas are the most numerous and influential. They are scattered widely over the hills and their villages amount to several hundreds in number. They are divided into four Nádus or districts, and are ruled by chiefs termed Gaudas. They live in a most patriarchal manner: all the branches of a family reside together under the same roof, under the rule of the head. The houses therefore are of immense size, like the tent of an influential Arab Sheikh; and often a few such houses constitute a populous village. The whole people are closely connected by caste and intermarriages: and form a compact mass almost impenetrable to foreign influence. Poor and low as they are, they have no less than nine grades of caste among them: and submit, like the Hindus of the plains, to the guiding tyranny of its rules. The idolatry of such a people can of course be only of the lowest kind: having its roots in the demon worship of India: but the brahmins have considerable influence, and the Badagas reverence Mahalinga and Gunga-ma. They are greatly enslaved by superstitious fear of demons and sorcerers who work in their name; amongst whom the Mullu-kurumbas on the slopes of the hills are most dreaded. It may be mentioned that all these hill tribes speak a rude kind of Canarese: and esteem the Tamil language, which they do not know, the language of true civilization.

Three large villages of Badagas, comprising about twelve hundred people, lie together in the very heart of the Nilgiris, in a peculiar basin, the name of which is KAITY. It is situated four miles to the east of Ootacamund, the European settlement. It is a beautiful spot, entirely surrounded by swelling hills, and having on its northern front, the full sweep of the mountain side of Dodabette the highest of the Nilgiri range. It is watered by several gushing rills: and the bright crimson rhododendron, the wild raspberry and blackberry, field marigolds, lupins, and numerous species of fern, both by their sight and sweet smell, call away the thoughts of English visitors to the land where they first beheld them. In this valley, with a design to benefit the poor ignorant Badagas, the late Mr. Casamajor fixed his seat, on retiring from the Madras Civil Service. He built a beautiful house, having a Badaga village close behind. He obtained first one, then another of the German missionaries to visit his people: and fairly set on foot a mission among them. Every day he received their sick and gave them medicines with his own hand. Every day he sat in his Badaga school, teaching the little hill boys the first elements of the gospel of Christ. He began also to translate the Gospel of Luke into their barbarous tongue. But it pleased God to take him away early: and he lived not to see his efforts meet with any success. By his will he left that house and property to the mission; a gift equal in value to Rs. 30,000: desiring that the whole establishment might be maintained after his decease.

The Mission was properly commenced in 1846 by the Rev. G. Weigle, who was then visiting the Nilgiri Hills for his health, and was completing his revision of the Canarese Bible. It was intended to serve a double purpose, viz. both as a station for the local mountaineers, and as a sanatarium for the numerous missionaries stationed in Malabar and Canara. In the latter respect, it has proved of great utility to the mission generally: while the former object has been also consistently kept in view. Mr. Weigle was soon joined by other labourers, and in a few years the settled staff at Kaity consisted of three missionaries, Messrs. Bühler, Metz and Moerike, who had made the Badaga language their special study. In carrying out their plans, the missionaries soon found that little opportunity existed for public preaching, and that they could best reach their ignorant charge by domestic visits and conversation. They have therefore maintained a constant system of itinerancy, and it is believed that but few of the natives on the hills have never heard the gospel from the lips of these indefatigable wanderers. They also established some schools; the scholars of which varied greatly in number with the fears or fickle disposition of their parents, or with the orders called forth by the policy of the heads of the tribe. To acts of kindness the poor are especially open: and the missionaries soon found that by gifts of medicine and attention to the sick, they had an access to the Badagas superior to every thing else. In one year they vaccinated no less than seven hundred children.

Hitherto they have received no converts, who have made a decided profession. Many have heard with attention, and many have expressed an interest in the truth. The name of Jesus has been uttered in prayer among their mountain torrents: and the New Testament daily worshipped as divine. By some the Saviour has been included among the number of their gods; by others he is feared as an enemy of their idols. The missionaries aware of these things, continue to visit and converse with the people, making their dim light clearer, and striving to remove their dense ignorance of every thing truly spiritual. They have recently added to their means of usefulness the translation of the Badaga Luke, begun by Mr. Casamajor and finished by Mr. Bühler. They still visit the idol festivals: and at the Badaga funerals, which multitudes are accustomed to attend, the missionaries are frequently present. So much is this the case, and so great is the increase of sound views, that the cry has recently been raised: 'You have ruined our country: why do you come to all our festivals: stay at home!' They have sown widely the seed of the kingdom: who can doubt that the harvest will at length be reaped.

The mission which has been now briefly described is not carried on by English missionaries, under a Government to which they naturally belong, and in a society of which they are born members. It is a mission established and maintained by foreigners for the welfare of the subjects of a foreign government. But to labours like theirs, what English christian will not extend a hearty welcome, and pray for a hearty blessing. Fellow-believers in the great truth of salvation only by Jesus Christ, they have become fellow-workers with us in seeking the conversion of Hindustan. Thrice blessed be their purpose: thrice blessed their holy toil! Cut off even more than others from home and fatherland, may they feel the sacrifice a thousand-fold made up by Him, for whom it is made. May their work be light, and their hands be strong. May their converts increase, and give them purest joy. May they soon find their sphere of labour brought entirely into the glorious kingdom of Jesus Christ!

LECTURE SECOND.

ON THE TAMIL MISSIONS

FROM MADRAS TO MADURA.

THE TAMIL COUNTRY.

The country occupied by the real TAMIL people is the plain which lies between the ghauts and the sea in the south-east part of the Presidency. It joins the Telugu land on the north; the river Kistna, between Nellore and Cuddapah, forming the boundary between them; and extends from that line southwards to Tinnevelly. This plain is nearly five hundred miles long and at its widest part, from Tranquebar to the foot of the Nilgiris, has a breadth of two hundred miles. Its soil is mostly dry, but several fine rivers, issuing from the ghauts run across it, of which the largest is the river Cavery. The country is watered twice a year. The north-east monsoon, blowing down the Bay of Bengal, brings large supplies of rain. The south-west monsoon, coming from the Indian Ocean in May, strikes the ghauts on the west coast and the high land of Mysore; and the rain thence produced, falling among the mountains, fills the rivers which run off towards the eastern coast: and thus the Tamil country receives large supplies of water for the second time without a drop of rain directly falling on it. This great plain contains some fine districts. The district of Chingleput, in which Madras is situated; as also Arcot and Chittoor, lie on its northern border. The districts of Salem and Coimbatoor lie along the ghauts, just under the Mysore province and the Nilgiris. Both are rocky districts and abound in various kinds of minerals. The province of Tanjore, between Coimbatoor and the sea is the most fertile of the whole. Its numerous rivers secure for the rich soil a larger supply of moisture than other provinces obtain: while again the value of this supply has been much increased by the canals and aqueducts which the Government has formed for spreading it over the widest surface. South of Tanjore and Trichinopoly, is the hilly district of Dindigul, and south of that again is Madura. Between them and the sea is Ramnad with the island and temple of Rameswaram. The Tamil country is in general flat, and in some parts appears sandy; but in many places it is pierced by detached and lofty hills, which give a most pleasing variety to the scenery. In this way appear the hill and fort of Gingee near which is a petrified forest; the Cheveroi Hills of the Salem district; the granite hills of Mahavalipuram, out of which the Seven Pagodas are cut; and the noble rock at Trichinopoly, with the French and Fakir rocks in its neighbourhood. Thus also have been formed the majestic hills on which the fort of Dindigul is erected, and those which surround the ancient city of Madura. Most of these hills I have seen and climbed with that peculiar pleasure, which is derived only from the contrast of a many years' residence on a perfectly flat and common-place soil.

THE TAMIL PEOPLE.

The people of this great Tamil plain are in most respects like other Hindus. They dress pretty much like the people of Bengal, except that all respectable natives wear a chapkhan or long-skirted coat above the dhoti or body-dress, and a turban of rather singular shape. The women are fond of coloured dresses, which they wear rather short; and often leave the head uncovered out-of-doors: a thing never done in Upper India. The workmen exhibit in some places the same ingenuity and skill which are found in North India. The goldsmiths of Trichinopoly, with their curious chains, their filagree work, bracelets and pens; the makers of pith-temples, mosques and figures; the carvers in ebony; the painters on talc; and the polishers of opal and marble, furnish illustrations of this fact. The people generally are divided into castes, as Hindus are in North India, but one great peculiarity distinguishes them from the Hindus of the north: namely, the existence of an immense class of *Parias* or out-castes. There are low castes in Bengal; as for instance the Doms, the Chandáls of Backergunje, the Háris of Burdwan, and the Báuris of Midnapore; these are however limited in number, and constitute compact castes of themselves. But the Parias of Madras are much more numerous, and from the consequent efforts made by respectable men to maintain the superiority of their own families, are much more despised and trodden down. The Sudra again, who is a nobody in Bengal, because the members of all castes form the bulk of the population, in Madras, as being a Hindu by birth, becomes, in contrast to the Paria, a gentleman and man of rank. This distinction between the races is carried very far throughout the Presidency: and we might be sure even *a-priori* that it would have an influence upon the christian church. Woe to the poor man who is born a Paria! However he may rise in wealth or learning, there is degradation in store for him all his days. The Parias form in many parts a third or fourth of the population.

Another peculiarity in the population, utterly unknown in North India, is the distinction into right-hand and left-hand castes. This distinction appears to have had entirely a political origin. It arose seemingly from a deep-rooted quarrel between the five castes of artizans and the brahmins. The goldsmiths, carpenters, blacksmiths, stonemasons and braziers, affirm that they are equal, if not superior, to the brahmins, and have full right to appoint their own priests: that the brahmins are usurpers, and did not exercise their present amount of authority in ancient days. A deadly feud exist between the two parties: and the brahmins in revenge declare, that these five castes with a few others are not proper descendants of Hindus at all, that they are of doubtful origin, left-handed castes; and that other Hindus, including the poor Paria, are right-hand or genuine. The disputes of the two have been sometimes brought by petitions even into the Madras Council Chamber, but the Government has refused to interfere.

THE TAMIL LANGUAGE.

The population of all castes speak Tamil. This language like the people, possesses peculiarities unknown to the tongues of the Bengal Presidency. It is evidently not of Sanskrit origin, like Bengali and Oriya: but is one of the indigenous tongues of India, and merely possesses Sanskrit words thrown in upon the top of it, which words are unknown to all but the educated classes. It has a most complete and extensive literature of its own, distinct from the Hindu Shastres; amongst which are celebrated books of poetry, of moral sayings, of philosophy and also of history. It is worthy of note that the older these books are, the more thoroughly free do they appear from any admixture of Sanskrit. It is evident from such facts that the Tamils were a civilized people, before the brahmins and sudras under Agastya Muni fell upon, and subdued them. Those who have studied the question best, consider that all the languages of South India, the Telugu, Canarese, Máleálim, and Tamil are of Tartar origin; and that a very close affinity exists between them and the Mongolian tongues, both in actual words and in the inflexions of nouns and verbs. It has also been shewn by Dr. Muller in his Bengali Grammar, that these parts of Bengali and Oriya which are not Sanskrit have the same affinity with the Tartar tongues. The Khond language is said to exhibit the best specimen of a Tartar tongue in the whole country. Thus the study of Indian languages enables us partially to trace the origin of the aborigines, whom the brahmins and sudras have enslaved, but who once roamed as lords over the soil of India. A portion of their numbers are still to be found in the lowest castes, or in the hilly jungles: traces of their original language also exist in the tongues spoken to this day; and where they have continued to be the largest proportion of the population, their language also has been less corrupted by foreign mixtures. The Tamil is the oldest of the South Indian languages: it contains all the roots of the Canarese and Máleáli tongues, besides others which they do not possess; neither do they possess such an extensive indigenous literature as the old Tamil has.

THE DANISH MISSION.

The first Protestant mission to India was commenced among the Tamil people. It was established by Ziegenbalg and Plutscho at Tranquebar in 1706; now a hundred and fifty years ago. When these servants of God reached India, nothing was known of the Hindu system, of Hindu caste, or the peculiar difficulties by which such missions would be met. But they gradually discovered them, and found too that the influence of their countrymen was also quite opposed to their own plans. They soon learned the Tamil and Portuguese languages, and began to prepare some small books for schools. One of their earliest letters contains mention of a plan for *buying* children for their boarding school: as 'they reckon the training of children to be of the greatest consequence.' They also think it necessary to lay some charitable foundations for the support of such heathens as by embracing the Christian religion are expelled from their possessions and for a time need help. These plans required considerable sums of money: and contain the germ of a system, which was partially continued during all the century. They next obtained from the Governor an order directed to all the Protestant inhabitants to send their slaves to be instructed, in order that they might subsequently be baptized. They then built their first church on the outskirts of the native town, and just on the sea beach. Their first baptism of *Tamil heathen* took place Sept. 5, 1707, when nine were baptized. I have read the entry in the church-book, having obtained a sight of the old registers, or a copy of them, during my visit to Tranquebar.

Three years after their arrival Ziegenbalg and Plutscho were followed by Mr. Grundler, a missionary of the same spirit as themselves; he laboured in the mission for eleven years with great zeal. A printing press and types, a printer and a physician, were also added to their establishment which they endeavoured to render complete. On returning to Europe for a time, Ziegenbalg found useful employment in directing the attention of English and Continental christians towards the infant mission. The royal families both of Denmark and England treated him with high honour, and gave him substantial aid for his labours. He lived but a short time after his return, and was soon followed to the grave by his colleague Grundler. They both lie buried in the large mission church, opened two years before Ziegenbalg's death: the one on the north, and the other on the south side of the communion table. Small slabs of marble in the walls above bear brief inscriptions to their memory. The antiquated building still exists unaltered. Their tablets and grave-stones; their old pulpit with its huge sounding board; the antique seats and contracted vestry remain standing to the present day. Long may it abide in testimony to that grace which made them such burning and shining lights in the days of dense darkness! Before their removal the New Testament had long been in circulation, and the Old Testament was printed to the Book of Ruth. Extensive itinerancies had been made through the villages around Tranquebar: many tracts and scriptures distributed; many children instructed: and great opposition and fear excited among the Roman Catholics especially the priests. Two large congregations had also been gathered, which were taught in the Tamil and Portuguese languages respectively.

The mission thus founded, was ably continued. At short intervals of three, five, and eight years, small detachments of missionaries arrived to take the places of those who died, or strengthen the hands and enlarge the usefulness of those who survived. The most able missionary, who immediately succeeded Grundler and Ziegenbalg was Dr. Schultze. He was a distinguished linguist, who had learned several European languages before his arrival: and soon made himself master of the Tamil tongue. He completed the translation of the Tamil Old Testament begun by Ziegenbalg, and having laboured eight years in building up the church at Tranquebar, was invited by the Christian Knowledge Society to found a mission in Madras. There he completed the second Indian translation of the Bible, that into Telugu; though as we have seen, it was never turned to account. His colleague Mr. Dahl, devoted his chief attention to the

Portuguese congregation, and continued his ministerial charge over them for twenty-seven years. What a vast amount of quiet, persevering effort, of patience and of trial must have been included in his toil, and in that of another colleague Mr. Bosse, who laboured for twenty-one years in the same sphere. Their very names are almost unknown, but the record of their service is with their Master who seeth in secret. At the same time with them, and after the departure of Dr. Schultze to Madras, the Tamil church had for its pastors, two very valuable missionaries, Mr. Pressier and Mr. Walther. The latter was an able scholar, and finding that the Roman Catholic priests, especially Father Beschi, were spreading extensively false reports concerning the mission, he drew up in reply, for the use of the converts, a work which he entitled *Ecclesiastical History in Tamil.* This book contains a masterly account of the rise and progress of the Christian Church; gives full and clear descriptions of the origin and conduct of the Jesuit Mission in India, and thoroughly refutes the many calumnies which the priests had circulated concerning the mission. It proved a powerful aid to the catechists and native converts: and was so unanswerable, that from the time it appeared, Father Beschi, the most able of the Jesuit writers then living, ceased to mention the Protestant mission in his works and argue against its so-called errors.

In the year 1733, the missionaries took the important step of ordaining one of their native catechists to the work of the ministry. The person upon whom their choice fell was named AARON. He had been from the first a pupil in one of their schools, had been appointed schoolmaster; then assistant catechist; and had finally become one of the three chief catechists in the Tranquebar mission. He was thirty-five years of age and had seen much experience. On his ordination, he was appointed to the charge of several congregations scattered in the neighbourhood of Tranquebar, but too distant for the people to attend the regular services in the mission church. He proved himself consistent and faithful: and upon his death another catechist, who had been his colleague for years, was ordained in his place.

The town of Tranquebar stands upon the sea coast, and has upon the land side, close to it, the great province of *Tanjore.* The town of Tanjore is distant from it only fifty miles; other important towns, like Combaconum and Mayaveram, are even at a less distance. During all last century, Tranquebar was under the Danish Government and Tanjore was ruled by a native prince. The missionaries had full access to the natives throughout their own territory, but found it difficult to do any thing in Tanjore.

Enquirers often came from thence, and the Raja himself at one time sent spies to bring reports concerning their religion and their plans. The gospel found entrance first into Tanjore through the means of a native military officer. His name was RÁJNAIKEN. Brought up a Roman Catholic he had been initiated into some of the outward forms of Christianity, but had never been taught its divine word and the depth of religious truth which that word contains. But God's good providence threw in his way a copy of the Gospels, and so delighted was he with the book, that, fearful lest the owner should take it away before he could understand all, he began to copy the whole out on palm leaves. Meeting with a man, who had been to Tranquebar, Rájnaiken enquired how more of these books could be obtained. The cunning fellow replied that he would get them for him; and Rájnaiken most gladly purchased several that the other had received as gifts. He soon found out the cheat, and went straight to the missionaries himself: from whom he received clear instruction in that religion towards which the Spirit of God was drawing his heart so powerfully. Upon his baptism, the most violent opposition was raised by the Jesuits and the members of his family: the latter however by degrees all joined him, and were received into the church at Tranquebar. Rájnaiken, immediately began a course of usefulness: and in order to increase it, he determined to leave the army and devote his life to preaching the gospel. He was settled, with his brother, in Tanjore; and was the means under God of bringing many in that province from the darkness of heathenism and Romanism to gospel light. The enmity of the Jesuits followed him unceasingly, but he remained firm. On one occasion his father was murdered before his eyes; and his brother nearly killed. On another occasion he was seized and beaten, and left for dead upon the ground. But the Lord preserved his life and usefulness to a good old age: and took him to rest after a faithful and remarkable missionary career of forty-four years.

The most prosperous period of the Tranquebar mission seems to have been the period of its first Jubilee, about the year 1756. Eight missionaries were then present; of whom three had been labouring nearly twenty years, and were men of great ability, respected by all around, christian and heathen. Swartz was at the time one of the junior brethren, having been at Tranquebar but six years. The whole number baptized during this first fifty years of the mission, amounts to about *eleven thousand*. The numbers added in different years greatly vary; sometimes they amounted to 300; 400; 550; 600; and in one year to 738. Deducting the children, the lists shew a large increase of adults: thus in 1747, three hundred were added from Hinduism, and eighty-eight from Popery and Mahomedanism. These numbers do not convey any great satisfaction to the mind, when we remember the principles with which the missionaries had set out, many of these so-called converts were slaves: others were people of low caste, who had nothing to lose and every thing to gain by being numbered among christians: others had been attracted by the pensions and charities freely bestowed upon widows and the poor: many had been children in their boarding schools. All enjoyed an improper freedom in respect to old customs and caste, which modern missionaries have justly endeavoured to put down. Often the missionaries found themselves deceived and saw apostates going back, whom only loaves and fishes had drawn to their side. Strong too were the prejudices still kept up between the higher and lower castes, the Sudras and the Parias. So strong were they, that the missionaries dared not to ordain to the ministry any but high caste men: although, as they confessed, on the retirement of Aaron, RAJNAIKEN, their zealous suffering Paria catechist, had from his sterling worth a claim to such office superior to all others. We may on these accounts not feel a complete satisfaction in contemplating this large number of converts during the first half century of the mission. But we must remember on the other hand, the many proofs which the missionaries had of the genuineness of piety in some of their converts; the calm and happy death, following the consistent life; and the patience under persecution to which many were at that time exposed. With these things before them, these servants of God, supported but feebly from the churches in Europe and living in India in troublous times, could not but thank God and take courage.

The first off-shoot from the Tranquebar mission was established at MADRAS by Dr. Schultze, at the instance of the Christian Knowledge Society in England. Its men were all supplied from Halle or from the Tranquebar station; but their salaries and other expenses of the mission were paid by the Society. Dr. Schultze laboured at Madras for fifteen years with fidelity and success. He founded schools, established a congregation and built a small church. The locality of his mission has been entirely changed in the course of years; but it long had small endowments of land, where the people lived rent-free and benefited by the same system of alms-giving which the mother mission had begun. Dr. Schultze's congregation gradually increased in numbers, receiving continual addition from the Roman Catholic and Paria classes. It soon lost however the benefit of his superintendence. In 1743 ill-health compelled him to return to Halle, and he retired from his mission work altogether: but the Tamil churches for many years enjoyed, in their completed Bible, the fruits of his Indian studies. Another missionary, Mr. Fabricius, arrived before his departure: and shortly after another, Mr. Breithaupt. These faithful servants of God laboured together in word and doctrine, and bore the burden of that increasing mission for nearly forty years. They were companions in the Lord's toil during life; and they died almost at the same time.

A third mission was established shortly after by the same English society between Madras and Tranquebar at CUDDALORE. Both the Madras and Cuddalore missions were on English territory; and to a certain extent were secured from the ravages of repeated war. Tranquebar was even safer; because the Danes kept themselves out of the political troubles of South India altogether. The former station, owing to the English wars did not always enjoy peace, but suffered greatly from the confusion of the times. Both had landed endowments, both cared much for their widows and poor; both therefore increased in numbers and always increased most in the years of the greatest scarcity. During the war, Madras was taken possession of by the French, under Labourdonnais, who immediately converted the church into a magazine, and otherwise injured the mission premises. Mr. Fabricius retired to Pulicat, but the native christians remained and lived in comparative quiet. On its restoration to the English a circumstance occurred, which had an important influence on the mission generally and on Mr. Fabricius's own fortunes. The Jesuit priests had acted throughout the war as spies for the French: and when the latter were driven away, the Government to punish the priests, confiscated their church at Vepery, and banished them from their territories. The church was then given over, with all its land and houses, to the Protestant missionaries, who at once removed their mission thither. Vepery lies out of Madras; that is, beyond the walls of the native town altogether: and in carrying thither a detachment of native christians and taking up their own residence with them, the missionaries exposed themselves to visitations from bands of soldiers and marauders, from which they would have been free within the walls themselves. Thus it happened that, ten years later, when Lally besieged Madras, though unable to get into the Fort, part of his native forces plundered the Vepery mission in the suburbs. They entered the mission houses, ransacked boxes and drawers, destroyed papers and books, and plundered property amounting to several thousand rupees, entrusted to Mr. Fabricius by various parties. Such evils happened occasionally: in the main the mission increased and prospered steadily year by year: so did also the mission at Cuddalore. The great confusion of the times kept the latter back, but it continued to grow till 1758, when the town was surrendered to Count Lally: the mission was deserted and Mr. Kiernander was compelled to leave the place altogether. On the restoration of peace in the same year, the missionaries, with one exception, all returned to their stations: Mr. Hutteman taking Mr. Kiernander's place at Cuddalore, Fabricius and Breithaupt returning to Madras; and the Tranquebar mission continuing as before.

Thenceforth the three missions ran forward together, conducted by similar men; who were born in the same country, were educated in the same place, and adopted similar plans. The TRANQUEBAR station was blessed with missionaries who were both able in their management and long-lived. Mr. Weidebrock, who died in 1766 is spoken of in the highest terms by heathen and christian! He lived there nearly thirty years. Mr. Kohlhoff senior, the first of the name, laboured fifty-three years: Mr. Zeglin, forty years; Mr. Klein, forty-five years; each steadily pursuing in his own sphere, either the Tamil or Portuguese, the particular duty assigned to his charge. To these succeeded three others, the last of the residents at the head-station: Dr. John, who came out in 1770, and lived forty-three years; Dr. Rottler, who began with Tranquebar, was transferred to Madras, and died in 1836, after a service of sixty years: and lastly Dr. Caemmerer, who arrived in 1790 and died after forty-seven years' labour. Their labours towards the end of the century were not of a very burdensome character. Stations in their neighbourhood, which had been off-shoots of the mission had then missionaries of their own: so that their care was required only for the churches in Tranquebar and the districts immediately around it. Their work was confined chiefly to the instruction of the congregations and the superintendence of the catechists. Of schools they had very few and those were very poor. Indeed throughout the history of the Tranquebar mission, the education of the converts' children had been greatly neglected. It was only towards the beginning of the present century that Dr. John, convinced of their importance, began to establish schools of a better kind: but the effort came too late and was soon retracted. The missions at CUDDALORE and MADRAS were carried on in the same quiet way; certain evils, connected with caste among the converts and with their pecuniary support, increasing in strength and becoming too influential for the missionaries to check them. An unhappy occurrence took place at Madras. After the death of his colleague, Mr. Breithaupt, Fabricius remained alone. He was a man of easy disposition, and therefore rather unfit to have the management of the extensive money-matters, which the care of the mission involved. Of the large funds in his hands, some belonged to the Mission Press, or arose from its land endowments: some had been borrowed in times of scarcity and not repaid; and some belonged to private parties. With a view to turn these funds to the best account, considerable sums not immediately required for current expenses were lent out: a large sum for instance was lent to the Nawáb's son-in-law at a high interest. Things went on prosperously for several years; but after the loss of several thousand rupees by the ravages of Lally's followers, clouds and difficulties began to surround Fabricius. By the repudiation of his claims on the part of several debtors; by the defalcations of one of his catechists, and by other calamities, the crisis at length came. A vindictive native threw him into prison, where he remaind fifteen months, overwhelmed with disgrace. He was of course compelled to resign his connection with the mission; and shortly after died at the age of eighty-one. Mr. Gerickè, who had till then resided at Cuddalore and Negapatam, took charge of the Vepery station. This distinguished missionary, the personal friend of Swartz, presided over the congregation for twelve years. He instructed and governed it with great wisdom, and in many ways greatly advanced its prosperity. The native christians declare to this day that his were the palmy days of the mission. To all external appearance it greatly flourished. He had ample funds at his command for the mission agents, both catechists and schoolmasters: and to the poor his liberality was unbounded. His labours however were not confined to Madras. He travelled extensively throughout the Tamil country, everywhere employing his great talents and influence in building up the church of Christ. His missionary career extended to nearly forty years.

It is time to speak with some detail, of the two youngest branches of the Tranquebar misson, the stations at TRICHINOPOLY and TANJORE. The celebrated missionary Swartz founded them both: and both were but the natural extension of the efforts steadily continued at the first station, Tranquebar. After a residence at Tranquebar of fourteen years, Swartz proceeded to Trichinopoly, then beset by the English troops, among whom he had some warmly attached friends; having found in that place a fresh opening for usefulness. In 1766, after the siege of Madura, whither also he had accompanied the army, Trichinopoly fell into the hands of the English, and Swartz took up his residence there. He built a house and school in the Fort; erected a church; and ere long was appointed, with a salary, chaplain to the English soldiers. He speedily founded a native church. In the first year, he baptized twenty persons; in the second year, twenty: in the sixth year, *five hundred;* the year following, two hundred: in ten years, altogether 1,238. At the end of ten years, he gave over the mission to an excellent and consistent missionary, Mr. Pohle, who conducted it faithfully till his death in 1816, a period of forty years. Swartz himself proceeded to TANJORE, with the view of founding a new mission. After some delay he succeeded in commencing it under favourable circumstances. I need not detail the history of this eminent servant of God, whose praise is in all the churches. He needs no commendation of mine: and it only remains for me to indicate two or three things which, it appears to me, had considerable influence upon his missionary success. His religious character was evidently of the highest order, and was the means of producing extraordinary confidence in him in native minds. His freedom from covetousness and from selfish aims, attracted all eyes. He was too a man of distinguished ability, of soundest judgment and wonderful prudence. But apart from his extraordinary private worth, his public position contributed to render his name great with the native population, ever anxious to secure a patron and a friend. His great influence with the English Government, who on several occasions expressed their high confidence in him: his successful embassy to the lawless chieftain Hyder Ali; his office as a member of the Tanjore Council of Government; his education of the young prince Serfogee; the influence he exerted on the Madras Government respecting his re-appointment to the throne, and the expulsion of the usurper, his uncle: the deference which the Raja paid him, when he remonstrated about his oppression of the peasants, and the immediate cure of that evil; and his occasional administration of justice in the Tanjore Court; all invested him with a political and public importance to which his brethren could lay no claim. The liberality he habitually exercised; his thorough knowledge of the Tamil language, and his ability to converse also in Persian and Mahrati: his celibacy too; and his position as a sincere and consistent religious teacher, were superadded, and raised his influence to a still higher degree. He made sincere converts, but it would have been strange, if such elements in his character and position had not tended with great power to draw many natives to him, to profess a belief in the christian religion as a means of rising in the world. Who can wonder that in the course of twenty years, he should have baptized two thousand persons, of whom he says two-thirds were of the higher castes: especially when he allowed the Sudra and Paria converts to occupy different sides of his church. The marvel would have been, that such men should not come at all.

One fact becomes at once patent, at the time of his death; viz. the extent of money that he was able to command for missionary purposes. The Tanjore mission received while he lived several gifts of land, including a large village; and at his death he left for its use no less than 85,000 sicca rupees. A few years later his friend Gerickè bequeathed to the Vepery mission in Madras, 67,000 sicca rupees. Thus, reckoning the money at its proper value at that time, we find that these missionaries alone left to the two missions over which they presided, a sum of money equal to £20,000. In life they had supported from these funds a large number of catechists, school masters and school children: and, at Vepery at least, Mr. Gerickè supported a large number of poor christians. To the same purpose the money was left on their decease, and the missions enjoy it to this day. The other missions had endowments also. That at Cuddalore had lands which at this time bring in about a thousand rupees a year. It is difficult to find out where all this money came from; our missionary histories have apparently not yet reached the bottom of the question. The stations constantly received gifts from individuals in the country, and especially legacies: but while their expenses must have been annually large, the supplies from Europe were but small; and a missionary's salary, in addition to a free house, was for a long time £50 a year, with a donation of ten or twenty pounds more; increased at least to £50; thus making a total of never more than £100 a year. In the case of Vepery, the Mission Press was a source of profit. However they arose, these large funds though they added to, and sustained, the agencies of the mission, could not restore its spiritual life. Before the close of the century, the churches at Tranquebar, Cuddalore and Madras had begun to fade; and when Swartz and Gerickè were dead, those of Tanjore and Trichinopoly followed them. A missionary or two remained at each place. Dr. John and Dr. Cœmmerer continued at Tranquebar. Pohle and Kohlhoff presided over the church of Tanjore. Dr. Rottler was at Vepery. No younger missionaries followed them to take their place as they grew old. The Evangelical Church at Halle, whence the strength of the South Indian Mission had been drawn, itself decayed and at last expired. Some of the later missionaries brought neology with them: and thus the missions lingered on and on till each of the old men was dead. Three of them survived till 1837: and one of them, Caspar Kohlhoff, died only in 1844. The total number of missionaries that had joined these several stations during the first hundred years of their history, is just above fifty: and their converts amount to more than fifty thousand. Whatever deficiencies there were, we must remember that the Lutheran missionaries were the very first to occupy the land: the first to find out what Hinduism really is: the first to oppose caste: the first to exhibit the peculiar character of Hindu converts; the first to meet the difficulties by which the work of Christ in India is beset. To the men then we must render high honour; as we admire the fidelity, consistency and perseverance with which they carried on their labours. They lived not in the days of missionary reports and platform speeches. No magazines chronicled their difficulties or sought sympathy on their behalf. Scarcely a man of them ever returned to Europe. They came to India young; in India they lived, in India they died. They lived amidst wars and raids, amidst plunder and confusion: they lived in an age of gross irreligion, and they fought their part manfully and to the last. Peace be to their ashes: honour to their memory!

The *conduct* of their mission and its long experience, convey to modern missionaries several lessons of great value. The attractions of influence and wealth increased the number of their converts. The missionaries being few in number, and latterly becoming fewer still in proportion to the demand for them, these converts were of course committed much to the care of catechists: especially as they were scattered in several places around the chief seats of the missions. With the strong prejudice which exists in South India between the castemen and those of no-caste, it was difficult even for the missionaries, and much more so for the catechists, to maintain among the converts the Bible doctrine of man's equality with man in respect to blood and race. That the missionaries did try to carry out the doctrine we know; but that the opposite doctrine did influence them, we also see in the case of Rájnaiken, who, though a more distinguished christian than his brethren, could not, because of his origin, be ordained to the christian ministry. With the introduction into the church, of men actuated by worldly motives, and with the increase of wealthy Sudras (as in Tanjore) holding important Government situations, the evils of caste-prejudice mightily increased. The influence of the missionaries was wholly carried away by it, and proved unable to stem the torrent of spiritual pride which was sweeping before it all the unity and even purity of the church. The dissensions of the Corinthians at the Lord's table were renewed in South India. The Sudra with the gold ring, the embroidered dress, and Cashmere turban, puffed up with pride of birth, was invited to sit in the high places of the church, while the poor christian Paria was bidden to stand in the doorway, taking care that he should by no means touch with his unclean body the garments of his holy superior. Such was the lamentable end of the first mission to India in its first stage. I have dwelt upon it long in order to put in a clearer light the present condition of the Tamil church. From this origin it sprang: out of these evils it emerged; and with these evils amongst others its missionaries are fighting to the present hour.

THE MODERN TAMIL MISSIONS.

The history of modern missionary efforts in this portion of the Madras Presidency needs only to be briefly sketched. These efforts have been put forth only since the commencement of the present century, and are therefore comparatively recent. Just as the light of the Tranquebar missions was fading away, the era of modern missions in England and America began. Attention was soon drawn and that most naturally to the country where they had so long been carried on. The first arrival of a stranger among the Tamil missions was that of Mr. Loveless, of the London Missionary Society, at Madras in 1805. As an interloper in the East India Company's territories, he would not have been allowed to preach to the natives, especially in those days of terror and fear of rebellion. Dr. Kerr therefore, the excellent chaplain of Madras, procured for him the mastership of the Madras Asylum by which he might procure an honourable livelihood, and prove useful to the community in general. After a while, Mr. Loveless erected a chapel in Black Town for the benefit of the East Indian population, then greatly neglected. By his gentle manners and unobtrusive goodness, he acquired great influence among them, and is remembered with affection to the present day. It was only after the charter of 1814, that missionaries were allowed to leave England for the Company's territories almost without restriction: but that charter once passed, the face of Indian missions rapidly changed. The Church Missionary Society began a mission in Madras under Mr. Rhenius in 1816, which was located in Black Town. Mr. Knill and others of the London Society joined Mr. Loveless; and commenced

Tamil services at Vepery and Persewaukum. The Wesleyan missionaries also entered the Black Town and Royapetta: and founded new missions both for Europeans and natives. Branches of these missions soon spread beyond Madras: and before the last Charter was granted in 1833, five stations had been established in the Tamil country, in addition to the old missions of former years, and to the stations also newly founded in the Telugu and Canarese territories. The progress of the Tamil missions was therefore but slow and gradual. Since the Charter of 1833, and therefore within the last twenty years, numerous additions have been made to all these missions. Several new Societies have entered the field; and many entirely new districts have been occupied. Within the same period, the old and decayed missions have been all revived.

At the present time the Tamil missions occupy a most important position. In the districts named above, no less than 67 missionaries are engaged either in the charge of christian churches or in preaching the gospel to the heathen. The catechists are 130 in number; and the native churches, include 16,130 individuals, of whom 4036 are communicants. The Vernacular schools contain 7100 boys and 2100 girls. The English schools contain 2840 scholars. The stations in which these missions are carried on occupy various localities, but are distributed chiefly into three groups; in the *town of Madras* and its neighbourhood, in the *province of Tanjore,* and in the *district of Madura.* Two isolated missions of some importance have gradually risen up at Coimbatoor and Salem, in the districts lying just under the ghauts on the borders of the Mysore. These two missions are distinguished by their admirable schools, intended both for christian and heathen scholars.

The town of MADRAS presents an aspect very different from that of Calcutta. In Calcutta the native population is concentrated in a solid mass of streets and houses, about six miles long and one mile broad. The native town is therefore compact and well defined, the river Hooghly and the Circular Road furnishing it with distinct boundaries. The suburbs also are similarly compact. But in Madras the native population is scattered over a wide surface, and appears in numerous separate districts. The part most densely peopled is the Black Town, probably the oldest of all the native settlements which make up Madras. It is situated close to the sea, having the suburb of Ráyapuram at its north end, and the Fort and Esplanade on the south side. It is a mile square, and is laid out with great regularity: the streets of the more respectable classes, the native merchants, being particularly clean and neat. One peculiar feature of the Madras houses contributes much to this neatness, the erection of the *piol* or covered verandah, which is placed directly on the road-side, and appears to occupy the whole front of the space in which the house stands. The *piol* does not appear in the brick houses of north India: though in the larger ones, there is provided a seat at the entrance for the door-keeper and his visitors. A small river running along the west side of the Black Town, quite cuts it off from the extensive suburbs; especially as there is also reserved to it a broad plain, where cattle are penned, sheep are fed, or rice is cultivated. Crossing this stream and plain by one of the numerous bridges, the visitor finds to the west and south-west, the important suburbs of Vepery and Pursewaukum, covering a large space of ground and containing a large population. South of the Fort runs the Mount Road leading to St. Thomas's: having on each side for some distance the best European shops. Between the Mount Road and Vepery is another populous suburb Chintadripettah, with a large bazar. Farther south are Royapettah and St. Thome. The European population, with the English churches, are scattered over this immense space of ground, greatly to the discomfort of visitors, who are quite lost in the bewildering similarity of winding roads, twin bridges, avenues and lanes.

The different missionary stations occupy the best spots in Madras and its suburbs; and several establishments have been founded in important villages and towns in the neighbourhood. As is proper for the chief town of the presidency, the residence of the heads of the government and of the mercantile community, the number of stations and missionaries is large: nor have they failed under the blessing of God to reap substantial fruit from their toil. The number of missionaries is thirty-two, supposing all present: and the stations amount to fourteen. The native churches include 700 communicants, in a community of 2,600 converts. As in Calcutta, the English missionary schools flourish more than in the country: they contain about 1,600 scholars. The vernacular boys' schools also contain 1,600 scholars; and the girls' day schools, 1,400 girls. The Auxiliaries to the Bible and Tract Societies are in a flourishing condition. The former has almost a larger sphere for its labours than any other auxiliary in India, owing to the great number of Tamil christians. The latter also excels many societies in possessing a very extensive variety of vernacular tracts, suitable not only to the Hindu and Muhammedan population, but also to the Roman Catholics.

The Black Town has received a larger share of missionary effort than any other portion of Madras: such effort having continued almost unbroken from the time of Schultz to the present day. The Church Missionary Society has under its charge five hundred converts and several vernacular schools. The mission occupies pretty much the site of Schultz's station in the division termed John Pereira's; in addition to another location of the society near Dr. Kerr's church. The London Missionary Society, in addition to its English chapel and the Free school attached thereto, maintains an English institution for native scholars. On the southern face of the Black Town also, the Free Church Mission has its well known institution both for male and female scholars and students: besides a branch school on the Mount Road in the suburb of Triplicane. On the sea-beach, the Established Church of Scotland has a similar institution, with a branch school at Egmore. These three societies have no less than 1,400 scholars and students in their institutions, in which as in Calcutta and Bombay, a thorough Christian education is imparted in the English language. Their day-schools for Hindu and Muhammedan females contain more than 700 girls, many of whom belong to respectable families: they are far superior to any thing of the kind to be seen in Calcutta. In the Black Town the Wesleyan Missionary Society has its principal English chapel: and there is a small native mission connected with it. Here also the American Board has its valuable press.

The suburb of Vepery stands next in importance not only in relation to the amount of its population, but also to the missionary labour expended upon it. The old Vepery Mission, founded by Fabricius and subsequently watched over by Gerickè and Dr. Rottler, is still continued by the Propagation Society: while the Leipsic Lutheran Mission has founded a separate station for a large body of native christians who sprang from the Vepery Mission, but disconnected themselves from it a few years' ago. In Vepery also and Pursewaukum, the London Missionary Society has its large native church, several vernacular schools, and the well known Girls' Boarding school under the charge of Mrs. Porter.

In Chintadripettah, lying between Vepery and the Mount Road, the American Board has its principal native mission, including a well-taught English school and several Tamil schools both for boys and girls. Farther south in Royapettah is the native mission of the Wesleyan Society, including a native congregation of a hundred and fifty persons and also several schools. The most southern mission is that of the Propagation Society at St. Thome, under the charge of Mr. Brotherton.

Every christian heart must greatly rejoice to witness the large amount of missionary effort exerted upon the native population in and round Madras, at these several stations; and to see the cordial manner in which the missionaries of different societies co-operate with each other. Many of them are labourers of long experience and great ability, who have grown grey in the Lord's service, and have spent their best years in promoting its interests. The history of their several labours, since the stations were established, is one of great interest: but deserves far more space than these few pages can allow: especially in view of the ignorance, blind bigotry, and opposition with which they have been met.

TANJORE AND MADURA.

The next group of missions embraces the stations established in the province of Tanjore, about a hundred and eighty miles south of Madras. The province extends chiefly from east to west, and comes down to the sea-coast. Three missionary societies are located here, all of which are comparatively recent, though the missions they have taken up are the oldest in the country.

The Leipsic Lutheran Mission has received charge of the churches and stations originally established by Ziegenbalg and his successors. Their first missionary, the Rev. H. Cordes, arrived in 1840, and was subsequently followed by several brethren. Their special sphere of labour embraces the two mission stations in Tranquebar itself, the station at Poreiar outside the town; and new stations at Mayaveram and Podukottah; all lying at the eastern end of the province. The native christians in these places amount to more than two thousand.

The Propagation Society entered first upon the two old stations at Tanjore and Trichinopoly, founded for the Christian Knowledge Society by Swartz: but as the missionaries increased in number, new missions were opened at Combaconum, Boodaloor, Canendagoody and other places, which had been outstations of the older missions or become the residence of the converts. All the congregations were found in a most low and formal state, with but little spiritual life among them; and greatly enslaved by caste prejudices which divided into perfectly distinct sections those who professed to be one in Christ. Measures were however taken to secure more efficient missionary instruction and superintendence: to raise the character of native agents, and to give a regular training to the young. The caste question also was taken up, and attempts were made to reduce its influence and correct its evils. It is satisfactory to know that everywhere improvement is visible, especially in the spirit and character prevailing in the new stations, founded upon better principles and with more watchfulness over special evils than the original ones. The greatest difficulties have been encountered among the more respectable converts of the older missions, who are unwilling to give up what they consider inalienable rights. These missions include more than five thousand christians in eight principal stations, with several schools, and a seminary for training native catechists in the neighbourhood of Tanjore. The Wesleyan Missionary Society has also two native missions in the Tanjore province at Manargoody and Negapatam.

The third group of Tamil missions has been established in the districts of Madura and Dindigul, lying between Tanjore and Tinnevelly. These missions belong to one single society, the American Board, and have been established and maintained on a regular system. The society has taken up the Madura district, determined to occupy it and it alone, until its missionary work therein is completely finished. The head-quarters of the mission are in the city of Madura, the former residence of Robert de Nobili and his celebrated Jesuit companions: and all the other stations, eight in number, lie round the city at greater or less distances, none being very far. The missionaries are thus always able to communicate with each other in times of emergency, and do not become hypochondriac from long living alone. All the missions are admirably placed. Madura, with its ruined palace, the residence of the powerful Telugu kings; its great temple and choultry; its numerous and influential brahmans, its well-built streets and large population, is the location of three missionaries, of whom one is a physician. Dindigul, with its mighty rock and large compact town, is the residence of two missionaries. At Pasumalie, just out of Madura, is the Mission Seminary, where the society is endeavouring to raise up both catechists and school-masters for the service of the mission. All these and the other stations of the society have village congregations attached to them, which occupy a large share of a missionary's attention, and by which the gospel is making progress among the people generally. These congregations have undergone considerable change since the mission was established. At first many people gathered round them after the example of the Tanjore christians, from very inferior motives. They came anxious to have the counsel of a European friend; to secure a means of livelihood; dissatisfied with their own gods;

wanting to be instructed, without any idea of what the gospel is. Of these many subsequently left. Perhaps the headman of a village died, and without him the christians were unable to withstand the opposition of their neighbours. Or perhaps a catechist was dismissed for conforming to the rules of caste, and in revenge took the people with him: or perhaps the rules against caste, or other means of discipline, were enforced among the people to their dissatisfaction, and with a view to *punish the missionary* (as they sometimes do in Bengal), they stopped away from church, took away their children from school, and gave up christianity altogether. Yet good has been done; and as the people have come to learn what the missionaries teach and what they mean to do, more steady congregations have gradually gathered around them, and a larger number of sincere, stable converts been admitted into their communion. The same change has come over their schools. At first they established schools for all classes, Hindus and Musalmáns. But as they enforced their discipline there also, and refused to recognise caste customs in the seats of their scholars, many left: the schools have by degrees been changed into schools for the especial instruction of the christian children of their own people. These missions, have in many ways, received tokens of the blessing of God; and amidst general prosperity, have observed in individual cases proofs of the exercise of his grace. Amongst such instances the following possesses points of peculiar interest.

There was an old Guru or priest, a few miles from Madura, a man of great influence amongst the people, who was consulted on all occasions of difficulty and regarded as the oracle of the country round. Clothes on which he had breathed or his hand been placed, were taken to the sick that they might recover: and mantras and charms were repeated by him in order to cure them. He was looked on by all the people as a man of great power, and to maintain his dignity and authority among them always had a silver wand carried before him. Amongst others he had heard of the missionaries in the district and was accustomed for years to read christian books which they had distributed. Indeed he had quite a small library, kept as usual in an earthen jar, but the words of truth had made no impression on his mind. One day, when walking in the bazar, he heard a catechist reading a passage from the Gospel of Luke. It struck him most powerfully. "What is that you read?" he instantly asked; "read it again." The catechist read it. "What a wonderful thing," exclaimed the guru, "where do you find it?" "It is written in Luke, a christian book, a portion of our Bible." "Why,

I have got Luke and have read it; but I never saw this statement, kindly read it again." The next day he sent for the catechist and requested him to read the wonderful passage once more. From that hour he received the gospel without reserve: experienced the greatest joy in his belief, and continued happy till his death. His religion however was not acceptable to his friends and disciples: his sons were perfectly aghast when he told them of his change of faith, and did all they could to induce him to give it up. "What a pity," said one, "that so much learning should make a man mad." They reproached him, and persecuted him continually. Often when he was on the way to the missionary, they would fetch him back and compel him to forego his visits. But he persevered, bore all the opposition with great patience, and looked forward with confidence to a secure repose in heaven. He lived thus for five years: his death was hastened by a chronic complaint, produced by some drug which he had taken in former days from a sannyási that he might be able to fly! He earnestly begged of his sons that he might be buried instead of burned: they complied with his request, and arrangements were subsequently made for putting a monument upon the grave.

A HILL MISSION.

On the western border of the Madura district lies a splendid range of Hills, the Pulneys, as large and as high as the Nilgerries. The eastern face is in one part a precipitous wall three thousand feet in height: and in other portions immense clefts exist by which the curious descend into a huge cave. These hills throw off numerous spurs towards the east: several ranges occur close to the foot of the Pulney Hills, two of which inclose a picturesque valley, called the valley of Dindigul. Detached hills also stand out in the very centre of the plain: as the Secundra Máli, near Madura: and the Rock on which the Dindigul Fort is erected. All these hills have been occupied as posts in war, and have played an important part not only in the history of the East India Company, but in the struggles of the different dynasties of the country, especially the Brahmins and Jains. Among the low spurs at the eastern border of these Pulney hills, the Society for Propagating the Gospel has a mission among a poor but simple people, remains of the aborigines. No obstacles to the gospel exist among them greater than their intense ignorance; and Mr. Coyle, their missionary, has received much encouragement in his efforts to instruct and enlighten them. They are quite simple and even patriarchal in their manners: and like things to be done with great form and ceremony. They are also great talkers, and at their meetings whether social or religious, one and another will rise to make their little speech. As an illustration of their manners, the following fact may be mentioned. One day Mr. Bower of Tanjore was preaching to them on the goodness of God's providence; and shewing how he orders all things well to his own people, who love him and pray to him. In the midst of the sermon a man stood up and requested permission to ask a question. The permission being granted, he said: "If God does rule over all as you say, and govern every thing for our good, how was it that my house was burnt down three nights ago to my great loss?" Mr. Bower was thinking how to answer him, when Abraham, a shrewd old leader among them, requested permission to ask the man a question in return: "Friend, he said, did you say your prayers that night?" The man looked down, then up, and confessed that he had not prayed that night as he ought to have done. "Well then;" replied his interrogator, "how could you expect to enjoy God's protection under such circumstances."

CASTE IN THE NATIVE CHURCHES.

I will conclude this notice of the Tamil missions, by a few observations on a subject of peculiar interest, namely, caste among the native christians. On this vital question to an immense extent depend the stability and purity of the churches in South India: and no estimate of their religious character, from which this element is omitted, can be of any worth. It has been often spoken of, written of, and discussed, but it still forms a difficulty to every pastor, and requires to be watched with a most vigilant eye. It is more to be found in connection with the Tamil christians than any others: and it is, because I think that the true key to the present condition of the Tamil churches is to be found in their past history and especially in the later history of the Tranquebar missions, that I have dwelt upon it at so much at length. Several circumstances must be remembered before the growth and subsequent great influence of the caste spirit among the converts can be truly understood.

1st. There exists in the Tamil population a very large proportion of a *Paria* or *no-caste* class, a people who are greatly despised by all other castes; and though having distinctions among themselves, are yet at an immeasurable distance from the Sudras and Brahmins. This is the root of the evil from which all the rest has sprung.

2nd. Throughout the Tamil country, the *Roman Catholic converts*, also called Christians and numbering many thousands of individuals, preserved among themselves the same distinctions of caste rank, which prevailed in the Hindu community. They did so from the very first; they did so all last century, and they continue to do so to the present day.

3rd. The Tamil churches at their commencement contained a large element of *nominal* Christianity, from the fact that slaves and others, with poor knowledge and no character, were baptized as Christians.

4th. The large bounty bestowed upon the poor added to the class of nominal professors especially at a later period in all the Tanjore and Vepery Missions.

5th. The small number of missionaries appointed to instruct these large and scattered christian communities, demanded an unusual amount of *native superintendence* and management. This was a great disadvantage, inasmuch as the highest purity of principle and the most vigorous arm were required to watch the evils beginning to arise.

6th. The increase of wealthy Sudra christians especially in the Tanjore kingdom tended to separate the different classes of christians still more: the worldly motives for which they changed their religion, preventing them from also changing the views they had previously entertained of their essential superiority to the Paria classes in blood and race.

7th. The moderation and gentleness with which the case was met, when first noticed, permitted the evil spirit to grow and increase. Though it was ever condemned, yet at the great stations, Tranquebar, Tanjore, and Vepery, no special measures were taken to put a stop to it.

When the modern era of missions in South India began, the new missionaries, wherever they settled, soon found themselves visited by native christians, the converts of the older missions or their descendants. They were found all over the Presidency: at Mangalore and Cannanore on the west coast: at Bellary, Dharwar and Secundrabad: at Bangalore, Cuddapah, and Vizagapatam: great numbers were connected with the army, and are so still. After a time, the missionary discovered in almost every case, that caste rules and customs were being observed by the native christians among themselves, though they might wish to conceal them or explain away their real force. The case, however, was taken up in novel fashion: these new missionaries anxiously endeavoured to check the evil and took measures for that end, not believing (as they were assured) that it would at length die out of itself. Mr. Rhenius and Mr. Haubroe both missionaries of the Church of England, were the first to take up the matter in earnest: and strove hard to effect a change in the views and practice of their christians: but the opposition was very great. The Vepery christians brought an action against Mr. Haubroe for interfering (as they said) with their customs: and many signed a covenant, binding each man to pay a fine of twelve rupees who should either attend his preaching or send a child to his schools. Dr. Rottler, Mr. Haubroe's colleague, and others advocated moderation—moderation: hoping that the evil would eventually cure itself: though it was evident that moderation had been tried long enough, and that the disease under such treatment was threatening to destroy the life of the Tamil church altogether. The christians, where there was the greatest moderation, were, in respect to caste, the worst of all. That fears respecting such a lamentable result were not groundless, will be seen from a contemplation of some of the forms which the evil has assumed. CASTE from its very nature, its origin, and the Hindu authorities by which it is expounded and enforced, declares both implicitly and explicitly, superiority in blood and origin of one class of men over another. It declares that Brahmins were created higher than Sudras; and Sudras higher than Parias: and to prevent their amalgamation, forbids intercommunion either by marriages or by common meals. This is the basis of the distinction, and the mode in which it is enforced among the Hindus down to the present hour. It refers to and includes social distinctions; but its origin, nature and authority are essentially religious. Among the native converts in the Madras Presidency in the worst days, it appeared in this way. The Sudra christians refused to sit on the same side of the church with the Parias. They would not drink at the Lord's supper *with* them or after them. They would not in common life eat their food, or drink their water. They would contract no marriages with their families, however wealthy or respectable they might become. They rather married into heathen families of their own caste, than among christians of a lower caste. A Sudra catechist would not enter a Paria house: nor could a Paria catechist preach to a congregation containing Sudras. At their weddings and feasts, the christians retained the processions, drummings and other old customs of heathen origin, in which their heathen friends and castemates took a part. They had changed the name of their religion, and the object of their worship, but they were still worshippers of themselves; and they set aside the beauty, the love and the gentleness of the gospel for their own heathen laws. It may be asked, did these christians apply to their missionary, a foreigner by birth, the same rules which they applied to their fellow-converts. They did apply them; and consistently regarded him as an outcast, a Paria, in all things except his instructions. They would not invite him to eat with them: nor could he invite any of them in return. In some cases christians have refused their missionary permission to draw water from their well. Illustrations of these facts, well known in the Presidency, are as follows. One of these Sudra christians wished to be ordained in the Church of England; and when Bishop Spencer spoke to him on the subject of caste, he asserted that he maintained nothing more than the civil distinctions which prevail between the higher and lower classes of society. To test the assertion, the Bishop replied: You must allow that I am in a social position higher than you, and especially, as a Bishop, am your ecclesiastical superior: come and dine with me, there can be nothing derogatory to your character in dining with your Bishop. Consistency forbade him to refuse the invitation: but when the day arrived, he complained of illness and went into the country. For a long time the Bishop refused to ordain him, though eventually he did so. To the brother of this gentleman, a missionary once used the following argument: "If your caste rules forbid intercourse with men of different origin from your own, you cannot eat with Englishmen even of the most illustrious name. You could not eat with Luther, or Calvin or Baxter." "No! he said; he could not." "More than all; if the Lord Jesus, your own Saviour, were to come down from heaven, as he once came, born among the Jews, you could not consistently eat with him!" He frankly confessed that he could not: so superior in his estimation was his vile caste to that of even our blessed Master! The same argument has been used with many other caste christians, and always with the same reply.

If SUCH be the conclusion to which caste principles consistently lead, can argument be needed to prove the mighty evil they must do to the Lord's church: or to urge on all pastors the necessity of rooting them out. Later missionaries in founding new missions have almost invariably begun on better principles than their predecessors. But great watchfulness has been required to see that the caste-spirit, always ready to spring up, made no head in the church. In some places, as at Chittoor, Bangalore, Cuddapah and Calicut, the attempt to free the church from the evil, has broken it up altogether: while in many others, it has produced continual disturbance. I heard several facts illustrative of its working in the Madura circle of missions. In the boys' boarding school, where all ate together, it was found that the Sudra boys kept to particular plates, in order to avoid eating from those, which had been touched by the Paria scholars. The Paria boys entered into the dining room by different doors from those which the Sudras used. The Paria and Pullar boys were made to sleep on one side of the room by themselves. When the missionaries mixed up both the boys and the plates, the school was cleared. Subsequently when their parents found that the missionaries continued firm, they allowed them to go back. Again some of the catechists would not go to Paria villages. One of them openly begged a missionary not to enter his house; alleging that as he was of high caste, it would cost him a considerable sum to get it PURIFIED! Worst of all, it was found that the Sudra catechists told the Parias NOT to become Christians. Before the missionaries they pretended to invite them; behind his back they threatened them with pains and penalties, if they agreed to do so. What a horrible state of things among missionary churches! All this has long since been put away from the American Mission. Various tests were employed, such as eating in common, by which the agents were proved: all caste catechists, school masters and church members were dismissed: and since then, the Lord has blessed the preaching of his word with great success.

Several years ago the Bishop of Calcutta, after visiting the Tanjore Mission, and observing the low condition to which its churches had sunk, determined to put down the caste observances there. His earnest letter tended much to arouse the attention of missionaries generally to the important subject: though numbers of the native christians refused to submit to the tests which he suggested, and refuse to obey his injunctions to this hour. More recently the Madras Missionary Conference and the Presidency missionaries generally, having taken the case into consideration, also agreed to act unitedly against it: and they are now endeavouring to enforce throughout their missions that glorious principle of the gospel; that "God is no respecter of persons; but that he hath made all nations of men of one blood." The fact that such a united effort should have been required only four years ago, exhibits clearly the extent of the injury which the caste-spirit has produced, the influence it continues to exert, and the tenacity with which the christian population hold to the system they have proposed to abandon. With truth may it indeed be asserted, that these efforts have not been made in vain. An improvement in the Tamil churches has been seen every where. In almost all missions, the various native agents, who are equal in social rank, are accustomed to eat together and associate on equal terms. The Lutheran missionaries at Tranquebar, who did not sign the Conference circular, though (as they assured me) they did not disagree with its principles, have recently laid down the rule, that no one shall in future be appointed to the office of Catechist, unless he abandons caste-customs. The number of the caste-christians in Tanjore and Trichinopoly, who have refused obedience to their Bishop's mandate, is not increasing but rather losing ground. And if all missionaries remain watchful and faithful, there is strong reason to believe, that the more open manifestations of the caste-spirit will ere long entirely disappear. Much remains to be effected, before the churches give up the more private influences of the old leaven, and retain nothing but the ordinary distinctions of social life among them. One can scarcely hope that the proud spirit will be easily eradicated: or that the missions will be thus thoroughly purified, so long as the large Paria caste exists all around them. I sympathise with our brethren greatly on this account, and feel that we in North India may be truly thankful, that the difficulty scarcely touches us at all. It seems to me that the only radical cure for so tenacious and deep-seated a disease is a *very, very high elevation* of the intelligence and the christian character of the Tamil converts.—May that be sought for, and speedily bestowed by the Almighty Spirit of God.

LECTURE THIRD.

ON THE MISSIONS AMONG THE SHÁNÁRS

IN

TINNEVELLY AND SOUTH TRAVANCORE.

Of all the Protestant Missions, which have been established in India, the mission in TINNEVELLY has been more extensively spoken of, and is better known by name among christians in general than any other, unless it be the mission in Krishnaghur. And many are the circumstances which justify the notice it has received, and the interest it has excited in the church at large. The great fact that in Tinnevelly there are thousands of native christians is quite true; but in regard to other points: such as, what sort of christians they are; why they became christians in such large numbers; and how the gospel is really progressing among them, not a few mistakes are prevalent, which it may be well to correct. During my recent visit to Madras I spent nearly a month among these missions and the kindred missions of South Travancore in their immediate neighbourhood. I saw much of the country and of the people; preached by an interpreter in several of the churches; examined many of the schools, and had numerous conversations with the resident missionaries upon various topics connected with their work. It was these two missions that I particularly wished to see, and my lengthened stay in their various stations has given me perhaps a deeper impression respecting them, than I received concerning any others. To understand a mission thoroughly, we should know something of its locality; the people among whom it is carried on; their former condition and history; their habits of life; the history of missionary effort among them; and its present character and fruits. I shall endeavour to notice all these subjects in the following sketch.

THE SHÁNÁR COUNTRY.

TINNEVELLY and TRAVANCORE are the two provinces which lie at the very southern extremity of Hindustán. They are separated from each other by a range of ghauts running from north to south between them like a huge back-bone. These mountains are in many parts high and precipitous, covered with jungle, and very dangerous to health. Their highest part is to the north, where they spring from the Nilgherry hills: the Pulney hills on the west of Madura here form a part of the range. As they advance to the southward they become lower, and passes easily ascended have been formed right across them. At length five ghauts appear standing alone, one after the other: the level ground runs forward quite flat for six miles, diminishing in width, and at last ends in a low reef of black rocks at Cape Comorin. TINNEVELLY thus lies between the ghauts and the eastern sea; TRAVANCORE, between the same ghauts and the Indian Ocean. The province of Tinnevelly, called by the natives PANDY, is about a hundred and fifty miles long; and in its upper part is seventy broad. It is a dry country, watered like Tanjore and the other eastern provinces of the Madras Presidency by rain at the end of the year and by the full rivers in May. Shut up on the west by these high and majestic ghauts, and lying only eight degrees from the equator, its climate is very hot, especially in April and May, the summer season. In many parts, broad barren plains spread out for miles and miles, covered with low bushes and grass, varied here and there by the graceful umbrella tree; and containing extensive swamps. Along the east coast, the sub-soil is chiefly sandstone, and being impregnated (like all the country from Orissa to Cape Comorin) with iron which is rusted by the air, naturally produces wide spread tracts of loose red sand. There are three such tracts of special note in Tinnevelly, called Tieris; of which two cover no less than forty square miles each. Except in the centre, they are covered with forests of palms. No roads are formed through these red deserts; foot-prints are every where visible; there are no standard marks to point one way more than another, and except by day, or during the clear bright night, it is next to impossible to travel across them to any direct spot. Almost all missionaries of long standing in Tinnevelly have at one time or other lost themselves in the sandfields and wandered about a whole night in the dense darkness. I crossed all three, and lost my way on two occasions. The north part of Tinnevelly is more suited for tillage than the south: and there is found the black soil, so favourable to the growth of cotton: of this district Tuticorin is the chief port. The great feature which distinguishes all central and southern Tinnevelly, especially near the sea, from other parts of the country, is the abundant growth of the PALM TREE: exactly resembling the TÁL, or fan-palm of Bengal. Wherever the traveller's eye turns he sees scarcely any thing but palm trees. In some places they closely cover such immense tracts as to become forests, containing many thousand trees. In others they are fewer in number and only appear as copses or topes. The red sand-fields are in great part covered by the palm forests. "God hath made every thing beautiful in its season." Even these sand-fields of Tinnevelly, that nourish only palm trees, feed thousands of human beings, to whom the trees furnish almost entire support. As I passed over their bare surface, I could not but think of their wondrous use, as well as admire their strange beauty and their intense solitude.

SOUTH TRAVANCORE, though adjoining Tinnevelly, possesses altogether a different soil and climate. It contains fine undulations and broad fertile plains. The mountains with their numerous streams and gushing waterfalls furnish ample supplies of water: in all the low grounds between the hills and the sea, rice is raised in abundance; on the slopes and higher localities grows the hardy palm. The wet and dry crops, of rice and corn, form a large item in the revenue returns, and more than a hundred thousand persons are employed in the pepper cultivation alone. Nothing but injustice, oppression and tyranny in the authorities, producing distrust and chicanery in the poor, prevent the people of this favoured extremity of India, from becoming as to worldly circumstances both rich and prosperous.

The difference between the two districts is produced chiefly by the different monsoons that prevail. Travancore enjoys the south-west monsoon, which blows with clouds and rain from the Indian Ocean, in the hottest months of the year. The climate is thus greatly modified and the heat tempered by the cool sea-breeze. At that same season, Tinnevelly is burning under a vertical sun, the ghauts like a wall intercepting the heavy rain clouds that pour their precious burdens upon Travancore, and preventing them from visiting also the neighbouring province. These rains on the west coast are much heavier than those of the Madras monsoon in October; more soil has consequently been washed from the hills: heat, water and fertile earth, the three chief elements of vegetable growth, are present in abundance, and if it were not for MAN, the country would flourish greatly.

TINNEVELLY and TRAVANCORE meet beyond the last ghaut, and the traveller can walk on level ground from one province into the other. Beside the passes between the last five ghauts, this level ground is six miles long and southward ends in the sea at CAPE COMORIN. I visited the Cape, when travelling among the out-stations of the Nagercoil mission, and was much struck by its numerous peculiarities. Near the shore is a fine group of palm trees; and close beside them stands a Hindu temple. On the very shore itself is a well-cut choultry, consisting of a corniced roof resting on twelve carved pillars, all built of stone. Directly in front of this choultry is the low black rock, which constitutes the last point of solid land in Hindustán. On the east side of the temple, there lies on the shore, a large mass of *purple sand,* which on examination, proves to be a collection of minute garnets, broken out of the granite rock of south India, in which it abounds, and strangely washed together in one spot. Close to the black rock is another curiosity; a mass of sand, each grain of which is as large as the ordinary grains of raw rice, whence it is called *rice-sand.* There is a singular legend told about its origin that may be thought interesting. It is told in various ways; but the following account is most common. It is said that the youngest daughter of the king of Pandy, named KÁNIÁ KÓMORI, was sought in marriage by a foreign giant named Vánásaram. She accepted his suit, and agreed to marry him, on one condition which she hoped he could never fulfil; namely, that he should, on the wedding-day, give the guests to eat, *rice* which had been sown, grown, cut, winnowed, and cooked upon that very day. Much to her astonishment, the ugly monster performed the task. Greatly enraged, she cursed the rice, which became stones; she cursed the chaff, which became sand: she broke down a bridge which the giant had built there for his convenience, and finally slew the giant himself.

THE SHÁNÁR PEOPLE.

The people who inhabit Tinnevelly and the southern part of Travancore belong, with few exceptions, to a single tribe and call themselves SHÁNÁRS. In locality, they immediately follow the Hindu Tamils of Tanjore and Madura, fill up all the south part of the Eastern continent, and, going round Cape Comorin, extend for thirty miles up Travancore. They are then followed by the Ilavas, a people similar to themselves. The whole tribe seems to number upwards of half a million of souls. In Tinnevelly they form about half the entire population of all castes, reckoned at 800,000: and in South Travancore they are set down in the Government census at a hundred thousand. The Ilavas number 180,000 people. Their legends declare that they came last from Ceylon, which lies immediately opposite to Tinnevelly; and RÁBON, whom the Hindus esteem an unholy giant, they look on as their divine king. On his birth-day is held their greatest annual festival. Their language is a rough, uneducated Tamil, without any mixture of Sanskrit, and furnishes a strong proof, cognate with others, that these Shánárs are another portion of the great aboriginal Tartar race, which first overran the soil of India.

They live in a singular manner. Where no rice or corn whatever is to be had, they subsist entirely upon the palm tree, whose latent riches long experience has taught them to develop. Where the soil is favourable to rice cultivation, or any kind of vegetables or fruit can be purchased, the produce of the palm forms only a part of their living. Of these two plans the latter is most common on the Travancore side. The people obtain their food from the palm in this way. The flower of the tree is contained in a large sheath, which when cut and pressed, furnishes a considerable quantity of fresh sweet juice. If newly cut and attended to every day, the juice is deposited daily; but if left for a couple of days, the juice thickens and the vessels in which it lies become hard and cease to secrete it. This palm-juice is the life of the Shánár population: and in order to get it regularly they are compelled to pass their life in painful and incessant toil. From forty to sixty trees are required to feed one family. The Shánár peasant furnishes himself with a large pot and several small ones, a staff with a cross at the top, and a pair of wooden pincers. Arriving at his tope of trees, he puts the large vessel on the ground, and hangs a small pot and the pincers to his waist. He next slips a small band round one of his feet: plants his stick against the tree, and, clasping the trunk with both arms, begins to climb. He first places one foot on the head of the stick: this is his start: he then slips both feet into the band, which prevents them from going apart, and clasping the trunk alternately with his arms and his bound feet, climbs speedily to the top. He there cuts the bud of the tree or plucks off a small strip; squeezes the juice into his little pot, presses it gently with his wooden pincers and comes down again. Pouring the contents of his pot into the large vessel, he climbs another tree, and another and another, until he has gone over his fifty trees. By this time, in the favourable seasons of the year, he has collected a large quantity of palm juice and returns home. In the evening, he goes the same round: and thus climbs full *a hundred times* a day. In the dry seasons, he must climb each tree three times a day; but he never does it less than twice. Most Shánárs take about fifty trees but some climb as many as SIXTY. Surely few people in the world can be reckoned more hardworking than they.

The juice taken home, the peasant's wife boils it continuously over a slow fire: the watery part is gradually evaporated, and a lump of coarse *black-looking sugar* is left behind. That sugar is the food of the people: with the very poor it is their wealth: and often is it put into the plate at the Communion table as an offering to the Lord. The following singular fact cannot be forgotten here. Though holding in their hands, on the largest scale, the means of making spirits, the Shánárs, as a people, do not allow their palm-juice to ferment: they are hence not at all a drunken race. The Ilavas, on the other hand, their neighbours in Travancore, who live on the cocoanut, always ferment palm-juice and do drink to excess.

Such is the common life of those Shánárs who stand on a level with the poorer classes of the labouring population: whose days are spent in excessive toil which yields them little more than their necessary food. They are distinguished among their tribe as Paniaris or climbers. All however are not so hardly situated. Some among them, constituting a better class, are Nádáns or land-holders; possessing small estates of their own. Such persons of course employ others to climb their trees: or if that be unnecesary, hire out their land for rent, payable in money or palm-sugar. Others, again have improved their circumstances by trade, especially among the christians; and it is always observed that the first thing done by a man, who is rising in the world, is to hire others to climb his trees. The Paniaris or climbers are of course the poorest of all.

THE SHÁNÁR RELIGION DEVIL WORSHIP.*

In religion the Shánárs are to a very small extent Hindus. They are of course not Hindus in caste; since they are not by birth and origin, members of the Hindu community: though in respect to their social position they occupy a higher place than the Parias. But they do pay some honour to several of the Hindu gods, of whom two or three

* An admirable account of the Shánárs and their worship, with that of the progress of the gospel among them, has been published in a little pamphlet, entitled *The Tinevelly Shánárs*, by the Rev. R. Caldwell; one of the most able missionaries in South India.

resemble their own deities; and especially attend the great annual festivals at Trichendúr and Alvar-Tinnevelly. Their own indigenous religion is of an entirely different kind. Of a Supreme God, creator and ruler of all, they have no idea whatever. In their oaths, they sometimes speak of *the Lord,* but the term conveys no meaning. During several years however the heathen Shánárs have become extensively acquainted with the notion of God, through the conversations and discourses of missionsionaries, catechists, and christians in general. Nor as heathen do they know any thing of a future state. They have no belief in transmigration (as all Hindus in North India have): nor in the immortality of the soul. They have no notion of a judgment and no sense of responsibility to a superior being.

The distinguishing feature of their religion is the direct WORSHIP OF DEVILS; that is, not merely of gods and idols, reckoned as such by christians, according to the statement of the Apostle Paul; but they worship beings who to them are actual bonâ fide devils. These devils are in their ideas connected with men, now dead, as if the disembodied SPIRIT of the dead man had remained alive to do all kinds of mischief. The character of these devils is believed invariably to be full of malignity, and hatred towards mankind. The people never appeal to them for blessings and gifts, they never attribute to them feelings of gentleness or compassion: they believe them only capable of doing harm.—How true a representation of those whom the Bible describes by that name!—These devils are believed to be of the same castes and classes, as all the dead whom they represent. There are male and female devils: high-caste and low-caste devils: bráhmin and sudra and paria devils: devils of Hindu origin and also foreign devils. In one village, an English officer, named Pole, was worshipped as such. They are supposed to reside in dark and foul abodes: in umbrageous trees, in uninhabited wastes; in dark and gloomy shades: in forests: in ruined houses: wherever in fact circumstances tend to inspire fear. All evil is believed to arise from their agency. It is they from whom spring losses in trade, failures in agriculture, and accidents to life and limb. They blast the rice crop, or the standing corn: they dry the juices of the palm on sultry days; or withhold the rain of heaven from the parched earth. They bring disease on men and cattle; or overthrow the forests by heavy storms. They frighten the timid in the dark night; the howling noises and shrill screams, heard in darkness among the trees on windy nights, are their voices: and it is they who revel in the awful hurricane. Sometimes also it is believed they possess men. If a man is affected with sunstroke, some devil has entered him: if another's head swims, the same cause is assigned. Hysterics, staring eyes, and epilepsy, of course, are attributed to their possessions. To drive such a devil away, various methods are employed. Sometimes a dose of medicine suffices. Sometimes a severe beating with a shoe or a broom is administered: or a plentiful supply of low abuse; sometimes sacrifices are resorted to.

To these devils NO TEMPLES are built. The most general form of building made in their honour is that of a pyramid of mud, plaistered and whitewashed, having the figure of a devil in front. Immense multitudes of these pyramids are found all over the Shánár country. A better kind of house is a small thatched shed, open in front; in which the people deposit some half dozen idols or devils, and various gifts of small value. Many of these figures are representations of Bhodrokáli, a form of terror among the Hindus. Others are formed with buffalo heads: most are females, and are represented in the very act of devouring children. These superior houses are for devils of bráhmin extraction or for the different forms of Kali. All these erections, whether of the better or more common kind, are termed pé-coils i. e. devil-temples. In the whole system there is not a single idea of beauty, or of mercy to a sinner's soul.

The service presented to the demons is of two kinds, DEVIL-DANCING and DEVIL SACRIFICES. The former is suggested by some ominous occurrence, and usually leads to the latter. When the former is required, the people assemble near one of the pyramids or devil-sheds, and after enjoying for a time the usual energetic beating of drums, proceed to sacrifice an animal, as a fowl, or sheep or goat, according to the peculiar taste of the devil to be honoured. Some one, usually though not exclusively a professional performer, then comes forward to dance. He puts on his feet a pair of tinkling bangles; wraps round him a cloth covered with figures of devils; sets free his long black hair; takes in his hand a jingling staff; and to the sound of drums and horns and the deep tones of the devil-bow, slowly begins to dance. After a time he will stop, drink off a large portion of the kid's blood just offered in sacrifice, and then, animated with fresh enthusiasm, his eyes staring, his long hair streaming in the wind, whirl round and round with mad excitement. To increase this excitement he will cut himself with the sacrificial knife; or lash himself with a formidable whip, until the proper pitch of frantic earnestness is obtained. After dancing some time, to the great joy of the spectators, who express their satisfaction by horrid yells, he sits down and is now consulted by the people as inspired. Questions are put to him, as to what devil has possessed a certain woman in the village with fever, or has blown down a cow-house, or frightened a child. The few vague murmurs that he may utter in reply, or the signs that he may make, are interpreted as sure indications of the cause of such evils. Generally he will mention by name some notorious person, recently dead, as the cause of the disasters: and declare that to appease him, a fowl or kid must be offered in the usual way. On a set day, the appointed sacrifices are presented. A number of cooking vessels are brought to the pyramid; there the fowl or kid is slaughtered, and with rice and the usual accompaniments is cooked and eaten on the spot. All who choose to come are permitted to share in the ceremonies and in the feast that concludes them. Missionaries have seldom been able to obtain a sight of these ceremonies, especially of the dancing. The people are ashamed of it: they hide their shame however under the avowal that their devils cannot cope with Europeans. A missionary was once building his house, exactly where a devil pyramid used to stand, in a place which was by the heathen still thought to be a resort of his. Soon after heavy rain fell, and the unfinished walls were somewhat injured. This was reported to be the devil's doing: but the missionary persevered. The rains again damaged it, as they will do in the rainy season: but he went on and in due time completely finished the house as he had intended. The heathen then reported that the devil, disgusted with the missionary's obstinacy, had left the neighbourhood. Strange and absurd as these things may seem to us, the poor Shánárs have believed them thoroughly, have believed them for hundreds of years. There is reason indeed to believe that this is the primitive worship of all the aborigines and has existed in India since the day they entered the land. What a proof does it furnish that, as nothing is too hard for the Lord; so there is no folly, no superstition, too low and too degraded for the settled belief of man.

As a consequence of such a religious belief, it will be readily understood that the Shánárs do not stand very high in a moral point of view. Having scarcely any sense of responsibility, they do not hesitate to follow the way of evil when open before them. Hence among them, as amongst other Hindus, there exist open, habitual, and shameless lying; vice and immorality of all degrees; fawning to the great, oppression of the poor; total disregard of truth and honour: no kindness to the brute creation, and no compassion towards their fellow-men. The Shánárs are a simpler people than the brahmins, and their lying is therefore not so smooth, so accomplished and so clever. Their knowledge too and their intelligence are not equal to those of the higher castes: still it is true "they are all gone out of the way: there is none that doeth good, no not one."

Their simple village life and the absence of caste *among* them, although they are treated by others as a separate caste, render them more open to the gospel than many other tribes in Hindustán. When they once feel the power of the gospel, they find few obstacles to a public profession of it: and the readiness of the people to act in a body tells even more in favour of the gospel than against it: so that when a man of influence in a village becomes a christian, he is almost certain to be followed by a number of families from among his neighbours. This gregarious feeling and the absence of caste bonds, will greatly explain the fact: that of this singular people no less than 52,000 are now under *regular instruction in christian congregations.*

FIRST SUCCESS OF THE GOSPEL.

The introduction of CHRISTIANITY among this remarkable people must be regarded as a matter of deep interest. During the flourishing period of the Tranquebar mission, nothing was done for the Shánárs, then far away from the missionaries' sphere of labour: their very existence I presume was unknown. Towards the end of the last century however, some christians from Tranquebar, and then from Trichinopoly, found their way into Tinnevelly and gathered a number of disciples in Palamcottah, its chief town. About the year 1780, Swartz himself visited the place and baptized a few from among the Romanists. In 1785, he visited it again, and finding that the congregation had increased to a hundred and sixty persons, left with them two catechists and a school-master. One of the catechists, named SATTIA-NADEN was an able teacher, a man of great personal influence and a consistent faithful christian. Under his instructions, the little church at Palamcottah increased in numbers, knowledge and strength: and such confidence did Swartz and the other missionaries place in him, that he was at length ordained by them to the ministry of that flock. Swartz gives him the highest character; declaring that for humility and disinterestedness, for love to souls and desire to benefit them, for great consistency and remarkable talent in teaching and preaching, he never saw his equal among the natives of the country. In 1791 a young and active missionary, Mr. Jænicke, newly arrived from Germany, was appointed to the charge of this increasing station, and set about his work with singular zeal; as if his mind had been taught from above that he could serve his generation for only a few short years. In discretion, in activity, in a readiness to devote himself to the salvation of the heathen, and, by repeated itinerancies, spread the knowledge of the gospel, he was second to none of the missionaries that had yet preceded him. He took up his residence at Palamcottah, and thenceforth Sattianáden and he, with the catechists of the mission, undertook regular and extensive journeys among the numerous and populous villages with which Tinnevelly abounds. Every where they were received with courtesy and listened to with attention: an open door was set before them among the Shánárs, and on their return to Palamcottah on one particular occasion, about thirty persons followed them determined to profess christianity openly. Mr. Jænicke's report of his journey concludes with words, since wonderfully verified: "There is every reason to hope that at a future period, christianity will prevail in the Tinnevelly country."

The west of Tinnevelly is bounded, as we have seen, by a range of high and precipitous mountains. At two places high up in these ghauts, named Courtállum and Pávanásum, are magnificent water-falls, regarded as sacred by the Hindus. In the hot weather these localities are perfectly healthy; and at the present day all the European residents in Tinnevelly wisely retire to them for a few weeks, till the greatest heat is past. In the cold weather however which immediately follows the north-east monsoon, it is dangerous to sleep two nights together in the hills; jungle fever following almost to a certainty. Ignorant of this fact, Mr. Jænicke in the course of his journey with several Government officers went into the hills to Pávanásum, whose three successive falls he discovered and described: but he took the jungle fever and was immediately obliged to quit the province. Returning to his labour he continued the same course for several years, the fever continually breaking out, and he was compelled again to leave the country. Returning once more with Gerickè, the two missionaries visited the whole of the numerous out-stations, opened a new church and station at Ramnad and baptized a large number of converts. Shortly after Mr. Jænicke sunk under his disease, after a brief but most useful missionary life of twelve years. Men like him can ill be spared in a country such as this; especially in those districts where peculiar facilities exist for carrying out the gospel plan of inviting all sinners to the cross. But the Lord seeth not as man seeth, and took his servant to rest in early life. The work continued to prosper, and was soon consolidated by a fiery persecution, carried on against the christians by the rebellious

Polygars, who then overran the province. A peremptory order from the Court of Directors, on the intercession of the Christian Knowledge Society, to allow the christians full liberty in professing the religion which they had embraced, compelled the persecutors to cease: and on Gerickè's travelling shortly after through the district, he baptized no less than thirteen hundred persons; while the catechists added to the visible church 2700 more. Published letters go far to shew that the people acted from many inferior motives in making such a profession; hoping, for instance, for remission of revenue or for more favourable consideration from the Government officers than the heathen could obtain. Be that as it may, they were formed into congregations and placed under a regular system of instruction and visitation. Such was the beginning of the present Tinnevelly mission.

The Shánár mission in SOUTH TRAVANCORE was closely connected with it, and sprang up about the same time. In 1805, a man from a family in Mylády, a village about five miles from Cape Comorin, went as a sanyási to Chillumbrum, in the province of Tanjore. He seems to have been a real enquirer after truth, and having heard of the celebrated temple at that place, set out in hopes of finding the true religion. He was, however, greatly dissatisfied with all he saw, especially with the bráhmins (the most pertinacious beggars in south India) and the numerous dancing girls; and felt convinced that true religion was not to be found among them. On travelling homeward, he passed through the town of Tanjore; and during a short rest there, one day saw Mr. Kohlhoff preaching in his church. He stood in the doorway and listened. Mr. Kohlhoff addressed a part of the sermon specially to him as a sanyási, and urged him to believe the gospel. The man attracted many eyes, and was invited by the people to stay a week and hear more of their religion. He was so satisfied that he stayed much longer, read several books and was eventually baptized. He then returned to his family in Mylády, and being unwilling to leave his native place with them to settle in Tanjore, he begged hard that a missionary might be sent to him. At that time Mr. Ringeltaube, who had arrived at Tranquebar as a missionary of the London Missionary Society, was looking out for a suitable sphere of labour: and deeming the man's invitation to be a call of providence, he agreed to visit the spot. The congregations in Tinnevelly, founded by Sattianáden and Jænicke, were at that time without European superintendence, and Mr. Kohlhoff of Tanjore, in whose charge they were left, himself a Lutheran missionary, invited Mr. Ringeltaube, a Lutheran also, to superintend them for a couple of years: on this condition, that all the increase in Tinnevelly was to belong to Tanjore and all in Mylády and Travancore to the London Society. Mr. Ringeltaube accordingly went down to Palamcottah; stayed for a time, and then took a survey of all the congregations, travelling onwards till he came into Travancore. He fulfilled his singular agreement well, and when the two years were completed, confined himself entirely to the Travancore mission. Col. Macaulay, then Resident at the court of the Travancore Raja, greatly befriended him and promoted the object of his mission to the best of his power. Mr. Ringeltaube was an extraordinary man, very eccentric but wholly devoted to his work. He cared little for the ordinary customs of civilized society: he seldom or ever wore a coat, except when a friend gave him one on his visits to Palamcottah or Quilon. He wore a common straw hat, and walked and wandered over Travancore, living in a common hut, but every where preaching the gospel of Christ. He made an extraordinary impression on the people, which remains to this day: indeed they believe him to have been inspired. Amongst other things he had no regard for money. The natives say that when he received his quarter's salary he would pay his servants the expenses of the previous three months and then give the remainder to beggars. He never, it is said, changed a rupee, but always gave it whole; an exaggeration, no doubt, of the real truth. He was a man of rather angry temper, and at times used to beat his servants and the converts in general, unmercifully. On one occasion when he went to Muthaloor, the first village mission in Tinnevelly, he was accused by an old woman of cheating, because his eggs were not paid for (probably through his servant's misconduct:) and became perfectly enraged at what he reckoned their ingratitude and extortion. The people declare that he cursed them and theirs; that he especially cursed the fowls; and that in consequence of his curse, the Muthaloor fowls for years laid fewer eggs than those in other places: by this time the curse has expended itself. With all these eccentricities he laboured hard for the Lord: and commended the gospel to the people most extensively. Thus he laboured for twelve years, and becoming hypochondriac and unsettled, went away to Batavia in 1817. One or two of his chapels are still standing as he built them, shaded by the cocoanut trees that he planted around their walls. In Travancore he founded six stations and left nine hundred christians baptized.

GROWTH OF THE SHÁNÁR MISSIONS.

The period of Mr. Ringletaube's departure was the time of trial to all these missions. The stations in Tinnevelly had received scarcely any superintendence whatever since 1807: and the christians had considerably decreased in numbers. Had not Mr. Hough, the excellent chaplain of Palamcottah, endeavoured to secure for them efficient instruction by means of native teachers, they might have suffered still more. The Travancore stations however were not deserted long. The London Missionary Society in 1817 sent out a second missionary, Mr. Mead, who soon took up Mr. Ringeltaube's labours and endeavoured to spread the gospel still wider in the province. A singular circumstance occurred at the time, that was not without its influence. Colonel Munro, then Resident in Travancore, finding no agents to carry out his enlightened views of government, recommended Mr. Mead to take the office of Judge in the district where he resided; and he held it for two years until the disapproval of the Directors of the Society obliged him to relinquish the office. Mr. Mead had honourably endeavoured to administer justice impartially, though his two offices were not exactly compatible with each other: and even when he resigned it, the natives did not consider that his political influence was gone. As a consequence in a short time no less than three thousand people placed themselves under instruction, in addition to Mr. Ringletaube's converts. Of course many of them subsequently went back; when they found that Mr. Mead did not always decide the suits in their favour; or that he would not interfere at all. Their retirement however was a benefit to the mission, as it rendered more definite the numbers of the sincere. In 1818 Mr. Knill joined Mr. Mead from Madras, where his health had failed; and the two brethren found ample work in arranging their enquirers into congregations, selecting catechists or readers, and otherwise providing for that agency by which the work of the gospel is continuously maintained. At that time the head station was removed from Mylády to Nagercoil, a beautiful spot in the very heart of the mission. The station is so maintained to this day. It has behind and on the west the high ghauts in several ranges, running out into the plains and inclosing extensive valleys where outstations exist among the very slaves of Travancore. To the east and southeast, its plain is bounded by the last of the ghaut range. Southward the plain extends for a few miles, till it reaches the sea. In the immediate neighbourhood of Nagercoil is the large native town of Kytar. Through the aid of Colonel Munro a very large chapel was built at the new station; towards which the Ráni-Regent, an enlightened princess, subscribed most liberally. Boarding schools were also established for the training of the young. On the departure of Mr. Knill, Mr. Mault and Mr. Miller with two assistant missionaries joined the mission. Of these Mr. Mault continues alive to this day, steadily and consistently pursuing his work as a missionary of Christ's cross. He has now laboured at Nagercoil for thirty-five years and has never been farther from his station than a hundred miles. Much honoured by the natives, he has lived to see the mission greatly prosper; to admit later and better trained converts into the places of the old; and to guide his younger brethren on their entrance into that sphere in which he cannot labour for ever. At the same time christian friends in England, who had heard of the opening for the gospel among the Shánárs of Travancore, forwarded liberal aid for the support of native catechists and school teachers. The missionaries were therefore enabled to enlarge their system of operations, and provide better for the instruction of their congregations than they had hitherto done. Village chapels were built; schools organised; teachers of various classes appointed; regular visitation commenced; and the whole sphere of labour divided into two districts having their head stations at Nagercoil and Neyoor. The difficulties met with by the missionaries were very great. Though they were troubled by caste-feelings much less than others, they had to meet obstacles of a different kind. Their people were intensely ignorant, their minds thoroughly untrained, their capacity of thought most narrow; the agents were in many cases men but little superior to the converts they instructed, because no better were to be had. The stations were numerous, the people willing; but the missionaries were few. Around them stood the brahmins, the ruling class in Travancore, possessed of political as well as religious authority, all watching with jealous eyes the efforts of Europeans to elevate those on whom themselves had for ages trampled in scorn. But the Lord helped his servants with sufficient grace. For twenty years they laboured on with steadfastness and zeal. Light increased and spread among the people. The young grew up better instructed than their fathers who first received the gospel. The small number of those who appeared truly converted received the most satisfactory additions. In times of trial from the heathen, the converts proved their fidelity in suffering, and died rejoicing in their Redeemer. The missionaries as they saw these signs of true improvement, thanked God and took courage.

In 1838 a considerable addition was made to the agency of the mission which resulted in greatly increasing its sphere of operations and their usefulness. Mr. Mead had been compelled to visit England on account of ill health, and so successfully pleaded the cause of the Shánárs, that the Directors of the London Society resolved to reinforce the mission on a large scale. Five missionaries left England with Mr. Mead: and on their arrival four new stations were added to the two already existing, as the residence of a missionary. Immediately after, two thousand persons placed themselves under instruction in one year. Mrs. Mault's boarding school was enlarged to 120 girls: and printing presses were established at Nagercoil, Neyoor and Quilon. A seventh head-station has since been founded at Santapuram.

It is impossible in this brief sketch to detail all the elements of the progress which these interesting missions have since exhibited: and which have greatly encouraged both the missionaries who labour and the friends who support their efforts. At the present time the London Mission in South Travancore contains seven chief stations, and about two hundred and fifty outstations; superintended and instructed by eight missionaries, and 105 catechists. The native christians so-called number 17,600 persons; amongst whom, owing to the high standard of admission into church fellowship, only 700 are reckoned church members or communicants. The boys in the Boarding Schools number 104; and the girls, 230: 6000 boys and 1000 girls are taught in day-schools. The three presses have lately been brought together at Nagercoil; in the hope that one well-managed establishment will better provide for all the printing which the mission needs. The various physical agencies required in such an extensive mission have long since been completed, though their preparation has cost both a large amount of time and anxiety, as well as a considerable expenditure of money. The out-stations have their village chapels and school-rooms. The head stations have the houses of resident missionaries; large, well-built chapels; and large school-houses for the boarding schools. In some cases a christian village has risen up at the station: in others, the christians are still mixed with the heathen population in general. To these must be added the three printing offices at Neyoor, Nagercoil and Quilon, that have already been mentioned. Of all the Travancore stations, two of the prettiest and most compactly built are Santapuram and James' Town. The former of these, "the city of peace," lies midway between Neyoor and Nagercoil, being about six miles from each. It lies opposite a noble hill which stretches far into the well-tilled rice plain. Its pretty parsonage; its neat church, already too small for the demands of the christian population; its flourishing girls' school, containing more than a hundred girls; its lace establishment; its almshouses for poor widows; its well planned village; and huge well; all reflect much credit on the perseverance and energy of Mr. Lewis, the missionary by whom it was founded. The station of James' Town, once rejoiced in the euphonious title of Pichi-gudi-iruppu. 'the town of the beggars.' It was then an out-station of Nagercoil; but on its establishment as the head of a district, it ceased to be poor, either in appearance or in fact, and received from its missionary a new name. In addition to the usual buildings the station has been planted with a large number of cocoanut trees. Among the out-stations of this district are the earliest villages which embraced christianity in the time of Mr. Ringeltaube. Mylády is one of them, Agateswarum another: another in the district of Santapuram is known by the singular name of Ananda-náden-gudi-iruppu. I shall never forget the happy faces of the Shánár girls in the school at this station, as they plied their merry spinning-wheels, and sang with glee, "Oh! that will be joyful, when we meet to part no more."

Little can the dwellers in English cities imagine how hard a trial it is to a European missionary to spend year after year of his tropical life, almost entirely surrounded by a native population. Who can wonder if hypochondria, low spirits, and stagnation of mind and body spring from the loneliness in which some are isolated. I was glad to perceive that the missionaries in South Travancore, in order to counteract such evils, were accustomed to hold frequent meetings at each other's stations: and also that they had secured in the hills around them a pleasant place of retirement for their sick members in the hottest season of the year. In the ghauts, immediately to the north of Nagercoil, and distant about fourteen miles, a few years back they discovered a series of water-falls. These falls are situated about eight hundred feet above the plain. Close at their feet is a platform of rock just large enough for a house, and having a fine view of the falls. Here a neat little dwelling has been erected, sufficiently large to contain two families; and in the burning season just before the monsoon sets in, the invalids of the mission are able to retreat to this retired spot, to enjoy its cooler air and the many natural beauties with which its scenery abounds. The upper fall comes down between two giant rocks, rounded and scored by the perpetual action of the mountain torrent, while trees and creepers of immense size, fed by its waters, gracefully shade and overarch the silver stream to which their own life is due.

From the platform the view obtained across the plain is one of the most exhilarating kind. Up the valley the rice-fields stretch away for miles; studded every where with topes of palms: and where hills project, their terraced slopes shew with what care and diligence the hand of man strives to obtain the fruits God showers on this world's soil. When I saw it, the people were every where reaping the golden rice harvest, but most of them were SLAVES.

The TINNEVELLY mission was revived from its lethargy by Mr. Rhenius, who with his colleague Mr. Schmid went down to Palamcottah as a missionary of the Church Missionary Society in 1820. Mr. Hough had endeavoured by the aid of Swartz's fund to carry on the missions of the Christian Knowledge Society, but the Society in England could not supply him either with men or more money. He then applied to the Church Missionary Society; and as Mr. Rhenius and Mr. Schmid were in Madras, prepared to enter on a new sphere, they were directed to proceed to Tinnevelly. Besides giving some attention to the older stations, they founded new ones for their own Society, and having started upon the sound principle that no caste distinction should be permitted in their churches and schools, they soon began to build up around them congregations both numerous and sincere. People came flocking to them for christian instruction in a way that had never been seen before: large as the influx had been at times in the province of Tanjore. New stations were soon formed, as Dohnavur, to which a third missionary, Mr. Schafter, was appointed; and Suviseshapuram, placed under another, Mr. Muller. In 1829, there were 6,000 persons under instruction; of whom however, acting more strictly than their predecessors, Mr. Rhenius and his colleagues had baptized less than 1,000. In that year, the Society for Propagating the gospel, which had taken up all the missions in South India held by the Christian Knowledge Society, sent to Tinnevelly their first missionary Mr. Rosen: and thenceforth the two Societies advanced side by side, engaging in their common work with common plans, and gradually increasing the agency by which they endeavoured to carry it out. It is impossible in this brief sketch to enumerate even the chief incidents illustrative of the history of the Tinnevelly mission. Time would fail to describe faithfully the zeal and earnestness of Mr. Rhenius and his brethren: the controversy into which they were led with their Society, and Mr. Rhenius's abrupt dismissal: the carrying on of two separate missions by the parties: the death of Rhenius and the gradual reunion of all the congregations to the Society again: the establishment of new stations to the west and south among the purely Shánár population, and their extension to the north among others more wealthy and independent: the proceedings of the Heathen Society formed at Trichendoor to put a stop to christianity; and the persecutions which at length they incited against the christians: the serious out-break which took place at Nalloor, (Mr. Schafter's station:) the trials in the Courts: the bitter feeling excited by Mr. Lewin's attack on the missionaries and their converts: the increased success of the mission following the failure of the persecutions; its continued spread to the north among the more independent people, especially the Retties near Sawyerpuram; the entire destruction of all the heathen temples or devil pyramids in some of the older seats of the mission, which have become altogether christianized:—the great increase of European agency of all kinds; the growth of many christian agencies and Societies among the native christians themselves for preserving their faith in their own families and spreading it where it is unknown:—these things constitute some of the striking features of the Tinnevelly missions, which have received their chief impulse and reaped their largest success during the last twenty years. At the present time there are 35,000 christians in Tinnevelly, of whom nearly 4,000 are communicants: 6,000 boys are under instruction in Vernacular schools: and excellent Boarding schools are maintained for the young, containing 360 boys and 490 girls. These agencies are great in number and well concentrated.

If we now make a summary of the efforts made for the *Shánár population* in general by the two Church of England Societies in Tinnevelly and the London Missionary Society in Travancore, the result will appear as follows. Of the whole Shánár tribe, half a million in number, about one-tenth, or 52,000, are under christian instruction and have means provided for securing to them regular instruction and worship: of this large number 4,600 are communicants: 12,000 boys attend the Vernacular schools: and the Boarding schools contain 500 boys and 800 girls. The number of chief stations is 25: of European missionaries, 24: and of native catechists and preachers, 254. Sixty years ago, scarcely one of these stations existed. A few natives only in Palamcottah were christians. Thirty years ago, the work had fairly begun, it has been continued with earnestness: new labourers have been added: and this is the great result: 4,600 adult communicants: 12,000 boys in day schools: 52,000 people under regular instruction. Of the number of devil temples, pyramids and idols destroyed in Tinnevelly, I know nothing: but in South Travancore, Mr. Mead assured me, that after extensive enquiry, it has been found that not less than 20,000 devil images and pyramids have been destroyed: while two Romish Churches with their altars and images have also been made over to the London Mission.

Had time permitted I should have liked to describe some of the christian stations in Tinnevelly among this interesting people: to point out the flourishing village with its rows of well-built houses; its green milk hedge; its gardens of mangoe and plantain trees; its extensive palm topes; its cocoanut and betelnut trees; its roads lined with trees; its fine stone wells: its Court house for the village puncháyat: its mission house and schools: and best of all the well-built Gothic Church, with its tall tower, appearing through the green foliage and by its pealing bell summoning the native christians morning and evening to the house of prayer. Or I might tell of the printing presses which supply the christian young with suitable maps and books of instruction: and then turn in contrast to the dark, low shed with the hideous idols, devouring their offspring, placed under the gloomy umbrella tree; might mark the small attendance on the annual festivals, the destruction of the devil pyramids and temples; and then impressed with the mighty contrast, exclaim in the language of the Bible: "What hath God wrought!"

WHY THE SHÁNÁR CONVERTS ARE SO NUMEROUS.

Having glanced at the history of the Shánár mission, it will be well to consider certain practical questions suggested by the facts of that history. The first of these enquiries is: WHAT PECULIAR CIRCUMSTANCES have caused so many persons to embrace christianity in Tinnevelly and Travancore, whereas the converts in other parts of India are so few? The great distinguishing fact which lies at the bottom of the case is, that the SHÁNÁRS, not being Hindus by birth, are only partially bound by the laws of *caste*. They form a caste by themselves, and as they occupy all together one great locality they can act almost as if they were not a caste at all. If then a Shánár become a christian, he does not become an out-caste from his people, and is not cut off from all intercourse with his friends, as a Brahmin is in like circumstances. The penalty paid for becoming a christian is in the case of the latter, the loss of every thing: in that of the former, little or nothing. Another fact is, that they are much accustomed to act together: and it is a general feeling in a family that what two or three influential members resolve on, the rest also will do. This has been proved in numberless cases in so reasonable a proceeding as giving up the devils for christianity. These two things shew the existence of facilities for leaving their own religion which are not common elsewhere in Hindustan. Why then did they embrace christianity, whereas they had not embraced Hindu idolatry. At the outset, in the days of their ignorance, no doubt inferior motives prevailed very widely. They hoped by becoming christians to get some immediate temporal good, with scarcely any idea of spiritual profit. The missionaries fully acknowledge this. In Travancore for instance, Mr. Mead, I have said, acted as judge, and numbers thought to get lawsuits decided in their favour by adopting the judge's religion. Col. Munro about the same time procured an order from the Rání, allowing the christians, slaves and all, to rest from labour on the Sabbath. Many tried to get the benefit of that order, who would otherwise have been forced by the government to labour on that day. In Tinnevelly persecutions broke out against the first christians, in which Gerickè and others interfered. The Court of Directors sent out peremptory orders to have them stayed. It was easy enough for other Shánárs when they saw the new christians possessing such powerful friends, to offer themselves also as candidates for baptism, in hope of obtaining the same boon. All this has passed away: the people have in the course of years learnt the truth that missionaries are not mixed up with the government and do not exercise political influence. They do see however that the missionaries and their catechists are the *friends* of the christians; their faithful religious instructors; their helpers in times of sickness, their advisers in difficulty: the mediators in their numerous litigious quarrels. They know as well as other poor people the value of such aid, and therefore feel a drawing towards christianity as likely to befriend them. On the other hand, they are dreadfully *afraid* of their *demons:* the sacrifices and fees to dancers are expensive: and as it is generally believed that the demons, called *Pesáses* in Tinnevelly as well as in Bengal, have no power over "the servants of God," many are found to give up the one system for the other. The christian *knowledge* also which the preaching of the missionaries and catechists has spread abroad, has shewn the heathen the reasonable character of the religion and morality which christianity establishes: the system of worship, the social order which prevail among the converts, are also before them. They have learned also in contrast the folly of their devil-worship, and they cease to defend it as a proceeding which their judgment can approve. They will never from very shame allow a missionary now-a-days to see their sacrifices and devil dances: what wonder is it then that those who do care for religion at all should prefer one which is so reasonable and which so many thousands of their fellow-villagers have already embraced. They may have also the general idea that as christians are no longer under the power of demons, they will get better crops of rice and fruit: and be preserved from danger. These are undoubtedly the kind of reasons for which the great majority of the unintelligent converts have placed themselves under instruction. If it be said, that many of the motives are of an inferior kind, the fact must be allowed: but it may be asked in reply,—Are these the only christians who have done a right thing from inferior reasons, where those of a higher character ought to have been foremost? The gospel is a system which confers a thousand benefits which only experience discovers. It is indeed profitable for the life that now is; and if its temporal blessings attract the eye of the ignorant who prefer sight to faith; and who come to the missionary, not to be supported, not to receive pensions and monthly doles, (for he has none such to give;) but to ask that they may be numbered among the christians, and may attend the instruction of the christian teachers, who is there, that with a clear conscience can forbid them. Especially who will forbid them, when the missionary understands their exact position, and without deceiving himself as to their being at once converted and perfect christians, takes them up where they are, and by careful instruction endeavours to lead both them and their children to the true and saving knowledge of the Lamb of God. The real value of the gospel as a truth "able to save the soul," the majority have had subsequently to learn: those who experienced it before they came, and some such have become converts, have been comparatively few.

WHAT KIND OF CHRISTIANS ARE THEY?

Few questions are more important than this, since a fair upright answer will shew in few words the real value of the Shánár missions in relation to the grand object for which missions are carried on. The materials however for giving such an answer have been amply provided. The missionaries in their annual reports enter into numerous details of the spiritual state of their flocks; and both Mr. Caldwell and Mr. Pettitt, in their accounts of the Tinnevelly stations, deal with the matter in the most straightforward terms. An impatient friend may ask: Do you mean to say that all the 52,000 Shánárs now called christians are converted men? Certainly not; the wildest enthusiast never imagined such a glorious fact: least of all has any one acquainted with the missions endeavoured to make such an impression upon the minds of their friends. The missionaries, who know the state of things thoroughly, tell us in their reports, and I heard the same thing from their own lips on the spot, that these converts are divided, in regard both to their knowledge of the gospel, and their personal character, into THREE CLASSES?

The *first* or lowest class includes a very large number of converts who are still *unbaptized*. These persons are candidates for baptism; who desire to enter the christian community, but at present know little of gospel truth. They learn the appointed catechisms; attend public worship; and are required to live in general as members of the christian community. But much cannot be expected from them as to spirituality of mind, or consistency of conduct. The *second* class are those who have *only* been *baptized*. They are reckoned as still under instruction; but it is generally seen that their conduct is influenced to a considerable extent by the Bible law. They of course possess much more christian knowledge; they have made an open profession: gross sins are not allowed to pass among them unreproved; and as they have a character to maintain in the community, they occupy a much higher position as to morality than they did among the heathen. A large proportion of this class are of course children. The *third* class the smallest of all, contains the *communicants*, called in some missions, the *Church members*. They number altogether 4,500 out of the 52,000, or about nine per cent. of the whole. These christians rank highest both in knowledge and character. They are spoken of in the same terms as are village converts in Bengal or the Mysore: and they are treated in the same way. All the missionaries watch carefully over the consistency and fidelity of those who are admitted into this body. The standard of admission is not the same in all cases. With some missionaries that standard is high. In the London Mission for instance it is so raised that the Church members form only four per cent. of the whole. Some of the Tinnevelly missionaries, as Mr. Cæmmerer, adopt I believe a similar standard; and administer a strict discipline. Good as many of their communicants are, they are all seen to be weak, especially the more ignorant; traces appear in their conduct of their old habits, old superstitions and old heathen rules. How could it well be otherwise, considering the origin whence they sprang, and the inveteracy of habit everywhere. Many of them live most consistent lives, and in contrast with their neighbours adorn the gospel. Catechists, schoolmasters and others of age and experience, appear generally as they ought to do the most consistent. Young men and women from the boarding schools, who have learned most, whose minds and hearts have been most cultivated, as a class, stand out higher than others, and it is hoped, will as they grow older become worthy leaders of the important community, to which they belong. During my visit, I had the pleasure of twice meeting Bible classes of young women at Nagercoil and Edeyenkoody, who displayed a very clear and complete knowledge of the Word of God. They were all trained in the boarding schools, and though they have now left them and have families of their own, they regularly attend these classes which are maintained specially for their benefit. All the girls' boarding schools that I examined gave promise of like success.

Anecdotes illustrative of the character of these christians could easily be multiplied. *Zeal for others* is not a distinguishing feature of native piety, but it has been exemplified among them. I will mention a single case, belonging to one of the newest stations. At Santapúram there is a poor man, a Pulliar of the lowest caste, who since his admittance into the Church has been very industrious in getting his own class to attend the means of grace. His wife and sister and another relative have, through his means, all been brought into the Church and two others have lately been baptized. His sister lately learned to read the New Testament: she is the only Pullian female of adult age that ever did so in Travancore. The man is like a father and priest among his people, warning, instructing and comforting them: and is greatly esteemed every where. At the same station there is a poor man who has three times fallen from palmyra trees. His chief peculiarity is that he has never been known to tell a lie or to deceive. So implicitly is his word believed, that in cases of dispute it is common to hear people say; "If Gúnamudeyan says it, I will believe it:" or, "Whatever Gúnamudeyan says, I will abide by."

NATIVE AGENCY.

An interesting topic connected with these missions is the *system of agency* adopted by the missionaries for the instruction and discipline of their multitudes of disciples: of whom each missionary has on an average two thousand. In these extensive missions, missionaries appear much more as the directors and superintendents of several congregations than of one: and much more as pastors of christian flocks than direct preachers to the heathen. The influence of each one of them is thus spread over a much wider surface, without being at all dissipated. The system of management is very complete throughout all the missions; and will, I feel sure, under God's blessing, tend to establish the converts in sound doctrine, and to apply the gospel widely and fully to the extensive district where they toil. This system has been the growth of years; and its elements have been suggested by the experience of actual wants. It is not invariably the same in form: individual missionaries making modifications of their own. All missionaries have a body of native catechists under their direction, who are employed in the charge of the various village congregations, connected with each head station. By some, all the catechists of a district are gathered monthly for three or four days at a time: by others they are gathered weekly on a particular day. On these occasions the catechists give in systematic reports of the state of the separate villages under their management. They report on the condition of the congregations and schools; the attendance at public worship; the sermons they have preached; the places they have visited; the burials they have performed; the number of converts added; the progress of enquirers; the number desirous of baptism; the applicants for admission to the communion: and so on. They also receive instruction; the missionary dictating a sermon to them, or reading regularly for their benefit through a book of Scripture. In some stations, the catechists preach sermons dictated to them by the missionary: in others they prepare sermons of their own and submit them to the missionary's criticism. Both plans have the same object, that of providing proper instruction for the out-stations. Similar reports are received from the schoolmasters. Again; in most cases, the agents of the mission pass through different grades of employment: as from assistant schoolmaster to that of schoolmaster. Thence they may pass to the office of assistant catechist: then become catechists: and finally may be ordained. This plan is found to work well, as furnishing a stimulus to exertion and improvement. In the Church Missionary Society, there are also superintending schoolmasters and superintending catechists, who have charge of several divisions of a district.

The work of the missionary in the complete and constant superintendence of the separate districts of each mission is by no means light. It embraces several distinct departments. First, a missionary is directly the pastor and preacher of the station where he resides. He also teaches the chief classes in the school of the station, especially in the boarding school and the Bible class. He has to receive the reports of all his native agents; to meet their difficulties; give them advice; or by them send advice to the people. He must also be prepared to see smaller or larger deputations arriving from all parts of his district at any hour of the day, to ask his assistance in settling quarrels, making up marriages, securing loans from the benevolent societies, or treating special cases of sickness. He has also to visit in turn the chief out-stations in the district: to examine and teach the local schools; preach in the village churches; meet the candidates for baptism; and settle a thousand varieties of miscellaneous business, which the people are certain to have on hand for his advice. He must also be architect and builder, not only of the mission buildings, but also superintendent of the village streets which spring up around his dwelling. How well these things can be done by devoted and energetic men, is proved by many examples spread over the whole province. Every station bears witness to their skill: but the villages of Edeyenkoody and Suviseshpuram: the establishment at Sawyerpuram; the beautiful gothic churches, built of stone, at Suviseshpuram, Pannivelei and Megnanapuram, display it in the strongest light. The districts to which they belong are also some of the most interesting, for the numbers and character of the converts, in all Tinnevelly.

All the Societies among the Shánárs have paid much attention to the raising of a thoroughly good *native agency*. Had they better materials, the results would be better than they now are, though still they exhibit a great advance on former days. Three SEMINARIES have been established for this purpose, at Nagercoil; at Palamcottah for the Church Missionary Society; and at Sawyerpuram for the Propagation Society. At each place a large number of promising lads and young men are subjected to a course of instruction, extending over several years and embracing the most important branches of education, with a view of being fitted for employment in the mission. Special instructors have been appointed to these institutions, and great pains are taken to secure the end for which they were established. The longer they are maintained, the greater will be the good influence which they exert throughout the Shánár Missions.

NATIVE LIBERALITY.

The last thing to be noticed in these missions is the practice early introduced among them, of leading the converts to contribute to the gospel which they have themselves received. In Bengal and other parts of India though a beginning has been made, native churches have been backward in this matter. The plan was I believe first introduced into Tinnevelly by Mr. Rhenius, and was then adopted at Nagercoil. In all the stations, contributions are sought for various christian societies. There are for instance the *Bible* Society and the *Tract* Society, both well supported by native subscriptions. In Tinnevelly in 1852 the christians contributed Rs. 900 to the Bible Society. From Travancore, they remitted Rs. 348. At Nagercoil and two neighbouring stations, the same year the collections and purchases in the Tract Society amounted to Rs. 670. At some stations there is a *Book Society;* at some a *Dorcas* or a *Poor* Fund. In the Nagercoil mission subscriptions are gathered as a contribution to the *Home* Society, and for several years they have amounted to a thousand rupees, enough for the support of twelve readers. Throughout Tinnevelly there are societies to aid the building of village churches. An immense number of such churches have been erected by their aid. They subscribe also to the founding of villages as well as societies, and are now endeavouring to establish endowments both by gifts of money and planting lands. Most of the christians are poor, particularly in the southern parts; yet even the poor give willingly. Many that have no money, contribute lumps of sugar: their coin however is very small: the copper *cash* having a very minute value; and many of these appear in the collecting boxes. The catechists and more wealthy men give liberally: and that too without boasting. In special cases many have frequently given a months' salary. One catechist in the Propagation Society's Jubilee gave four month's salary; and when Mr. Cæmmerer objected, thinking it too much, he said that he must give it in thankfulness for what he had received from the mission and for the education of his children in the knowledge of the gospel. The same man on collection days has been known quietly to give his two boys two rupees each to put into the box. Richer men do more. In Mr. Tucker's district, where the Shánárs are wealthy, some have frequently given *five, four,* or three rupees at one time: and one man on several occasions has given twenty-five. Let but the principle be understood and the habit established; and why may not the same be seen in other parts of India?

Through the kind aid of the Rev. W. Clark of Palamcottah I have obtained a carefully prepared statement of the sums of money contributed by the Tinnevelly Christians to their different Christian Societies during the last four years. The statement is not quite complete: but it proves the astonishing fact, that the christians of eleven stations, 21,000 in number, contributed during that period for the various benevolent objects above mentioned, no less than seventeen thousand rupees. If we reckon those of the seven other stations, containing 14,000 people, as liberal in an equal degree, it will exhibit the sum total given by the whole Christian community in the province, as amounting to more than TWENTY-EIGHT THOUSAND rupees in those four years.

At nearly all the stations, numbers of WIDOWS were found by the missionaries to be continually dependent on their charity. In one district, that of Santapuram, Mr. Lewis found *a hundred and fourteen.* Mr. Rhenius many years ago secured for their benefit the establishment of a *Widows' and Orphans' Fund*, at Palamcottah, intended especially for the catechists and other agents of the mission. The same plan has been acted on elsewhere. The societies have been formed on the principle of an Assurance Company: monthly subscriptions are paid; the fund is lent out on interest: and the widows of subscribers receive pensions in proportion to the amount subscribed. These societies have proved exceedingly useful.

Another plan for the benefit of this poor class was devised by Mrs. Mault of Nagercoil. Finding a number of distressed women in the mission she thought of introducing among them the art of LACE-MAKING. She procured materials from England, taught them, and sold their work very advantageously. The women learned it immediately; their taper fingers being admirably suited for the delicate process. At present there are no less than three establishments of this kind; two at Santapuram and Edeyenkoody, with the original one at Nagercoil from which they sprang. Patterns, pins and thread are obtained from England, but the pillows and bobbins are made on the spot. Instruction in the art is reserved for poor but respectable widows, or the very best of the school girls. To the latter it is quite a dowry: and great is the competition among the young men to secure as a bride one of the favoured few who have acquired the skill. It is astonishing what beautiful work they can turn out, and in what comfort they are supported. More than this, the respectability and cleanliness of the employment react upon the mind and character of those who pursue it: and tend to preserve their intelligence and self-respect. Many of them are church members and consistent christians. To many may be applied Cowper's beautiful lines on the English cottager pursuing like employment. They are another specimen of what the gospel, the despised gospel, is doing to elevate the character, and control the principles of the christian poor: and though sceptics may doubt, and infidels oppose, that gospel shall not be without its triumphs even among the happy lace-makers of Nagercoil.

LECTURE FOURTH.

ON THE SYRIAN CHRISTIANS

OF

NORTH TRAVANCORE.

When the Portuguese first landed on the long-sought shores of India, amongst the strange sights that met their eye, there appeared a people, who declared themselves Christians in religion, led the wandering visitors into their churches, and laid before them numerous manuscript copies of the Word of God. The fact of their existence had long previously been published in Europe, but the navigators knew nothing about the matter; and soon turned their wonder into disgust when they discovered that these Christians were heretics who knew nothing of his Holiness the Pope, and were innocent of all belief in the blessings of image worship or the saving efficacy of transubstantiation. The origin of this singular and isolated body of christians is lost in the depths of antiquity. So early as the year 325, a Bishop from India was present at the first council of Nice: and as the creed which the body have held in later times contains neither image-worship, nor transubstantiation, nor Papal authority, nor the sacraments of marriage, of extreme unction and confirmation, it is thereby proved to have had an origin earlier than the period when those doctrines became settled errors in the western church. Cosmas, a celebrated Egyptian merchant, visited them in his voyage to India in 547, and describes their tenets as agreeing much with those of his own church, the Nestorian. He says too that at that time they were accustomed to receive their bishops from Persia. Whether their church began by conversions of the natives of Malabar, or from a Colony of Syrian families, who had settled there for trade, it is now impossible to say with exactness, Most likely the latter notion is the more correct; traditions respecting it being clear and confirmed by collateral circumstances. One thing is quite plain, that the christians in very early times received from Chandra Perumal, king of Kerala or Malabar, high political privileges; which were recorded upon tablets of copper, and were enjoyed undiminished for many centuries. The old copper plates still exist: and a few years ago were carefully translated by Dr. Gundert, one of the German missionaries at Tellicherry. It appears from them, and from the *Kerala Utpotti,* the great chronicle of the Malabar coast, that in ancient days there were four communities of foreign merchants in Malabar, held in high repute; namely, Jews, Manicheans, Nestorians and Arabs. The whole trade of the west coast across the Indian ocean was in their hands: and all were treated by the Kerala kings, with a kindness, liberality and respect, which foreigners do not always enjoy. The Jews appear to have been the oldest settlers, and grew important enough to receive high privileges from the Raja: recorded also on similar plates. One of their number, Joseph Rabbon, was presented with a large estate at Cranganore, was made head of his community, and appointed councillor and commercial manager to the king. Next, one of the Manicheans was elevated to the Lordship of a district and dignified with the title of "grand merchant of Kerala." His people are now numbered among the Sudras. Subsequently the Nestorians received a grant of land near Quilon with the rights of nobility: but they were not so honoured as their predecessors. The Arabs followed, obtaining less distinction still. All these classes are termed MAPILLAS, or moplahs; i. e. people of high rank: being distinguished from one another as Yihudi Mapillás, Nasrani and Suriani Mapillás, and Yavana Mapillás. The privileges which the SYRIAN CHRISTIANS received were very valuable. They took precedence above the Náirs, the highest caste of Sudras: they could have enclosed porches to their houses; and could even ride on elephants, a dignity belonging only to the royal family. They were allowed freely to enter the courts of justice, to walk boldly along the highway with the best of the population, and to enjoy the free exercise of their religion. They were permitted also distinctly to extend their religion by making proselytes; and all their converts, of whatsoever caste, were admitted to the same rights, the same social rank, as the first christians enjoyed. Their Bishop had extensive authority in civil as well as ecclesiastical matters; they were trained to the art of war: and at one time endeavoured to seize the rule of the country. When the Portuguese arrived, the Syrian Christians possessed upwards of a hundred churches, resided in many important villages and were carrying on considerable trade. Their doctrines much resembled, and resemble still, those of the Nestorian Churches in Mesopotamia: they however, reckon themselves as belonging to the SYRIAN CHURCH, so-called; and to this day look for their bishop from Mosul or Mardin where the Patriarch of that Church resides. In tenets they were in some respects evangelical; though their ritual contained many forms and practices deemed erroneous by Protestant Churches: such as, prayers to saints, baptismal regeneration and prayers for the dead. They were, moreover, without spiritual life and had become greatly paganized. Their zeal for the conversion of the heathen had long since cooled: and instead of rejoicing at the introduction of degraded idolaters into the church of Christ, they feared for their own respectability, and had become tenacious of their rank. They seem to have been far more dead than their sister churches in Mesopotamia; as much so as the Armenian, Greek and Coptic churches were only a few years ago. Their scriptures and liturgy were entirely in the old Syriac language, and public worship was rendered totally unprofitable.

It was impossible for the Pope and his emissaries to leave the Malabar christians alone or to refrain from efforts to introduce them into the Romish system. For forty years, however, only measures of conciliation were employed with a view to secure an object so desirable. A college was established to teach their young priests Syriac; the missal was translated into the same tongue and circulated every where. But the priests and people refused to receive images in their churches: to believe in transubstantiation, to follow processions in honour of the Virgin Mary; or to compel their priests to live in celibacy. In 1595, the celebrated Menezes was appointed to the Archbishopric of Goa, and he determined to crush their opposition with a strong hand. He visited their principal churches, and when, in discussion with him as to the origin of their Church, the Syrians appealed to their ancient records, he seized and burned those valuable papers before their eyes. Multitudes of documents, including doubtless many ancient copies of the scriptures, were thus wantonly destroyed. The bishops of the Syrian church were seized and imprisoned; and a new bishop who arrived from Mosul was drowned in Cochin harbour. At length the Archbishop offered to submit the matter to a Council to be assembled at Diamper; and the Syrians agreed to the proposal. Full of guile, he took care to pack the council with men suited to his own views: he disputed loudly and dogmatically with them; and there being no priests whose learning could cope with such a foe, he speedily procured a vote, uniting the whole body to the Church of Rome. For fifty years this unrighteous system of oppression was carried on, adding another black page to the history of Popish persecutions; and pouring upon the earth fresh blood from the saints and martyrs, whose death an angry God has promised to avenge. One can scarcely read these awful tales without crying out in agony: Oh Lord, how long?

The union to Rome remained unbroken for only a few years. Many of the priests and people submitted in silence but with hatred; determined to take the first opportunity of casting off the galling yoke now placed upon their neck. A few Nestorian priests found their way into their midst, and animated by their presence, many churches in recesses among the mountains refused to follow the Romish ritual, and placed themselves under the authority of a former bishop, who had escaped from confinement. On his death they renewed their connection with the patriarchate of Antioch and the intercourse recommenced has been maintained to the present day. In this way the Syrian christians became divided into two bodies: the SYRIANS who remained independent, upholding the doctrine, ritual and practice of the ancient Church: and the ROMO-SYRIANS who adhered to those of the Portuguese Catholics of Goa. The former in all their struggles with the Papacy, appealed not to that divine strength by which alone they could overcome: they asked not for that grace which alone would have rendered their persecution a blessing. They wielded no sword of the Spirit, and they won not the victory of faith. God spared them yet for two hundred years; but in spite of their renewed independence, they improved nothing in doctrine, worship or character. They seem rather to have become infected by the errors into which their neighbours and brethren had fallen, and to have sunk deeper into ignorance, formality and decay. In 1836 the Syrian christians were reckoned as 120,000 in number: and the Romo-Syrians, 60,000. The latter are now declared by the catholic authorities to be 158,000.

Their ecclesiastical system is this. Over the whole church presides a bishop called *Metran,* who is appointed by the Patriarch of the Syrian church at Mardin. The bishop appoints to the different churches *cattanars* or priests, who perform the services of baptism and the communion; read the liturgy, celebrate marriages and bury the dead. Attached to each church are a number of *deacons,* as a lower order of clergy. Many of these deacons are mere boys: who have been ordained solely for the fee which their ordination secures to the bishop. Their churches are strange old buildings, with sloping roofs and gable ends: unlike that of English churches, the chancel is both wider and higher than the rest of the building. Inside the church there are figures of the crucifixion: in the chancel are hung large pictures of similar subjects in bright colours. In front of the altar a lamp is always burning.

The service consists in reading the liturgy with its responses, in the old Syriac language: but the lesson for the day is read in the vernacular Malealim. It was with great pleasure that on the reading desk of several of these Syrian churches I found the Syriac New Testament of the British and Foreign Bible Society: it has been in use for many years. In the Romo-Syrian churches there is of course no such wise instructor to give even one lesson each day. These latter churches retain much of the old fashions of the primitive churches; but have superadded numbers of Roman Catholic emblems. Crosses, pictures of the saints and of the Virgin Mary, are very common: the outside is adorned with figures, standing in niches, of the apostles and saints. The tomtom, fireworks, and incessant firing of guns, attend the weddings and festival processions of these people, as they do of the heathen. The service is still read in the old Syriac language, and not in Latin: but the native cattanars know nothing beyond the routine of their mass book. All the people are excessively ignorant and their religion consists in nothing but forms. Near Cochin are the head-quarters of the Romo-Syrian mission in the island of Verápoli; where the vicar-general resides. Two seminaries and a large establishment of priests are maintained there. From the harbour of Cochin no less than seven of these Catholic churches are visible. Pleasant indeed do their white walls and turrets appear, peeping from the rich foliage by which they are surrounded: but the incessant din of cannons, and the sight of niches for saints, dispel the illusions of fancy, and exhibit them to the christian mind as embodiments of real heathenism, remembrancers of dire acts of oppression, and illustrations of that "other gospel" of antichrist which ruins souls for ever.

The country in which these Syrians are settled, is one of the richest in Southern India. It lies partly in the dominions of the Cochin Raja and partly in the northern districts of Travancore. In shape it is long and narrow. From the sea on the west coast for a distance inland averaging ten or twelve miles, it is pretty flat or marked only by gentle undulations available for cultivation. Beyond this tract low hills occur on which flocks are pastured; and at the back of all, runs the great chain of ghauts between Travancore and Tinnevelly, covered with forests and with dense jungle, in which the tiger, the cheeta and the wild elephant abound. The inhabited part of Travancore, before reaching the highest hills, is on the average twenty-four miles in breadth. Abundance of water is supplied to it from the ghauts, and by the great monsoon in June. Innumerable streams flow towards the sea, among the slopes and on the level plain; so frequent are they and in parts so continuous, that a great part of the country may be traversed by their means, as are the Sunderbunds and southern districts of Bengal near Calcutta. At a short distance from the sea shore a continuous stream of water, narrower or broader in different places, runs along the whole coast. It is called the Backwater, and is extensively used for transporting the inland produce from north to south without the dangers of coast navigation. Owing to this abundant supply of water, the whole country is green all the year round. In the low lands are raised extensive fields of rice: on slopes and drier spots, fine crops of corn and other grain are reaped. In sandy parts the cocoanuts grow in profusion: in the most southern districts are the palm-topes already described. Pepper, and other spices cover the land; in the jungles the teak, the dark anjeli, and the ebony tree are very common: and give to the range of mountains their sombre and desolate appearance. Wild flowers spread over the land in profusion; the mangoe-bird and others of variegated plumage adorn the leafy jungles; the flying-lizard and flying-squirrel are met with in the woods: the otter and alligator possess the waters; while among the reptiles may be found every kind, from the little goldsnake that sleeps in the kúldeva flower to the great boa constrictor that hides in the forest shade. There are many points from which the traveller, as he passes through this richly endowed country, catches the most delightful prospects. One of the most beautiful that I saw was from the astronomical observatory at Trevandrum.

The population of TRAVANCORE according to the census of 1836, amounts to 1,280,000. Of these 28,000 are bráhmins. The Nairs, Sudras, and other high castes number 450,000, one third of the whole. The Shánárs and Ilavas amount, as we have already seen, to 290,000. The SLAVES are 128,000. The bráhmins are very powerful and exercise more influence on the government in this little state than on all the rulers of the rest of India put together. They are divided into three classes; the Nambouris or native Maleali bráhmins; the Puti or Canara bráhmins; and the foreign bráhmins from other parts. Of these the Nambouris rank highest of all. They and the Canara bráhmins are ten thousand in number: of the foreign bráhmins, there are about eighteen thousand. The temples throughout Travancore are almost all meanly built; even the best of them can make not the slightest pretensions to architectural beauty: although some bear a celebrated name. They are altogether about 4,000 in number: amongst them three hundred are dedicated to Vishnu and

Siva. They are all reckoned so holy that no Europeans are allowed to enter them: or to build their churches within a considerable distance of the road along which their worshippers march in procession. The annual festivals in Travancore are of course celebrated with great pomp and spirit: especially the Wonum, at which the people observe a general holiday, decorate their houses with flowers, and illuminate them at night. One important feast, the Murájabam, is celebrated at Trevandrum only once in six years. It lasts fifty-six days, and all the bráhmin population of the province, who join in its ceremonies, are hospitably entertained by the government during that period. Again, for the special benefit of the bráhmin population, there have been established in various parts of the province, Uttupárás, or public inns, where free meals are given to such of the bráhmins as choose to accept of them. These places are forty in number: at one half of them, food is prepared twice a day: at the other half, only once. And so numerous are the priestly applicants for the royal bounty, that their maintenance costs the government no less than £25,000 a year. The other religious institutions and temples swallow up £51,000 more; and thus the bráhmins obtain from this petty state, with a revenue of £370,000, no less than £76,000, or one-fifth of the whole. As another illustration of the strength of bráhminism in Travancore I may mention that it is the rule, when a new Raja ascends the throne, to weigh him with golden weights. The process completed, the amount is coined into very small gold coins, and distributed to all the bráhmins, male and female, young and old, that are found in Trevandrum on the auspicious day. A story is current that the present Raja on his accession to the throne was a thin man, and the brahmins fearful of losing their accustomed douceur, purposely delayed the ceremony till he had attained a respectable size.

Their sway, however, over their august monarch is not confined to this undignified but profitable ceremony. They make a gain of every circumstance that occurs in his person or his family, and compel him to observe all the private and public ceremonies of Hinduism with rigid punctuality. On not a few occasions, does he walk barefoot on visits to the sea or to the great temples, in token of his holy zeal for the faith to which he is enslaved. The bráhmins too lord it over Europeans as far as they can. If a procession is moving towards a temple, or holy food being borne along the streets, Europeans are ordered to get out of the way, that they may not pollute it. The government is chiefly in their hands, and is as full of corruption as it can well be. Being independent of the East India

Company, it contains very few Europeans. The Raja, his Dewan or chief minister, the Judges of the supreme and inferior courts, are nearly all natives and possess the whole authority. The Government of India merely appoints a Resident, who is bound to give advice to the Raja in all important cases, while the Raja is equally bound to follow it. The native government maintains for itself a small body of troops called the Nair Brigade, consisting of two battalions drawn from that caste, containing 1600 men; they are disciplined and commanded by English officers. The present Raja is in education and capacity of mind far ahead of his predecessors: he speaks English well, is a great chemist, and is fond of getting all the new inventions that he hears of. His Durbar hall contains a great variety of English curiosities. In Trevandrum he, several years ago, established an English school and placed it under the care of a master of decided piety: it was at first a pay-school, but was at length made quite free. Mr. Roberts, the master, after some time, cautiously and with much prudence introduced the Bible into the school, making the study of it quite voluntary. Many held back at the outset; but soon, as a matter of curiosity, some offered to enter the Bible class: others joined; and from that time till now, during several years, the Bible lesson has been given without any objection. The school has prospered and been useful: it might have become much more so, if those who hold authority had extended to it that fostering care which it deserved at their hands. It is under this native government that the greater part of the Syrian churches reside, and it is with influences naturally springing from an authority in which Hinduism possesses such a large share, that the missions planted among them have had to contend.

The first effort of modern times to penetrate the ignorance in which these Syrian christians were enveloped was made by the Rev. Dr. Kerr, who at the desire of Lord W. Bentinck, then governor of Madras, proceeded into the Máléáli country, and made minute enquiries concerning them. He sought and obtained valuable information concerning the history of their church, the doctrines believed, their system of worship, and the persecutions to which the papists had subjected them. Dr. Buchanan of Calcutta, a few months later, proceeded to the same spot, on the appointment of Lord Wellesley, to make similar enquiries, especially in reference to the use of the scriptures among them. The object of both was, to see how far a union could be effected between the Syrians and the Church of England. Dr. Buchanan's sympathetic imagination was greatly excited by the sight of this ancient people, and he wrote in his

"Researches" a glowing account of them and of their wrongs. He found among them 55 churches, acknowledging the patriarch of Antioch as their head, but otherwise forming an independent body of christians. Having gained their confidence, he succeeded in procuring a number of valuable manuscript copies of their Syriac version of the Bible; and engaged (if they would give them up to him) to return in their stead a hundredfold printed copies of the same, from the Bible Society, for the use of their churches and cattanars. From these, I believe, the first modern copies of the version were published. The Metran or bishop of the church, at the time, was a man well disposed towards the gospel, and quite ready to allow the circulation of the scriptures among his people. Under his sanction a Máleáli translation of the scriptures also was commenced; but being badly executed came to nothing. Col. Macaulay, and after him Col. Munro, both Residents at the court of Trevandrum, took a deep interest in the revival of these churches; and the result of their measures, and of the kind treatment of the Ráni, was a great improvement in the general spirit of the people, in their circumstances and political condition. They secured amongst other things a consideration and protection which they had not enjoyed for years. Col. Munro endeavoured also to heal their dissensions; but his plans were frustrated until the death of their bishop and the appointment of a successor; when comparative peace was restored. His next step was to apply to the Church Missionary Society for agents who should give the Syrians the religious instruction which they so greatly needed. Accordingly Messrs. Norton and Bailey proceeded to Travancore in 1816, and in the following year Mr. Bailey opened the valuable mission at Cottayam. In 1819, three missionaries had entered on that important station, Messrs. Bailey, Penn and Baker: they reported that no less 50,000 or 60,000 christians were immediately accessible to them, and expressed it as their purpose unitedly to keep up the most close and intimate intercourse with the Syrian bishop and his cattanars, with a view to elevate and establish their religious views, and thus ultimately elevate the people at large. The theory looked well, and was carried out with patience and energy for many years. The missionaries found at Cottayam the college which had been established in 1815 by Col. Munro, and been liberally endowed by the Ráni with lands and grants of money, including Rs. 5,000 at the very outset. They joined the college with hearty zeal and endeavoured so to organize its system of instruction and government, as to render it an efficient training establishment for the Syrian clergy. In addition to the superintending missionary there were two Syriac professors (Malpans): a Hebrew professor, and teachers of Sanskrit, Latin and English. Between forty and fifty students soon joined the institution: their ability seemed high, their spirit and conduct excellent: their desire for learning not inferior to what is found in English lads of the same age. The whole Syrian population were reported as looking to the college as the eye of their body; and it was fondly hoped that, under God's blessing, in ten years fifty or a hundred learned priests would be found, "in this venerable church," nourishing their own flocks and spreading the triumphs of the gosple among them.

At the same time three Seminaries, on the plan of Free Grammar schools, were projected for the three divisions of the Metran's diocese: from which the more promising lads were to be advanced to the college. Parochial schools were next established all over the district and in a few years, there existed no less than 37 of them, containing 900 scholars. The missionaries also prepared religious tracts and elementary works in the Máleáli language. A translation of the New Testament was soon required; and was commenced by Mr. Bailey, who devoted to it all the energy and knowledge of his active and persevering mind. He translated also a great part of the English Liturgy into the same language. A press to print these works was soon found to be essentially necessary to the success of these literary labours. But Mr. Bailey could not get one: he was promised a fount of types from the Government Press at Madras, but when they arrived they were found to be quite useless. Mr. Bailey however was not a man to be put down by difficulties: he began to cut the matrices for types with his own hand: made his punches from them: invented moulds; cast a fount for himself; and finished it off for use. He then made a printing press, taking his model from some Cyclopædia; finally he taught a lad in one of the schools to set up the types. Thus it was, he brought out his first edition of the Máleáli Testament. The translation, the types, the printing, the press, were entirely the work of his own laborious hand. The printing-office at Cottayam flourishes still: it has convenient rooms for composing, pressing and storing both materials and finished works. Numerous native compositors are employed there; it possesses ample supplies of beautiful type; new type is cast whenever needed; the printing is performed with the efficient iron presses so common now in India. But though the Columbian and Stanhope presses are elegant in form, are instruments of great power, and complete their work rapidly, to my mind, as I passed over the establishment, the most interesting object amongst all the printing apparatus, was the old original press, with its huge wooden beams, now laid aside; a monument of patient industry and self-devoting zeal.

The officials of the Syrian church were at the outset well-affected to the new order of things. They saw the great interest felt in the church by English people: they saw also that the missionaries made no aggressions upon their own rights and privileges: that they wished only to revive the spirit of the people at large; and being well disposed towards the gospel, cordially promoted the plans which the missionaries had adopted; especially as they found the secular and political interests of the people were advanced through the powerful friends who had risen up to protect them. The Metran of the day was Mar Dionysius, a man of amiable deportment and religious tone of mind. He resided in the college, was associated with the missionaries in its management, and was always consulted on every plan and measure intended to enlighten and instruct the people. He was thus made not only head of the church but of the mission likewise. He sympathized with the efforts of their English friends and both he and the clergy about him expressed their gratitude for those efforts to the society which had originated them. Thus things went on for several years. The press, the college and the schools were maintained efficiently. One missionary after another joined the pioneers; new stations were established in important localities, as at *Cochin, Trichur,* and *Mavelikurray;* in numerous out-stations public worship was performed and schools maintained, with the same hope as animated the Society from the outset. By degrees however the missionaries gained a clearer estimate of their true position. They saw that in relation to the Syrian church they were absolutely without authority; they were mere volunteers in the attempt to get rid of existing evils; they were physicians ready to assist the cure of a disease of which they had clear perceptions; but which the patient scarcely felt, and in regard to which he might at any time decline their services in toto. They found that when the novelty of the thing had worn off, the old Adam in the people had greatly revived. They saw that the spiritual worth of the church and the task of raising it up, had been much overrated. They found the people careless about real religion; they found the priesthood unconverted; looking after their fees, formal in their service; the whole body was lifeless and cold. They found enmity gradually excited, especially in persons of influence, by their pure doctrine. While they preached Christ crucified; the priests in power taught regeneration by baptism, and the efficacy of prayers for the dead. By those prayers the priests gained their chief support, and they were of course opposed to a system of doctrine which diminished their gains. They found themselves and their usefulness entirely in the hands of the Metran: all the priests were ordained by him; all their priests, all their scholars and students were under his ecclesiastical authority. If any were obnoxious to him, or to the priests generally, by peculiar excellence or fidelity, he could refuse ordination, or he could forbid them to preach; or by himself he could keep up the error already existing of ordaining boys as deacons. As head of the mission he could check or alter, or refuse to sanction, measures for the improvement of the people. In the course of time all this opposition was experienced in fact; an irreligious Metran was appointed, who cared nothing for the spiritual progress of the church: and on more than one occasion, a missionary in charge of the college, returning suddenly to his class room, after going homeward, caught the Metran or one of the native Professors in the very act of teaching some doctrine, the very opposite of that which he had just laid down—and purposely undoing all the good which the missionary had just endeavoured to do.

After submitting to this opposition for a long time, and seeing the labours of the missionaries set at nought, the Bishop of Calcutta a few years ago, resolved to disconnect the Church Missionary Society from the Syrian Church altogether. The missionaries left the college; their assistants left the Syrian body: their converts did the same: and the whole drew off from the decayed church, exactly as converts in Bengal or Tinnevelly separate themselves from the heathen. These converts and the missions founded for their benefit have since greatly prospered; large congregations exist at every station: including no less than 4000 persons young and old: of whom 1000 are communicants. Fifty day-schools exist for boys; and 150 girls are instructed in the boarding schools. The chief stations are six in number of which five are in most important localities among the Syrian christians. *Trichoor* contains 12,000 Syrians: *Cottayam, Mávelikáre, Tiruwilla* and *Pallam* are in the very heart of the churches, and are advancing in usefulness every year. Their handsome Gothic churches, their school and mission houses, bear testimony to a purer faith and purer missionary zeal for the true Head of the redeemed church, than their dull neighbours, the venerable buildings of former times.

As a body, the Syrians remain very inactive, irreligious and formal. Yet their knowledge of the gospel has been greatly increased, both by its preaching among them and the spread of the printed word. Numbers possess and are able to read that word for themselves. They have much less faith in prayers for the dead than formerly; and many priests have in consequence been obliged to give up their work in the church in order to get a livelihood by other means: some are employing themselves in so undignified a pursuit, as the making of embroidered fans. The mind of the people has been greatly unsettled by the disputes concerning the office of the Metran: three or four rivals have claimed authority together for years: and they look all the more to the quiet and prosperous missions of the Church Society for true help and guidance. The heathen too are coming nearer. Several cases have occurred in which high brahmins, nairs and sudras, have come forward to profess Christ: and a remarkable progress has been made among the wild hill people, especially the Chogans and Araans, living in the jungles near the ghauts. Thus is the wilderness made glad: thus the parched desert becomes like the garden of the Lord.

LECTURE FOURTH: PART SECOND.

THE JESUIT MISSIONS
IN
SOUTH INDIA.

When the Portuguese first arrived in India, they obtained possession of the town and territory of Goa. As became good catholics, they soon had an archbishop appointed by the king with numerous clergy: but they did little for the heathen for many years: the scandalous lives of the Europeans high and low, giving their native subjects the lowest idea of their moral and religious character. The first really missionary efforts were made by Xavier, who landed at Goa in 1542, now three hundred years ago. Directing his attention to the state of his own countrymen, he set his face against their shameless wickedness, and it is said by his instructions and personal influence, produced a considerable reformation in Goa. He next went and visited the fishing villages farther down the west coast, especially in the southwest of Travancore; and coming as both their political deliverer and religious instructor, enrolled thousands as disciples of Christ. Passing onward and round Cape Comorin to the gulf of Manaar and the Pearl Fishery coast, he baptized thousands more of the same class, remaining among them for five or six years. His chief church is still at *Kotar*, a mile from Nagercoil; and is celebrated for the miracles wrought within its walls. An annual festival in his name is maintained to the present time. The fishing villages to which he went, are situated all along the two coasts of India, at intervals of two or three miles. They are not very large and are inhabited by people of the lowest kind. On the west coast they are termed Mukúas; on the east, Paravers. To this day thousands of these people call themselves christians. As the traveller passes through their village on the sandy beach, he sees a large cross or two, and a very common hut, very like one of the Shánár devil-sheds, but of considerable size. This is the church. I remember especially a village and church of this kind close to Cape Comorin.

In Tinnevelly all the Paravers are catholics, and hundreds are found in different localities all up the east coast as far as Pulicat. They are in the lowest state of ignorance and degradation. The very morning that I left Madras, I had a painful illustration of this fact. In going on board the *Hindostan* in the Madras roads, we had to pass through a very rough and wild surf, which now and then broke right over the boat. In all their difficulties and dangers, the boatmen uttered but one cry "*San Javier*;" "*San Javier*." During the many pitchings and rollings of our stormy trip, they had but one talisman to trust to, the name and intercession of their patron saint, "*San Javier!*"

When Xavier left the country other Jesuit missionaries entered on his work. The most celebrated among his successors were the missionaries of Madura. Their head and founder was *Robert de Nobili,* the nephew of Cardinal Bellarmine, who began a new mission entirely on a new plan. The energy, the self-denial, the hardship and privations endured by his followers were very great: but according to their own account the results correspond to their efforts; the mission being vaunted as the most successful in all modern times. With a view to overcome the repugnance of the natives to familiar intercourse with Europeans, Robert de Nobili after a successful study of the Tamil language, disguised himself as a brahmin, and before brahmins in Madura swore on oath, that like them he was descended from the God Brahma, and had obtained a revelation of the true divine law. After a time many came to him fully believing that he was not a European, but a genuine brahmin from another part of India: his successors kept up the same system and maintained it against all opposition for a hundred and fifty years. They assert that they never baptized till after careful examination of their candidates; that their converts were christians of the most spiritual views and the most holy lives; that for weeks together they might hear their confessions without finding one guilty of mortal sin: that their disciples had a perfect horror of idolatry and all its accompanying rites: that they were even desirous of persecution and under it upheld their faith most nobly: that even the devil acknowledged the excellence of their mission and could injure none of its weakest members; while the fear of the devil so drove converts into the church, that he might be termed the best catechist in the mission; that tigers also refused to injure christians passing through their jungles; that numerous miracles were continually wrought especially in Xavier's church at Kotar: and that their people were on the whole a most excellent and angelic body of converts. Such is their own account: but there is evidence of the clearest kind from their own pens and from Papal records, that the whole plan was a LIE; that it began in lies and perjury: that in perjury and lies it was maintained; and by lying and deception was utterly ruined in the end. From the outset Robert de Nobili and the others denied with oaths that they were *Feringis* or Europeans, asserting boldly that they were real brahmins; they dressed, bathed and ate like brahmins, wore the sacred thread, put ashes on their breast and forehead; wore the native wooden shoes; and slept upon a tiger's skin. Themselves assert that their whole attention was given to concealing the fact that they were Feringis, since they augured the complete destruction of the mission from its discovery. Yet after all they failed to bring in the brahmin class for whose conversion their system was adopted. Sudras came; but the majority of their people were Pariás. Thousands on thousands of this class were baptized: but they were never elevated, and the missionaries kept up as great a distinction between them and the higher castes after their profession as before it. They also baptized by stealth thousands of dying heathen children; their catechists and christians would go to the sick under pretence of giving medicine, and knowing the baptismal formula, administer the rite unknown to the parties themselves. In this way, they boast of immense numbers of converts. In managing their converts, they kept up the same system of deception and compromise. They allowed them the same cars and idolatrous processions as before, the Virgin Mary taking the place of the Hindu god: the christians too in certain cases *joined the heathen* in their idolatrous ceremonies. In their marriages the heathen emblems, the heathen rites and customs as to food, were all kept up still: in their bathings they still repeated the same formulas as before, uttering the name of some god as they touched each successive limb. In fact, except as to name they were, exactly and in every respect, the same heathen Pariás as they were before. Hence as a matter of course in the Tanjore persecutions in 1701, thousands at once apostatized: and in later years in the Mysore, under Tippoo, of 60,000 catholics, says the Abbe Dubois, *not one* had the courage to die for his religion.

As soon as Pope Gregory heard of these proceedings, he commanded the priests to desist from them. They received his command in silence and went on as before. The Cardinal de Tournon was despatched to India to examine into the matter; and after ascertaining every particular from the confessions of two leading missionaries, passed a decree forbidding the continuance of all or any of these practices. They remonstrated and *took oath* that to deprive their converts of any of their customs in marriage, bathing, processions or feasts, would be to endanger their souls' salvation! What an awful confession from these blinded men; that to give them the pure gospel would ruin their souls; while to continue their heathen practices would ensure their salvation! Yet these men called themselves ministers, not of heathenism, but of Christ. Failing in Europe to get the decree reversed, they yet in one of their churches, "called the body and blood of Christ to witness" that it had been annulled and the forbidden practices allowed. "Obstinate and impudent" (as Pope Clement styles them,) they would not obey the papal decrees sent to them again and again. At length according to the Brief of 1734, they vowed and swore on the holy gospels, that they would obey; and at once without delay they perjured themselves by persisting in their former contumacy. As a last resource, Pope Benedict ordered that any one of the missionaries who should refuse to carry out his oath, should be transmitted to Rome immediately. They were compelled to stop, beaten at every turn, and in 1773 the Society was dissolved.* Of all misrepresentations of missionary labour, theirs was the most awful: of all deliberate rejection of the gospel, for heathen rules in preference, theirs was the most voluntary: of all the lying and perjury, which have been committed by men of knowledge and education, theirs were the most deliberate, most unblushing, most continued, that the world ever saw. Such was in deed and in truth the system of the famous Madura Mission: a mission full of scandalous wickedness from its beginning to its end.

For nearly sixty years, i. e. from 1773 to 1830, scarcely any care was taken of the catholic missions and of their numerous converts. The older missionaries gradually died out, while none arrived from Europe to fill their place. The Paris Seminary for Foreign Missions was destroyed in the revolution of 1793: and thus in 1802 the whole of the French Missions in India had but one Bishop and fifteen European priests, several of whom were old men. So great was the disproportion between them and their flocks that many congregations could not be visited even once a year. In 1807, the priests were reduced to five. In 1830 some Roman Catholics went over to the Protestant Missions, and as the number of Protestant Missionaries was greatly increasing, an appeal was made to the Society for the propagation of the faith

* Calcutta Review, II. pp 77—115.

to send Jesuits again to their former sphere. The offer was accepted, and at once the whole of South India was parcelled out into different Vicariates, as were other parts of Asia. In 1837 four Jesuit priests arrived at Pondicherry: and five more in the next two years: in ten years, sixty-four arrived, and were spread throughout the missions, so as to render their services as efficient as possible. One of the first matters which attracted their notice was, that the Goa clergy had, during the days of neglect, quietly taken possession of many of the Jesuit churches: and assumed the pastorship of their congregations. The Portuguese crown entirely opposed the right of the Pope to appoint Vicars apostolic to these dioceses in India; the right of patronage having been conferred on it in former days by Pope Leo. To this claim the Jesuits reply that Portugal is unable to maintain the ancient bishoprics, and that having an archbishop at Goa is a mere farce. A deadly feud exists between the parties: and in numerous instances expensive lawsuits have been carried on by the new comers in order to oust the Goa "schismatics" from their territories. In many cases they have succeeded; in others they have been foiled. All the catholics of South India are in the Jesuit almanac divided into *Orthodox* and *Schismatic*.

A peculiar circumstance which for many years distinguished the modern mission was the repeated deaths of young and promising missionaries. Totally inexperienced in the influences of an Indian climate and having no elder associates to give them advice, these zealous men from the time they arrived gave themselves up to a life of hardship, starvation and toil. They spent a large portion of the year in travelling through their districts; walking long distances and putting up in mud huts, eight feet square, totally unfurnished; they generally slept upon the damp ground, and contented themselves with little food. They were accustomed to eat nothing but rice and fish curry. Meat or wine never passed their lips, and the taste of bread was almost unknown. As a natural consequence of this severe and entire change from that diet to which they had been accustomed in Europe, they began to fall with fearful rapidity: cholera became quite common among them; and several were seized with it at the very altar, while performing mass, after a night spent almost entirely in listening to the confessions of their people. In ten years twenty-one priests died out of sixty-four; the majority of whom had not reached thirty-five years of age. These facts are mentioned in a little work, entitled *the Jesuit Mission in India*, published in 1852 by the Rev. W. Strickland, a Jesuit priest at Trichinopoly. It contains numerous facts most condemnatory of the system it describes. In 1841, Father Clifford, an English Jesuit, brother of Lord Clifford, joined the mission. His plain English common sense discerned at once the folly of the system which they were pursuing, and from the time of his arrival, he remonstrated again and again with the Superiors of the mission in France, assuring them that it was far more expensive to send out new and inexperienced missionaries, than to take proper care of the experienced men already in the country. The repeated deaths of his brethren, especially in 1843, convinced the Superiors that he was right; and permission was given for the missionaries to take a small quantity of wine daily, of bread a moderate portion, and meat every day except Fridays, Saturdays and the fast-days of the church. From the time when the new rule began to tell upon their constitutions, the mortality was greatly reduced, and for several years has not been much greater than in healthier spheres of labour. Father Clifford did much to build up the modern Jesuit Mission, during his short career. He seems to have been a man of great zeal, and to have acted from very high motives. His spirit was full of affection, and he was a powerful preacher. He was stationed at Trichinopoly for the double reason, that it is a large Civil station; and in addition to the officers of two Native Regiments, has a European Regiment and Artillery. His work therefore was, as an Englishman of rank, to influence the English: he was greatly beloved by the Catholic soldiers and much respected by Protestants as an upright and consistent priest of his church. In 1844 after a short career of three years in India he was drowned in the Coleroon. His successor at Trichinopoly, also an Englishman, was a great hunter, and used up all the hacks of the town in his enthusiastic sports: he soon dissipated the good feeling which Father Clifford had excited towards their church. One of the chief objects which the latter earnestly aimed to accomplish, was the establishment of a College at Negapatam, which should serve both as a boarding school for young catholic boys and as a training school for native priests. The college was founded in 1845: and its present large building was opened two years ago. I went over it in the course of my journey, with one of the priests, and also over the Jesuit Church and Seminary in Pondicherry. Two other institutions of the kind have long existed in the pleasant and well cultivated island of Verapoli, the head-quarters of the Romo-Syrian mission in North Travancore: another has been established at Quilon; and there is a sixth seminary at Mangalore.

At the present time, the Jesuit and Roman Catholic missions are spread very widely throughout the Madras Presidency. We have nothing like them in North India, except in the neighbourhood of Dacca, at Hussingabad, Furreedpore and Pubna, where there is a Catholic population of 13,000 souls. It will be useful to sum up the Roman Catholic population as given in the *Madras Catholic Directory* for 1853, a work published on authority, *permissu superiorum.* A similar statement, taken apparently from the same authority, was handed in to the recent India Committee in the House of Commons.

Vicariate.	Catholics.	Schismatics.	Regular Priests, Jesuits.	Children under instruction.
Madras,........	41,400	8,334	17	1600
Hyderabad, ...	4,000	250	6	... 5 schools.
Vizagapatam, ..	6,250	...	12	70
Pondicherry, ..	96,550	...	41	
Mysore, ...	19,000	...	12	... 6 schools.
Coimbatoor,....	20,000	20	11	...
Madura, ...	150,000	...	38	...
Quilon, ...	44,000	9,000	18	...
Verapoly, ...	69,180 Latin. 158,826 Syrian.	...	41 Natives. 397 Natives.	... ...
Mangalore, ...	13,052	18,000	5 + 17	...
	612,258	35,604	160 + 455 natives.	

This table compiled from the *Directory*, gives the very large number of 650,000 persons as followers of the Roman Catholic Church, either as schismatics or genuine catholics. Such may indeed be the fact: yet it is acknowledged that the Jesuit missionaries still make converts, or as they call it, still "save souls," by the plan, "adopted so largely in all our missions," of baptizing dying children. But what sort of christians are these so-called converts? The missionaries do not preach; they have never once given a copy of the Bible to their people; they have few schools, or none; they only administer the various "sacraments" according to rule; their time is spent chiefly in hearing thousands of confessions; the converts observe the distinctions of caste which are very strong throughout the Tamil country: many heathen customs are still retained by them, in weddings and feasts: in great festivals the priests accompany the catholics at night as they draw their car through the public streets with tomtoms, shouts, torches and fireworks:—what can they have learned under such circumstances; what can they, under such a system, know, of all the high requirements of the law of God?

Uninstructed, without the Bible, what can they understand of the minuteness with which the holy law of Christ enters as a guiding principle into every thought and act and purpose of a christian's life. If those who are constantly instructed from our pulpits, and who, educated in good schools, read for themselves intelligently the word of God, still feel that for warning, exhortation and comfort such study and such instruction are daily required to counteract the heart's evil,—what must be the degraded condition of the poor Paravers and Mukuas and Romo-Syrians and Parias, who are called christians indeed, but are full of heathen notions, are never taught to read or write, never preached to, and are encouraged in their heathenish practices by their teacher himself. Is it not a mere matter of course, that we find them as they once were, with only the names of their deities changed, while their thoughts, belief and conduct remain as degraded as ever. That this is really the case, has been declared by Protestant missionaries over and over again; when they have met these native catholics in retired villages of the country: *perfect heathen in every thing but name.*

I think that in India, Protestant missionaries have nothing to fear from Roman Catholics; even with the skill and policy for which the Jesuits are celebrated. Their converts help to draw away fallen and outcast christians, and are a great scandal in the way of the heathen; but otherwise it seems to me there is little cause to fear their injuring us among the natives. The Hindus have gods of their own and need not the Catholic Saints as intercessors. They have a ritual of their own and need not the Papist beads. They have their own cars and ceremonies and processions; why should they join a people who have borrowed them from them. More than that, if there is one thing which has distinguished Protestant Missions in India more than another, it is that they have fearlessly spread the Word of God, and have widely established schools to illustrate that word with all the reasons that an enlightened mind can grasp. The Roman Catholics flourish in ignorance. The Protestant missionaries have gained their 100,000 converts by hard battles with the sword of wisdom. The one has invoked darkness to its aid; the other light. The one has trusted to human policy; the other appeals to the converting grace of God.

Nor do I think that the Jesuit missionaries deserve above Protestants praise for their self-denial. I allow that they dress simply, eat plainly, and have few luxuries at home. I allow that they travel much, are greatly exposed, live poorly and toil hard. I have heard of a bishop, living in a cave on fifty rupees a month, and devotedly attending the sick when friends and relatives had fled from fear. But all this is much easier on the Jesuit's principles, than it is to be a faithful minister on the principles of the New Testament. The Jesuit missionary's chief care is to administer baptism and the mass rightly: to hear confessions and prepare for the communion. He studies not the Bible to find lessons of instruction suitable to the condition of his people: if he finds among them gross sin, the next absolution wipes it all away. He does not mourn over the heathen practices of his converts; he upholds and encourages them. Their blind ignorance of God's truth is no burden to his mind; firm faith in the church is amply sufficient to secure their salvation. Nor is his own condition simply one of discomfort. The church teaches him that self-denial for its service is a ground of religious merit; which the saints will not forget; and for which he will be amply rewarded in another world. To such a motive, human nature is peculiarly sensitive. History proves that to obtain merit there is no depth of suffering and misery to which a human being will not submit. Hindu sannyásis suffer enough; but the anchorets of Mesopotamia in the early church suffered immensely more. Far different is the belief of the christian and the christian minister. He fights against his very nature from the first: he cuts away the root of human pride and of self-righteousness by acknowledging salvation only by another. And when he labours, he labours with this conviction, that when all has been done that was appointed, he is only an unprofitable servant. A Protestant minister too is not contented with the mere performance of a line of ceremonies. He looks not to baptism, to the Lord's Supper, and to extreme unction, for his people's salvation: he is not contented to leave them in ignorance, relying on these things and knowing nothing of their Saviour. He makes it is his first duty to warn and teach, to exhort and invite, to comfort and cheer his flock. If he finds gross sins, he mourns over the signs of an unconverted heart and feels that those who call themselves christians are in the gall of iniquity still. These things constitute the grand difference between the two parties. The one throughout his course acts with human nature; the other fights ever against it. The one submits himself to the smooth doctrines of the religion of man; the other, to the humbling precepts of the revelation of God. Which of these is the easier: which of them is the greater burden. The physical privations of a Jesuit, (and he has no other), supported by his motives of self-righteousness, are not to be compared to the mental anxieties and griefs of a faithful Protestant pastor. They are as much lighter to bear, as it is easier to crush the body than to mortify the soul. Because the gospel of the New Testament finds these spiritual evils to contend with, while all other religions yield to and adopt them, I take the fact as a clear indication that that GOSPEL IS FROM GOD.

LECTURE FIFTH.

GOVERNMENT EFFORTS AMONG THE KHONDS.

When visiting in 1849, the missionary boarding-schools at Cuttack and Balasore in the province of Orissa, my attention was specially drawn to a class of children, who but for the humane interference of Government would have been brutally sacrificed upon the blood-stained altars of heathen gods. These children were termed Merias. They belonged not to the Oriya population, amongst whom they were then living, but had sprung from the *Khonds* of the distant hills, and for very safety had been brought by the officers of government down into the Orissa plains. Their dark complexion, broad face, and flat nose, shewed them to be of different origin from that of the Hindus; while the position they had occupied, and the horrid death from which they had been saved, invested them with a peculiar interest; and rendered them objects of peculiar solicitude to those who are interested in seeing the fruits of christian humanity developed amid oriental barbarity and crime. Surely every christian heart will join in the prayer, then mentally offered, that these dear young people might be brought by the Spirit of God to "present their bodies a living sacrifice" to the Saviour of sinners; as the most "reasonable service" they could render to Him for saving them from a cruel and bloody death in ignorance and sin; and for bringing them out of the darkness of idolatry into the gospel's marvellous light. Much has been written of late years concerning the human sacrifices prevalent among the Khonds: but I have thought it advisable in order to complete these sketches of Missions in the Presidency of Madras, to describe them somewhat in detail: and to sketch the history of those measures which have been employed for their suppression.

THE KHOND COUNTRY.

The Khonds are an aboriginal people inhabiting the hills which border the southern portion of the country of Orissa: their territory lies almost entirely within the Presidency of Madras. Till a few years ago, nothing whatever was known concerning them. In the year 1829, when Lord Bentinck abolished the rite of Suttee, no one could have informed him, that within four hundred miles of Calcutta, their existed numerous tribes, who were then perpetrating human sacrifices and destroying their female infants, without one thought that they were doing wrong. Even by the Supreme Government of India, the thing was absolutely unknown. It was in 1836, when the Raja of Goomsur, who had long been tributary to the East India Company, rebelled against the Government, that a military force was required to occupy his territory and to subdue the Khond tribes of Upper Goomsur, to whom he had fled. The Government and the Khonds then became intimately known to each other for the first time; and then for the first time all the barbarous practices of the latter stood revealed to the wide world. The enquiries then and subsequently made by the Government officers, brought to light the manners and habits of these hill barbarians; the character of their country; the constitution of their Societies; the relations in which they stood to each other and to the Zemindars of the country near them; their domestic, social and tribal feuds; their mode of life; the amount of their civilization and knowledge; their religious superstitions; and the objects and method of their worship. Thus was it found that in extensive districts human sacrifices were practised; in others, female infanticide; in others, both these evils; in a few others, neither of them. This information contributed chiefly to the Madras Government, by many officers and during several years, appears in the most complete form in the ably-written Reports of Capt. Macpherson, the first of which was published by Government, in 1841.

The Khonds inhabit the hill districts on the borders of Orissa and Ganjam. Their country naturally divides itself into two parts; lying as it does partly above and partly below the Ghát range, of which we have so frequently spoken. In the lower districts the hilly wastes, clothed with deep woods and interspersed with extensive valleys and undulating downs gradually come down to the level plains of Orissa, near the sea. From these the higher districts are separated, by the steep and precipitous Gháts; and form an extensive plateau above them, somewhat similar to that of Mysore, stretching far away into the territories of Central India. These hill regions termed Máliás, are distinguished by different names. Bordering on the Orissa territory and the river Mohanuddy, lie the *Boad* Máliás; next toward the south the *Goomsur* Máliás, including *Hodzoghoro*, the *Bara* and *Atháro* Mutahs, and *Chokapad;* south of these are the *Surádá* and *Corada* Máliás; and west of these, the extensive Máliás of *Chinna Kimedy*. These are the chief divisions of the Khond country. Of these only the Surádá Máliás entirely, and Goomsur partially, lie below the Ghâts: the rest are entirely above them.

The country thus divided presents a varied aspect to the traveller's eye. Below the Ghâts, the villages are somewhat scattered; the valleys appear poor, bleak and barren; water is less abundant than in the higher lands; the country displays no varieties of scenery; and the hilly slopes under the great range are thickly covered with the Dammer tree and the bamboo. The districts on the plateau above are far more picturesque. The table-land is much broken by valleys sometimes deep and rugged; and is crossed by ridges of hills of varied height some being 4000 feet above the sea. Many parts are bare of wood; in others are groups of forest trees; in others a jungle rich in flowers; the valleys and glens furnish sites for the villages and fields for culture; while in the higher and deeper recesses of the hills thick forests grow inhabited by the tiger and the bear. In the Máliás of Chinna Kimedy a thick forest of timber trees covers the whole surface and extends westward without a break for more than a hundred and forty miles. Portions of this forest have been cut down by the people, and the cleared land in the valleys cultivated. The soil is every where fertile; and if the land were all cleared and the numerous waterfalls and springs properly turned to account, it would yield the most abundant harvests. Numerous vegetable products are raised, which furnish materials for traffic in the plains. In Chinna Kimedy alone, besides what is consumed by the people, more than ten thousand bullock-loads of turmeric and four thousand loads of mustard, pepper, tamarind, arrow-root, honey and wax, are carried to the markets below the Ghâts to be exchanged for cloth, brass and iron vessels, and beads. The routes by which the traffic is carried on from the higher land to the plains are most difficult to traverse. Till lately they were merely the natural openings through the mountains, unimproved by any aid of art: one of them however, leading through the heart of Goomsur, has been greatly improved by the Government, and rendered a safe and easy pass.

THE KHOND PEOPLE.

The people are in general divided into two great classes; those living on the lower ranges of the Ghâts, and those in the districts above them.

The former are called *Bennia* Khonds; the latter, the *Máliá* or highland Khonds. The Bennia Khonds were apparently permitted by their Hindu conquerors to retain their lands on a rent tenure or on that of feudal service to their zemindars. Living nearer the plains, and in subjection to Hindu governors, they have of course been brought into constant intercourse with the Hindus who people them: they attend the markets and bazars, and witness much of a life and habits different from their own. The consequence has been a partial adoption of Hindu manners. The most changed among the Bennias are very like the Hindus; and between them and the pure Khonds may be seen all grades in the change from the habits of the latter to those of the former. They wear the Hindu dress, speak the Oriya language, build houses after the Hindu plan, use the Oriya plough, refuse to cultivate turmeric, drink milk, eat ghee, and abstain from the barbarous practice of dancing, of which their less refined countrymen are extravagantly fond. They have even adopted *Káli* as one of their deities; while the Hindus in the same districts have adopted the Khond god and call him *Khondini.* In the worship of the deity both people unite together; while the Khond priest and the bráhman serve together at his altar. In this way while they retain many of their original customs, the Bennia Khonds have departed from the thorough barbarism of their highland brethren and become assimilated in some measure to their Hindu neighbours. The process of assimilation is still going on; and will advance, perhaps with accelerated speed, now that the East India Company are rulers of the whole country, and more frequent intercourse has been established between its different localities.

The *Máliá* Khonds on the other hand, living on the plateau and in the vallies above the ghâts, exhibit all the characteristics of Khond society in their purest form. They have, it is true, always been in intercourse with the zemindars of the lower country; sometimes making a raid or foray into their territories to levy black-mail, but acting usually as independent allies and friends, never as subjects. Separated from the Hindus of the plains by the broad belt of hill zemindaries, filled with men like themselves, and shut out by their inaccessible hills and jungles from all attempts at conquest, they have remained the same people in manners and pursuits for many hundreds, it may be thousands, of years. To some particulars concerning these manners, let me briefly direct your attention.

The *dress* of the Khonds both male and female is very scanty, and resembles that of the poorer Hindus. The men wear their black and shiny hair in a knot fastened by an iron pin above the forehead or on the side of the head: both men and women wear ornaments of iron or bone, or of dyed wood. *Agriculture* is considered the only honourable employment, and, drawing to itself the people's greatest energy, is exceedingly productive. The land of every community is apportioned into a great number of petty free-holds; and each proprietor cultivates for himself. Several kinds of rice, yams, millet, turmeric, tobacco, and mustard are the staple produce. They possess large herds of buffaloes, bullocks and swine, numerous fowls, and flocks of goats. But the people are also *warlike:* from early youth they are trained to use the sling, the bow and arrow, and the *tangi* or hill-axe; and so constant are their quarrels as almost totally to suspend cultivation at some periods. No indigenous *manufactures* are produced among them: the employment is considered low. The cloth and brass vessels which they require, as well as their salt, they procure in the plains, in exchange for the produce of their fields. Various Hindu outcasts have from time immemorial acted for them as potters, blacksmiths, weavers and distillers, and have performed various menial services. Their *houses* are made of strong boards, well fastened, and are sometimes plastered inside; the roof is thatched. Forty or fifty such houses arranged in two rows, with the doors fronting the street, constitute a village. These houses are all alike for rich and poor. The Khonds never repair them; but when they grow old, as they do in about fourteen years, a new village is built of entirely new materials. *Intellectually* the Khonds are rather quick in perception, firm in their resolutions, and good-humoured. They have an unconquerable love of personal freedom and are very impatient of restraint. They are faithful to their engagements when made; but have no idea of any rights except their own. Hence their readiness, both singly and in bands, to make a foray on others' territories or districts, and seize "whatever they like best" (as they term it): which means, the most valuable property of others. They are selfish, ferocious, and dreadful drunkards. Like the Arabs, they are remarkable for their hospitality, and rather suffer loss and danger than violate its sacred rites. *Marriages* only take place between the members of different tribes. The women, though they do not eat with their husbands, are yet treated with some respect; they attend to domestic duties; hold ammunition for their tribe on the battle field; and by their advice exercise much influence on their Councils. A wife can quit her husband's house and return to that of her parents when she likes; (in which case her dowry must be repaid); and if she choose another man for a husband from among the unmarried men of a tribe, he is compelled to marry her. The license thus allowed to the women is productive of great evil. Their *judicial* customs are very simple. Murder, manslaughter and wounding are generally settled privately according to the law of retaliation, which in the case of blood is binding on the nearest relative: (as was the law of the Goel or blood-avenger among the Hebrews.) Important cases are settled by the Patriarchal Council. Witnesses are then examined and many kinds of ordeal appealed to. At the close of all trials, the members of the tribunal are well feasted with rice, meat and spirits, at the expense of the losing party. Throughout their *social and political constitution*, the *Patriarchal principle* prevails. All the members of a family are subject in every thing to the supreme control of its head, called "Abbaya." A collection of families makes a village, over which is a village abbaya, selected from the abbayas of families. A collection of villages is called a mutah or district, over which is a muliko chosen from the village Patriarchs. A number of mutahs make a tribe, which is governed by a tribal muliko. Tribes are grouped together in a confederacy, over which is appointed a *chief federal Patriarch*. This is the form of their constitution; but breaks and anomalies here and there occur, produced by the disorganisation which wars and other events have produced among them. These Patriarchs of various grades possess authority to settle disputes in the sphere over which they are respectively appointed: and in difficult cases they consult with those of their own rank what is to be done. They receive no emoluments. At these councils, the members of each society may be present and vote, though they do not speak. Upon very important public matters a General Council of the whole people is held, when the matter is discussed by the Abbayas of mutahs and tribes; and the votes of the whole assembly are taken to decide it. The chief Federal Patriarch stands at the top of this social pyramid. His first duty is to consult the interests of the whole people by maintaining as far as possible the closest union between all the sections into which they are divided. Boundary questions are his especial care; but as he has no force at his disposal to compel submission to his sentence, tribal feuds arising from them are constantly bursting out. This Federal Patriarch has been hitherto the channel of communication between the Khonds and the zemindars in the lower Máliás: and through him all arrangements have been usually made. His position is therefore a most important one both to his people and to the zemindars. In relation to this position and the duties it involves, the Patriarchs receive a distinctive name. In Boad, they are called *Khonro*: in Suradah, *Majee*: in Goomsur, *Bisaye*:

in other districts, *Muliko.* Their immediate descendants also bear the same name. The Bisayes of Goomsur are a family of Hindus, who long since ascended above the Ghauts, and settled in the district of Hodzoghoro. Sám Bisaye, so often mentioned in the correspondence of the Government officers, was formerly Federal Patriarch of the Goomsur tribes: and Chokra Bisaye, who occasioned the rebellion in the Boad Máliás, was his nephew.

THE KHOND LANGUAGE.

As may be well imagined from the circumstances of the people, the Khond language is not a single fixed tongue, like Bengali or English, which all the people speak. As we survey the whole extent of their country, it seems to have more than one chief dialect with many local varieties. Unwritten languages naturally fluctuate much, according to the different degrees of intercourse which are maintained amongst the several branches of the tribes that speak them. A very interesting example of this change is thus described by the Rev. R. Moffat, in connection with a servile portion of the Bechuana nation, termed Balala.

"Connected with each of the towns among that people, there are great numbers of what are called 'Balala,' poor ones, who stand in the same relation to the Bechuanas in which the Bushmen formerly stood to the Hottentots, and whose origin doubtless was of the same nature. These Balala were once inhabitants of the towns, and have been permitted or appointed to live in country-places for the purpose of procuring skins of wild animals, wild honey, and roots, for their respective chiefs.

"The dialect of the Sechuana spoken by these people, especially in districts remote from the towns, is so different from that spoken by the nation generally, that interpreters are frequently required. In order to account for this, it is necessary to become acquainted with their habits. In the towns the purity and harmony of the language is kept up by their pitchos or public meetings, at which the finest language is spoken; by their festivals and ceremonies; as well as by their songs and their constant intercourse. With the isolated villages of the desert, it is far otherwise. They have no such meetings, no festivals, no cattle, nor any kind of manufactures to keep their energies alive. Riches they have none, their sole care being to keep body and soul together; to accomplish this, is with them their 'chief end;' they are compelled to traverse the wilds often to a great distance from their native village. On such occasions, fathers and mothers and all who can bear a burden, often set out for weeks at a time, and leave their children to the care of two or more infirm old people. The infant progeny, some of whom are beginning to lisp, while others can just master a whole sentence, and those still farther advanced, romping and playing together, the children of nature, through the livelong day, become habituated to a language of their own. The more voluble condescend to the less precocious, and thus from this infant Babel proceeds a dialect composed of a host of mongrel words and phrases joined together without rule, and in the course of a generation the entire character of the language is changed."

The Khonds are not so uncivilized a nation as these poor Balala; in social rank and in civilization they are rather like the Bechuanas from whom the Balala spring. They too have their tribal meetings, their consultations, and speeches: and thus a knowledge of the higher terms in their language is preserved. But a change in the common language must gradually take place in the course of years: the differences between the expressions of the more distant tribes and those of the lower classes of the people increasing to the greatest degree. Where there are no authorities to determine style in the choice of words, to define their pronunciation and to maintain their grammatical relations, the wonder is not that such changes are introduced into a language, but that it can for hundreds of years maintain so many of its original forms and terms.

The Khond language remained unwritten till the people became known to Europeans. During the Goomsur war some of the military officers occasionally recorded some of the words in Oriya characters in order to facilitate their intercourse with the people, when meeting them in the markets below the ghats: or making known to them the wishes of Government: but no systematic effort could be made to study the language, till the country had been well settled for some time. Dr. Cadenhead, when Assistant in Khondistan, was, we believe, the first who made any endeavour to reduce it to writing and prepare for imparting information by its means in the education of the people. Amongst other things he planned the commencement of a translation of the New Testament. His residence in the country was however too brief, and his engagements too onerous, to allow him to devote much of his time to the important subject; no practical results followed from his plans, and he was unable to print any thing before he left the Agency. The honour of first making a thorough study of the language, of reducing it carefully to writing, of developing its grammar and printing the first Khond book, belongs to Capt. Frye. This able linguist after considerable intercourse with the people, drew up a vocabulary, a spelling book and other elementary works suitable for the young, which were all received with great delight by the Merias in the mission schools; and was preparing other works when ill health compelled him to leave the country. The Khond Grammar was naturally expected from his pen; but sickness delayed its appearance: and it was recently drawn out by one of the Orissa missionaries.*

* In the *Calcutta Christian Observer*. May and June 1853.

The language appears to be regular in its structure. A survey of its roots and forms at once shews that it is not, like Oriya and Bengali, of Sanskrit origin. It has a greater resemblance to the Telugu; that is, to the pure and original Telugu, freed from the admixture of Sanskrit. It is therefore connected with the most ancient tongues of Southern India, those of the aboriginal population, whose words, grammatical forms and idioms pervade the Tamil and Telugu, the Canarese and Maleali, throughout the whole of the Peninsula. Competent scholars too have declared it to be the best specimen of an original Tartar tongue to be found in all India. The conclusion is natural that the Khonds once occupied the plains at the foot of their mountains, now held by the Oriyas in the north and the Telugus in the south: and were driven from the lowlands, by the irruption of the brahminical armies that hold the soil to this day. In manners, customs and language, they greatly resemble the other hill people who are their neighbours. Mr. Inglis says, they are like the *Sourahs* on their south border, and the *Koles* on the north: and a friend assured me that a description of their manner of life will extensively apply to the *Santals* of the Bhagulpore hills. Who can wonder that with their fierce spirit, freebooting has been a traditional custom among them, and that they now delight in making forays upon those plains, from which their forefathers were long since driven. May they not say like Roderick Dhu, as from their elevated homes above the ghauts, they survey the lowlands of Orissa:

"These fertile plains, that softened vale,
Were once the birthright of the Gael:
The stranger came with iron hand,
And from our fathers rent the land.
Where dwell we now? See rudely swell
Crag over crag, and fell o'er fell.
Pent in this fortress of the north,
Think'st thou we will not sally forth
To spoil the spoiler as we may,
And from the robber rend the prey?"

Here I cannot help hazarding the conjecture, based upon the existence of these aborigines from the banks of the Ganges down to Cape Comorin, that they have had much to do with peopling the islands of the South Pacific. These islands, it is known, are occupied by two different races, of which one is the Malay. The Malay Polynesians occupy the islands to the eastward, the Navigators', Hervey, Marquesas and Society groups: and are of a fair complexion. The other race occupies the great islands to the west, of which New Caledonia and New Guinea are the chief: they are of much darker complexion and have somewhat woolly hair. It seems probable that the Malay Polynesians started from Burmah and Siam by the Peninsula of Malacca, and thence made their way to the eastern Pacific. Whence sprung those of the darker race, if not from the aborigines of India? Any one who has seen a band of *Dhangor Koles* cleaning the streets of Calcutta will at once acknowledge their perfect resemblance to the natives of New Guinea; and that any one of the former people could have stood as a model to Captain Erskine, for the sketches which he has given of the latter, in his recent work on the Pacific. May it not then be, that it was from the aborigines of India pushed forward by their Hindu conquerors, that the Archipelago and Western Pacific received at least a portion of their swarthy and barbarous population: and that coming last they drove before them to the eastward such of the Malay-speaking islanders, as they found already there?

THE KHOND RELIGION.

The Khonds, being ignorant, are excessively *superstitious.* All internal diseases (the chief of which among them are fever, enteritis and small-pox) are treated as the fruits of the displeasure of the deity. To effect a cure no medicine whatever is taken, but various incantations are performed by the priests. They thoroughly believe in witchcraft, magic and sorcery: and various punishments, even to death itself, are inflicted on those who are supposed to injure others by magic arts. All tigers which kill men, are considered to be men who, through the agency of a god, have transformed themselves into the shape of that animal. Ugly old women are, among them, as elsewhere, often set down as witches.

The Khonds, though a barbarous tribe, possess a religion; though unlike the mythology of their neighbours, the Hindus, theirs is rather simple. They worship many inferior deities; amongst whom several of the Hindu gods and goddesses seem to find a place. But a few particular deities occupy the chief share of their veneration, and are the chief objects of their worship. The earth being the great source of subsistence to the Khonds, they reckon the *Earth-goddess* as one of these chief divinities; and the functions, attributed to her, are just such as express the fears and desires of an agricultural people. As constant quarrels arise between the tribes for the possession of land, it is natural that they should have, like the Romans, a *god of boundaries,* in order to define with the highest sanctions the borders of each tribe. The *Sun* and *Moon* from their position and uses, are of course constant objects of worship. Continually engaged in wars and feuds, they honour most highly a *god of war:* every village has a grove to him, wherein his appropriate symbol, a piece of iron, is buried. Partly dependent on the chase for their support, they have a *god of hunting*. Liable to the small-pox, they recognise, as the Hindus have done, a god presiding over that disease and offer sacrifices to appease him whenever it appears. Like causes have given rise to a *Forest god*, a *god of Rivers*, another of *Fountains:* each hill and each hamlet have their separate deities. Thus we see that the causes which gave rise to such divinities in olden times, have produced them likewise among the Khonds. "As face answereth to face in a glass, so doth the heart of man to man." The priests among the Khonds form a distinct class, and they alone can perform all the ceremonies appointed in public or private worship: at births, sicknesses, marriages and deaths, they alone can officiate. They receive no fees, and no rank: even their share of the land is tilled by themselves: honour is professedly their only reward: but their very position, as the leaders of superstition, cannot fail to give them a predominant influence in the councils and proceedings of their tribes.

HUMAN SACRIFICES.

One particular of their worship, already alluded to, demands a special mention. It forms a most important item in their opinions and practices, and indeed is one of those essential points, whose influence is felt throughout the whole framework of their society. The *earth goddess*, on whose favour (as they think) their very subsistence depends, is worshipped with HUMAN SACRIFICES. "Once," it is said, "the earth was an unstable mass, unfit for cultivation: the goddess said, 'Let human blood be spilt,' and a child was sacrificed. The earth became fertile, and the goddess ordained that man should repeat the rite and live." By this legend the sacrifice is dated from the very origin of agriculture, and the Khond believes that its continued observance is essential to the produce of his food. Hence the pomp and ceremony with which it is celebrated.

These sacrifices are performed both publicly and privately. The public sacrifices take place in the spring when the earth is sown, and at harvest, when it is reaped: others also are offered while the crop is growing. The occurrence of a great pestilence in society; the ravages of wild beasts; or any thing which happens peculiarly unpropitious to the person, the family or the property of the various Patriarchs of the tribes, are all circumstances which call publicly for these dreadful offerings. They are offered privately by a particular family for similar reasons: fear, not love, prompting their performance.

The victims, which are of both sexes are known by the name of MERIAS. They are not native Khonds of the district where they are sacrificed; but are usually children from the plains or from distant localities. They are procured by some of the servile Hindus already mentioned as settlers among the Khonds, viz. by those of the weaver caste. By the Khonds these persons are called Dombango; by the Hindus, Panwa. Some of this class are attached to every Khond village and perform various offices for the community. They weave, trade in cloth and steal; they are the public messengers and musicians; and are always employed to procure Meria victims. These Merias they sometimes steal from the Oriyas; sometimes they buy them; sometimes they get them from distant sections of the Khond themselves in times of scarcity; sometimes they get them from families of Panwas like themselves; and not unfrequently they *sell their own children.* Many of the children that I saw in the Cuttack and Balasore schools were said to be of this class: and two or three in Balasore are apparently Sontals. The victims, when procured, are brought blindfold into the village where they are to remain: those intended for public sacrifice are lodged in the house of the abbaya. They are not immediately sacrificed; but are kept and fed with great care, it may be for several years. Males are sometimes married to females like themselves, in which case their offspring are born to the parents' condition. In some cases they are married not long before the sacrifice, and the marriage is merely nominal. If possible, the actual position and prospects of these Meriás are concealed from them; so long as they are unsuspicious and live contented in the family which has charge of them, they are free and honoured: permitted to wander every where and welcomed as sacred in every house. If however, they exhibit any signs of fear or any desire to escape, they are chained up. One boy in the Cuttack school who had been thus confined before the officers delivered him, had a ring on his ancle, so tight that it could not be taken off without being filed through. Another informed us, that being afraid after seeing a sacrifice, he was told by the people with whom he lived; "Why should you fear; nothing will happen to you, you are our son: we shall never kill you." It is not easy, however, to keep such a matter thoroughly secret for any length of time, and before the sacrifice at least, it becomes openly known to the victims themselves.

The public sacrifices are always arranged by the patriarch and the priest. All the community gather together to celebrate them; all feuds are forgotten and all labour is laid aside. The manner in which the sacrifice is performed appears to vary in certain details in different districts; but substantially it is the same in all. The great festival of the year, called *Tonki,* occurs at the full moon in the month of Poush, about the end of December; it lasts for three days; and the sacrifices are more numerous than on other occasions. On the first day the whole community give themselves up to feasting and riot. On the second, in one district, as preliminary to the chief sacrifice, a victim is suspended by his neck and heels lengthwise over a trench, is then gashed by the priest in six places, then beheaded, and buried on the spot. In most places, however, on the second day, there is a grand procession. The appointed victim well dressed, is led forth to the Meriá grove; all the people, decked out in their hill finery, with their bear skins and peacock feathers, accompany it with drums, dancing, shouting, and singing some sacred song, in which the victim is devoted to the earth-goddess. One of these songs was sung before us by the Khond boys in the Cuttack school: it contained among other things the following unmistakeable announcement; "We have fed you long, we can support you no more; to-morrow you will be cut to pieces." The second night is passed, like the first day, in revelling and feasting. On the third day, after a renewal of the rioting, the whole village bring the unhappy Meriá forth to the spot already pointed out by the priest as a propitious one. A split bamboo is planted in the ground; and the victim, quite intoxicated and unconscious, is fastened within the cleft, either by the throat or chest, the crowd standing eagerly round. On a given signal, they rush on the wretched being, and with their knives and axes, cut out small pieces from the living sufferer, taking care to avoid any vital parts, until death takes place. The whole process occupies about twenty minutes. Each piece cut from the victim is immediately carried by its possessor to his fields and deposited in the earth. Great value is attached to the first piece and a proportionate eagerness is evinced to obtain it. Such is the account which we heard in Cuttack from the lips of a rescued Meriá, who had seen the sacrifice five times.

The *number* of Meriás yearly sacrificed before the British war in Goomsur, must have been very large. It appears that nearly the whole of Khondistan is more or less infected with the evil: and that it prevails to the greatest extent in the districts most removed from the influence of the East India Company. Not only the Maliás above named, and which are best known to the English, but Jeypore and the country southward as far as the Godavery, are all involved in the awful crime. Westward again by Bustar, the Khonds go far into Nagpore and into the state of Hydrabad: and they have carried the rite with them. In Bustar it is known that the sacrifices have been enormous. On one occasion about the year 1826, when the Rájá set out to visit the Rájá of Nagpore, *twenty-five grown men* were all sacrificed at one time. In all this immense extent of country stretching far away to the westward, not one voice was ever raised against its horrid barbarity. A variety of causes also have been allowed to call for this sacrifice. It is not only a single annual festival, that demands its performance, but public and private calamities of various kinds, in addition to the regular return of the seasons of sowing and harvest, have been held to justify it. It would seem then that *hundreds* of Meriás have been annually required to meet this large demand; and the great number, found on different occasions and given up to the Government officers, confirm such a supposition. Three hundred have at one time been brought away even from small districts. Thanks be to God that this dreadful form of human guilt is now drawing to a close!

The horrid rite of human sacrifice does not prevail throughout every single district of the Khond country. It seems that in the Maliás below the gháts it is not observed at all. In the northern Maliás above the gháts, that is, in Boad, the Bara and Atháro Mutás, in Hodzoghoro, it seems very general; as well as in some parts of Chinna Kimedy, and also in the unknown territories stretching far to the west. In the southern districts, another practice pretty generally exists, of a different, but not less destructive kind, that of FEMALE INFANTICIDE. Apparently the latter custom has no reference to religious feeling or law: but finds its root in the civil institutions of the people, especially in the expenses connected with marriage, and the great freedom of divorce allowed to the Khond wives. The Khonds of these districts always allege poverty as the cause; as did the Rájputs of Upper and Western India, who till lately practised a similar custom. A *thousand children* at least must have been destroyed annually, in two or three of these districts alone. Whole villages have been met with, without a single female child.

Such are the appalling facts, and such the horrid practices which were revealed to the Government of India by its zealous officers, who superintended the Khond country: practises which existed unknown and unchecked, till less than twenty years ago, in a country within four hundred miles distance of Calcutta. Some errors may have crept into the description; but these are the main features of the character and habits of the Khond tribes. "It is no easy task," says Col. Campbell in his Report of 1849, "even in a civilized land, to glean from the more intelligent members of the community a narrative of the origin and progress of innumerable customs and observances, which are nevertheless most rigidly and superstitiously adhered to; how greatly is the difficulty augmented, when we have to deal with a people, whose moral and intellectual nature has yet to be developed." It is only after Europeans and Natives from the plains have acquired the Khond language, or Khonds have acquired Oriya or English, that all the details of their customs will become fully and correctly known.

GOVERNMENT EFFORTS TO SUPPRESS THESE RITES.

No sooner was the Government informed of the appalling evils existing amongst these newly conquered barbarians, than they adopted measures with a view to suppress them. And from the date of the first war in Goomsur to the present time, they have continued an agency among the Khonds, not merely for the purpose of promoting civil and social order, but for checking and bringing to an end, if possible, the horrible rites we have described. In this humane purpose of the Government, every Christian heart must rejoice. How seldom has such a sight been seen! We have had in this country, and still have, cause of difference with the Government for the position it occupies in some points, with respect to religion, (such as its endowment of Jogonnáth and its connection with the idol temples in Bombay and Southern India;) but its benevolent efforts for the social welfare of the Khonds deserve from all right-thinking men the highest praise. These efforts have been fully described in successive numbers of the *Calcutta Review*, and numerous extracts have been therein published from the official reports of the several officers employed. It is from these extracts and others contained in a pamphlet on the Khond Agency, that the following summary of their measures has been compiled. It is impossible, in reading these reports, and the orders which they called forth from the various Governments in India, not to admire the deep interest taken by all concerned in the suppression of these barbarous rites. Two officers of the Madras army have especially distinguished themselves by their hearty zeal in this good cause. Both have received the warm approbation of the Court of Directors and both deserve the honour of the community at large. These officers are Colonel Campbell and Capt. Macpherson.

The Hon. Mr. Russell, Special Commissioner in the Goomsur war, was the first to bring the evils existing among the Khonds to the notice of the Madras Government. In doing so, while he laid bare the facts of the case, he acknowledged there were great difficulties in the way of their removal. He distinctly showed however that as the people knew so little of the Government, coercion was out of the question; that only slow and gradual means could be employed; that an effort should be made to convince them of our good intentions; to treat them as friends, and then to enlighten them as to the real character of their superstitious customs. For the promotion of intercourse with them, he also recommended the revival of the old markets, to be plentifully stocked with articles which the Khonds desire. The Madras Government adopted these views, and instructed the Collector in Ganjam to make further enquiry into the matter; to take all opportunities of convincing the chiefs of the heinousness and folly of these practices, and to assure them that the Government had determined to put them down. The *first victims rescued* were saved by Captain Millar in the early part of 1837, while the troops were serving in the country. With blunt candour he demanded these victims and by force and intimidation compelled their surrender. Seventeen others were given up to Mr. Russell. In December of the same year, Capt. Campbell, finding the season of the great sacrifice drawing near, proceeded to visit the Upper Máliás of Goomsur, with the distinct purpose of opposing its celebration. Having summoned the heads of the different districts, he explained to them by an interpreter the abhorrence of the Government at these rites; endeavoured to convince them of their barbarity and inutility: and declared that the Government would no longer allow the sacrifice, and peremptorily demanded all their victims. He received after some trouble no less than 105. Oaths were then taken from the chiefs after the Khond fashion, that their Meriá sacrifice should henceforth be at an end; and that any one who performed it should be deemed worthy of severe punishment. Capt. Campbell sanguinely believed that in these Goomsur Máliás, the sacrifice would henceforth cease. The following year he visited the Mutáhs again and reported that the sacrifices had greatly diminished in comparison with former times; only three had been performed on the borders of the districts. He also seized two notorious kidnappers, and sent them for trial to Ganjam. At the same time, Mr. Bannerman, the Collector of

Ganjam, proceeded to a more southern portion of the Khond country, the Máliás of Chinna Kimedy. He came upon the people in the very midst of their ceremonies; and having obtained the meriá whom they were about to sacrifice, stated it to be the determination of Government that the rite should be performed no more. He also reasoned with them about the heinousness of the crime they were committing and urged them voluntarily to abolish it. With their usual independence of feeling and manner, they at once replied; That they owed no tribute and no allegiance to the East India Company; that the sacrifice was an old custom: and that without it, their fields would yield no crops. They also shewed themselves on all sides armed, and seemed half inclined to attack the Collector and rescue their victim. He retreated however successfully: and brought to Ganjam altogether nine meriás.

The Khonds of Goomsur who had become the direct subjects of the British Government, enjoyed a peculiar advantage above their countrymen. In their superintendent, they had a central and controlling head, able to hear and settle the endless disputes and feuds which arose among them; and which till that time, under their own system, no authority among themselves could finally determine. One or two most important cases arose very soon after Capt. Campbell received charge of the province, and were satisfactorily settled. So sensible were the people of the value of this reference, that they constantly brought their disputes, from trifling matters up to blood-feuds, before Capt. Campbell, and when his cold-weather tour among the hills was finished, they followed him with the same object to the plains.

These measures were steadily maintained during the next two years. Peace prevailed in the Goomsur and Suráda Máliás. The confidence of the people in their new government increased. They continued to bring to the agent their boundary disputes and the endless quarrels produced by their women: and they attended in large numbers the fairs opened for their use. Capt. Campbell also continued to visit the districts above the gháts; especially at the important seasons of the great sacrifice, and to argue with the chiefs and people against its continuance. Nor were his visits by any means fruitless. The people, however unconvinced, were at least over-awed, and the number of sacrifices openly performed was decidedly lessened. He found, however, when visiting Upper Goomsur in January, 1841, that the Khonds were still much attached to the old system, and though no public sacrifices had been made since the British troops entered the country, yet twenty-four victims had been purchased during the year 1840. This circumstance cannot be regarded as unnatural; a superstition believed to lie at the very root of social prosperity, and observed unbroken for ages, was not to be eradicated in four years, with no greater coercion than the brief imprisonment of a few kidnappers; especially when all the neighbouring districts sacrificed meriás without let or hinderance. The subsidiary agency allowed to the officials was of a very imperfect kind. The time subtracted from other duties for attention to the one great evil was but small: their visits, owing to deficiency of carriage, were few and beset with obstacles: while one great means of bringing the Khonds into constant intercourse with the lower districts, viz. the road through Goomsur to Sohnpur was not even begun. Efforts were almost entirely confined to a single district. The Government of Madras dreading another collision with the barbarous tribes, acted timidly: and while Capt. Campbell was urging that measures should be taken for abolishing the rites in Boad and Chinna Kimedy, as well as Goomsur, no notice was taken of his appeal. At length, however, after repeated representations from Capt. Campbell that additional means must be employed, on the recommendation of Lord Elphinstone, amongst other plans, an officer was appointed to survey the line of a road through the hill tracts and to raise a body of hill Paiks as a semi-military police. His whole time was to be devoted to the subject: and better means of carriage, with a separate establishment, were allowed him than his predecessors had enjoyed. Immediately after Capt. Campbell accompanied his Regiment to China, and Capt. Macpherson received the appointment he vacated, with the increased powers and more efficient agency mentioned.

The important districts of BOAD and DUSPALLA, lying to the north of Goomsur, did not share in the efforts we have now described. Being under the jurisdiction of the Bengal Government, they were superintended by other officers. In 1837, Mr. Ricketts, the Commissioner of Cuttack, marched through them both and having ascertained the existence of the sacrifices amongst their inhabitants, he demanded from the Khonds of Duspalla, the surrender of their Merias. For this purpose he summoned the Raja and the Khond Chiefs: and having spent days in reasoning with them upon the wickedness of the practice, induced them to sign a paper, engaging to give them up and confessing that any who should perform them again would be justly liable to punishment. Mr. Ricketts next visited the chief Khonros of the Boad hills; but they, being more independent and less afraid of punishment, declined to sanction either the surrender of victims or any engagements for the future abolition of the sacrifice. Mr. Ricketts brought away in all 24 merias. At a later period, Mr. Ricketts's successor despatched a native officer with a small guard, into the same districts, in order to demand the surrender of merias and report on the present state of these rites. He brought away eight children, but reported that the Boad chiefs, though they attended his summons, refused to give up seventeen victims whom they acknowledged to be in their possession. In 1844 Lieut. Hicks, the Commissioner's Assistant, visited the two districts again, arrested one of the kidnappers, and succeeded in rescuing twenty-five merias. He also met the Khond chiefs and induced twenty-six of them to renew their agreement that the inhuman rite should be abolished. It was with great reluctance, and only after long delay, that many of the chiefs consented to visit him: and when urged on the best grounds to abstain from their sacrifices, they only replied that they were ceremonies received from their ancestors. The year following, Mr. Hicks repeated his visit, which in Duspalla apparently had the best effect. It was found that the rite was losing its publicity and was perceptibly on the decline: the customary processions were omitted and secrecy was courted in its celebration. The Boad chiefs, however, he found as obstreperous as before, and almost inclined to drive him from the country by force. Entering one of the districts, by a most precipitous and formidable pass, he found that the people had all fled; the few chief men, who presented themselves, came to him intoxicated; and it was only after many refusals on their part, that he succeeded in bringing away twelve victims. He learned however with satisfaction that even amongst these fastnesses of Boad, the revolting sacrifice had been considerably checked: only thirteen victims had been sacrificed, where formerly hundreds had been slaughtered, and that here also the rite had been performed in private that the perpetrators might not be known.

A third series of Khond districts, farther west along the Mohanadi river, were under the jurisdiction of the South Western Agency in Bengal. Col. Ouseley, hearing that numerous merias were held by the people in the Zemindaries of Sohnpore, Patika and other estates, sent prompt orders to the Rajas who governed them to send all merias to him instantly; to give notice of all persons who retained them or purposed to sacrifice them; and to inform the Khond chiefs under their jurisdiction that all who should sacrifice for the future were liable to be hanged. He however expressed his fear that owing to the seclusion of the Khonds amongst their jungles and fastnesses, to their comparative independence of the Rájá's authority, and to the distance of his agency from the districts where they resided, this plain order would be but little obeyed. What was the result of Col. Ouseley's efforts, and whether they have been continued by his successors, I am unable to say.

Such were the early measures adopted by the Governments of Madras and Bengal for the suppression of the dreadful Meria sacrifice: and such the kind of success which their plans met with during the first few years. Begun in the upper Maliás of Goomsur, and its several mutahs, they had been continued there for four successive years: and partially extended to Chinna Kimedy. Boad and Duspalla had been really visited for only two seasons with any thing like a persevering determination to put the evil down. Immense tracts of country, and numerous branches of the Khond tribes, had not been visited at all. Some of the effects of these visits had been immediate: and some had an influence upon the practice of the rite which would be exhibited only in future years. The *first* result of the Government enquiries was to reveal the actual fact of the Meria sacrifice, the ground on which it was maintained by the people, and the revolting barbarities with which it was accompanied. Then, the deeper the enquiry went, and the greater the variety of the modes of investigation, the more appalling did the sacrifice appear, from the immense extent of territory over which it was celebrated unchecked; its perpetrators ignorant of its dreadful heinousness, and its victims every where awfully numerous. Then too did men learn the many difficulties by which the efforts to suppress it were surrounded. It became evident that the Khonds who had first learned the might of the Government in a disastrous war, and were ignorant of the humane principles by which these efforts were suggested, were suspicious of all interference with their peculiar customs, and doubted the motive by which the rite had been so earnestly attacked. Endued with the warmest love for liberty, they feared, in these efforts, underhand attempts to bring them into complete political subservience to this new Power around them. It was seen also that their political relations to the Government were unfavourable to the decided measures which their case seemed to require. In only one case, was the East India Company a direct ruler, in the districts of Goomsur: in others, there was a Rájá over the Khonds, who paid a small tribute to him: while he alone had any direct dealings with the Government. Far to the west, other districts were even more independent than these. Again, the physical difficulties in the way of the Agent's progress were very great. The passes from the plains to the Maliás above the ghauts are few and hard to travel: the districts are cut off from each other, by lines of hills, precipitous valleys, and immense tracts of forest and jungle: in some cases, as in Boad, the routes could be entirely closed, the valleys blockaded, and all intercourse with other parts brought to an end. Malaria and fever are very prevalent at some times of the year; the heat and rain are obstacles at other times; so that the period of each year in which Europeans could safely visit the hills was reduced to a very limited time. Added to these things was the fact that all the agents employed were amply engaged in other duties and that but little leisure could be spared from them, to devote their attention to the important work of saving merias and humanizing their barbarous sacrificers. Happily these difficulties were not all insurmountable: they did not therefore prevent all good: they served to call forth the zeal, energy and self-denial of all engaged in the good work: so that in spite of all disadvantages attempts were made to meet the evil and to meet it with success.

The good really effected during the few years mentioned can scarcely be reckoned small. In addition to the knowledge acquired of all the circumstances that had to be dealt with; two hundred and forty victims had actually been rescued and safely placed under Government protection. Repeated conferences had been held with the Khond Chiefs; in which principles of humanity had been expounded, the revolting nature of their sacrifices explained, the horror of the Government at their cruelty been declared, and all had been informed in the plainest terms that the Government had determined to have them abolished. Such explanations were indeed but steps towards that suppression, but they were absolutely required for a clear understanding of the proceedings of Government, about which the Khonds were suspicious. They had also an immediate effect upon the people, in checking the sacrifice, which till then they had never hesitated to perform; this gratifying result is shewn in several ways. First the sacrifices became much more private: secondly; they became less numerous: and thirdly; the people were inspired with a wholesome fear of punishment for what had now been declared to be wrong. I quote two very interesting illustrations of this last fact from the statements of rescued children. They reveal several painful elements in the private preliminary history of these horrid crimes; as well as exhibit the influence of the Agents' visits:

"*Deposition of Susta, of Boad, aged about twelve years.*

"About three years ago, Rotna Panwa, of Putka in Boad, sold me, for I know not what sum, to Sugaib Mullick Khund. He had previously brought my mother to live with him. I went with her; he then kidnapped me. I was employed in fetching wood. Last October, the paiks of the village in which I was, went to call the priest to sacrifice me, but the priest would not attend. He told them to wait until all the Government servants had left the district, and then he would sacrifice me. There was no other meria in the village but myself. Upon the occasion of sending for the priest, I first knew of the human sacrifices. My mother is still alive. The man who sold me, I have heard since my release, has died. I beg to be sent to my mother, who is in Ulut in Boad.

"*Deposition of Subdee, aged fifteen years, of Duspulla.*

"About five years ago, my father and mother went to Patka in Boad, for the purpose of getting mangoes, as it was a time of scarcity; they took me with them; and when in the jungle at that place, Peenka Panwa, of that village, took me away and sold me to Gobur Naik, who employed me in fetching wood. Two months ago I was covered with turmeric, and then I heard from the villagers that I was intended for a 'meria.' The villagers sent for one Ruthee Gooroo, a priest, but he refused to come, as the Government servants were in the district and had forbidden the custom."

Beyond these direct results of their interference, the Government officers had acquired valuable experience respecting the greatness of the evils to be dealt with, the difficulties to be encountered in suppressing them, and the means demanded for their removal. The measures suggested by them for the future, in order to attain a more secure, speedy and complete suppression of the meria sacrifice, were both *direct* and *indirect*.

1. The *indirect* were such as would remove obstacles to the exercise of more extended influence, and would aid in humanizing and civilising the barbarous people. They were measures calculated to secure increased intercourse with people of better habits and better views of the laws which govern society at large. For this end it was essential to have good and easy roads formed through the various districts; a difficult work, owing to the precipitous passes which shut off some localities, and the dense forests which covered others. Capt. Campbell suggested that the chief road should be formed, from Aska near Ganjam, up the Koorminghia pass, and across the districts of Gomsur and Boad to Sohnpore on the Mohanadi. This is the high road from the coast into Nagpore; and as it would run through the very heart of Khondistan and would carry immense traffic both to and from the sea coast, it would not only prove

of the greatest use to the Khond trade, but would bring the hill tribes into constant communication with the plains. For the same reasons it was recommended by Capt. Hicks, that a similar road should be formed leading from Cuttack through Duspalla and Boad, up the Burmúl pass, then almost impracticable. In all the districts other roads might be opened, leading from the main routes. Thus trade would be carried on with ease, the people of different districts be no longer isolated, communications be secured both with Nagpore and the sea coast; and best of all, unity be imparted to the various branches of agency among the Khonds which they had never yet enjoyed. It was also suggested that markets should be maintained, and fairs established, for the purpose of facilitating trade, and that they should be amply stocked with all the articles which the Khonds are anxious to buy. It was proposed also that a body of Khond police should be raised and permanently maintained in the Goomsur territory, in order to keep the peace. The value of these measures as subsidiary to the higher purposes of maintaining political and social order, of humanizing the wild people, and above all, of suppressing the dreadful rites of their cruel religion, will be readily acknowledged. It must be regretted however that several of them, especially the completion of the great routes, were not accomplished for several years; and thus the other plans of the Government were needlessly impeded in their progress.

2. The most important question which arose from the experience of the first few years, related to the *principle* on which DIRECT measures for the abolition of the meria sacrifices and infanticide should be based. By all the Government officers, who were men of judgment and well acquainted with the country, the case was felt to be exceedingly difficult. Here was a barbarous people, extremely ignorant of the Government, extremely ignorant of the first principles of true morality, engaged in the constant commission of the most brutal murders, without one thought of their heinousness, and convinced that by their means they were securing the favour of the gods and the fruitfulness of the soil. These people were to be taught the real character of their rites and to be induced entirely to abolish them. Was the Government to turn missionary, and strive to get rid of the evil merely by producing an entire change in the moral and religious opinions of the Khonds? Or was it to turn despot, issue an ukase, denouncing the sacrifices, and despatch a military force to crush the rite with bullets and the sword? Or was it, in assuming the rule of the country, to recognise the sacrifices as murders, and steadily

punish the perpetrators with imprisonment and death. It was felt that something must be done, and done on system, to meet the evil as extensively as it existed: and accordingly from the first, the local officers in submitting their own views of the matter, asked direction from their respective superiors as to the RULE by which they were to act.

a. On one point all the officers were agreed. All rejected as impracticable and cruel, the despotic plan of crushing the system by bullets. All felt that the ignorance of the people claimed compassion, and that the kindest *persuasion* must be employed to induce them voluntarily to abstain from their repeated cruelties. All felt that justice and mercy alike required that the most earnest endeavours should be made to convince the people of their guilt; to explain the true nature of their human sacrifice; to exhibit its brutality, its cruelty, its utter uselessness; to shew how those who did not sacrifice, fared in their harvest as well as those who did: that the people of the plains also needed no such dreadful rites to secure the harvests by which they are fed, and that on the contrary, such sacrifices are horrid crimes which alike meet with the reprobation of men and with the anger of an offended God. Such persuasions therefore were offered from the very first, and such considerations were laid before the Khond assemblies, year after year, to convince them that their rites were both wrong in themselves and injurious in their results.

b. But this was not all. The various officers of Government, civil and military, were agreed also that some degree of force must be used in its suppression. All were agreed that the sacrifice should be treated as a CRIME, and that those engaged in it, either as principals or accessaries, should not only be declared worthy of punishment, but have that punishment inflicted upon them. This suggestion was a most natural one. Even in the professing church of Christ, which occupies the highest stand of morality, the motives to holiness embrace not only the love and gratitude due to the Redeemer, but appeal also to the fear of his punishment and the rebuke of fellow-christians. In the most civilized communities all great vices and crimes are checked, and the cause of order sustained, by inflicting punishment upon offenders. At this very time, the burning of a Suttee, human sacrifice at Kalighát, the sacrifice of a child at Gunga Sagor, are all crimes in the eye of the law, and are punished as deliberate murders. The Government of India regards these acts, though professedly religious, as crimes against society; and not content with mere persuasion, endeavours by the effect of punishment to suppress them. The officers in Khondistan wished the same rule to be promulgated among the Khonds. The Government was however timid in so soon declaring an extensive custom a public offence, and it was years before even the kidnappers were openly and regularly dealt with, as men guilty of acknowledged crime. The difficulty lay in securing to the Government sufficient authority to enforce a law that should forbid the sacrifice by inflicting such punishment for it as the law might threaten. Ultimately such authority was secured by the experience of a second war in all the Hill tracts of Boad and Goomsur; and the fears of the people have since compelled them to yield obedience to the law, accompanied as the penalties have been, by constant endeavours to convince them of the real heinousness of the forbidden crime. Lord Auckland thus concisely expressed the two principles on which it was proposed to conduct the Khond Agency, and by which all civilized Societies are practically governed:

"The working of a moral change among the people by the progress of general instruction and consequent civilization, can alone eradicate from among them the inclination to indulge in rites so horrible. But though the entire suppression of the practice of human sacrifice among this wild and barbarous race must be the work of time, yet much may be done even now, and no proper exertion should be omitted towards checking the frequency of the crime by the terror of just punishment."

The best plan was however adopted to meet the difficulties which the case presented. Goomsur was made the basis of all operations against the sacrifices. In Goomsur the war had occurred, its people knew the force which the Government could command, when it liked: and Goomsur was directly under Government authority. In this important country therefore thus impressed, the work was begun, and had steadily continued; considerable success was attained: and a foundation laid for extending efforts into the other provinces. The work of abolition was immense, and patience and perseverance were required in the measures adopted to secure it.

In the commencement of 1842, Captain Macpherson succeeded Major Campbell, as principal assistant in Khondistan. He was in many ways, eminently qualified to succeed that distinguished officer. Possessed of great energy, and great ability, he had applied himself for a considerable time to the study of Khond affairs: and had recently presented to the Madras Government an elaborate Report upon the subject of the country and customs of the people. This Report is exceedingly interesting, and gives a remarkably clear and complete account of the habits, and manners; the tribal relations, the government, and religion of the Khonds. All the subsequent Reports presented to Government by their author are distinguished by the same power of analysis and the same clear and forcible language. In entering upon the duties of his important office, Capt. Macpherson adopted a peculiar theory as to the best mode of inducing the Khond tribes to give up the sacrifices which had so long prevailed among them. It is often repeated in his valuable Reports, and is so different to the plan adopted by missionaries for civilizing as well as converting idolatrous nations, that it is worth while to say a few words respecting it. Capt. Macpherson entirely repudiated in these efforts of the Government any resort to force on a large scale; though like others he fully allowed that at the right time the sacrifice must be declared a crime, and those who engage in it, especially the procurers of every class, must be subjected to severe punishment. His clear intellect however saw that to secure the efficient execution of such a law, it was necessary to obtain strong authority for the Government, and a spirit of obedience to that authority on the part of the people. This authority he hoped to secure in several ways. The personal influence of the agents had already been exerted for it, and should be so still: influence acquired by free intercourse with the tribes, and by the exhibition of a deep interest in their welfare. Grants of land from the wastes of Goomsur and Boad might be made to those of the people who had little or none of their own. On the chief Patriarchs might be bestowed a home in the low country, that they might familiarise themselves with the customs and notions of the plains. Grants of money and cattle, titles of honour, and privileges might also be given to deserving chiefs. They might be appointed to various offices in the public service; a body of troops also might be raised in the country. The chief means however which he proposed to employ in drawing the regard of the tribes upon the Government was the administration of justice, which amongst themselves, they were ill able to enforce. He thought that if the Government gave them this boon, the tribes would exercise confidence in the Government, and allow it to exercise authority in return. That is, out of gratitude for securing them justice, the tribes would give up a measure of their loved independence, and in obeying the Government orders, even surrender their long cherished sacrifices. In this way these sacrifices would eventually be abolished. This theory at first sight looks well, being both ingenious and novel: but it is fairly open to criticism. In the *first* place it hopes to obtain a great effect from a small cause. Religious feelings are the strongest of all human impulses; and religious practices are more tenaciously adhered to than any others. Liberty and independence among the Khonds are most highly prized. Justice was no doubt a want among them: but it would be felt only by individuals in times of dispute: and the administration of it, even by the best courts, contains too many defects to be attractive even to the most civilised community. The love of liberty, and the love of the sacrifice were universal; yet it was hoped that this complete independence and this exercise of a universally practised rite, would be set aside for the boon of justice, which only individuals, at various times, would need. Again: *gratitude* is a Christian virtue, and even when felt towards God by his own children, is far from securing that perfect obedience which he requires. To expect it then from a Khond for such a benefit, and to expect it, when his ancient superstitions were in the way, was to secure certain disappointment. Besides, the authority permitted to the Government, and the obedience consequently paid by the tribes, were to be voluntarily tendered. On the one hand, it would take a long time before the independent tribes would surrender their liberty: and on the other, they would be prepared to throw off such allegiance whenever they were displeased with the proceedings of Government. That this consideration is a sound one, is proved by the fact that the tribes in Boad actually did resist the agent in the case of their sacrifices and retook their merias from him by force. Lastly, the theory was really inapplicable to the only part of the country where it was tested for more than a short time, viz. Goomsur. In Goomsur the tribes could not tender to Government an allegiance which it had already won by the conquest of the country. The administration of justice on the part of the Government was also not a boon, but a duty which it owed to the tribes, and which, as such, had been performed by Capt. Campbell for four years, as a part of his official labours. Apart too from all these considerations, it is a lamentable fact, that the theory was utterly ruined by the native members of the Agency. By their bribes and extortions, they so perverted justice, that they became personally the objects of intense hatred, and the occasions of a lamentable and disastrous war.

Capt. Macpherson however, was no mere theorist. Thoroughly interested in the welfare of the people, whose habits he had studied for years, and deeply anxious to aid in totally suppressing the horrible meria sacrifice, he conducted his Agency and discharged his important duties with energy, fidelity and zeal. He saw clearly that the best way to root out the evil was to secure for the Government a greater amount of authority than it then enjoyed, and a more complete submission to its will than the people had yet given; and both by his personal influence, and by his devotion to the good order of the tribes, endeavoured as far as he could to obtain the desired ends. His first visit was paid to the non-sacrificing districts of Goomsur, and the districts in which female infanticide was practised. Returning to the plains, he summoned to his office at Nowgaum the chiefs of the Bara and Atharo Mutahs, and strongly urged on them the propriety of totally abolishing the bloody rites to which they were still clinging. He at the same time assured them that the Government was determined on the abolition, and so long as they were obedient to its authority, would, as a duty, give them justice and protection. The chiefs then renewed to Capt. Macpherson the pledge which they had previously given to Major Campbell. On visiting their villages the following year, Capt. Macpherson found that only four sacrifices had been publicly performed; although the longings of the people were evinced by the fact that numerous merias continued to be purchased and reserved for future opportunities. Of these, no less than one hundred and twenty-four, who were valued at twelve thousand rupees, were surrendered, and taken to Ganjam. In Chinna Kimedy and Boad, the districts that had been little visited, the sacrifices continued to be numerous.

In 1844, Capt. Macpherson brought away one hundred and forty-two victims from Upper Goomsur; and again received pledges from the Khond chiefs that the sacrifice should be discontinued. It is however, to be regretted that, on misrepresentations made by his subordinates, he was led to recommend the removal and imprisonment of Sám Bisaye, the Federal head of the Goomsur Malias: and, as a consequence, found the district of Hodzoghoro, where the old chief lived, in great dissatisfaction and disorder. The same year, he renewed his efforts to secure the abolition of infanticide in Suradah and Pondacole, and finding a deficiency of women in the tribe, gave to various individuals in marriage, fifty-three of the female merias whom he had saved from Goomsur. He gave them as wards of Government, hoping that their husbands would, from their relation to the Government, have nothing to do with the cruel practice that had hitherto prevailed. It was subsequently found however, that the girls, which sprang from these marriages, were all destroyed!

The usual visit above the ghauts was paid, in the commencement of 1845, by Dr. Cadenhead, the able Assistant of the Agency; Capt. Macpherson having visited Calcutta in order to expedite the passing of an

Act for putting all the Khond districts under one system of management Dr. Cadenhead reported that there still existed among the great body of the people an intense longing to return to their old customs. They said that they had appointed chiefs who might represent the matter to the Government and secure permission for them to sacrifice again: this had been in vain; and they were wishing to appoint others who might further their cause more effectually. They were assured, however, that such a permission the Government could not give. This was the only point on which the people were dissatisfied. The country, said they, is happy: but the Government has not yet permitted the sacrifices.

In February, 1846, a new district was brought within the range of the Agent's operations. Capt. Macpherson in that month proceeded to the Boad Malias, and after a short delay induced the Khonds to surrender one hundred and seventy merias. But the infamous extortions and corrupt practices of the native members of the Agency, which had long drawn towards them the dislike of the people, had become so bad, that the Khonds of Boad hastily jumped to the conclusion, that the Government intended not only to take the victims, which had been surrendered, but to subdue their country and punish the chief men for having sacrificed in former years. A mob at once rose to arms and demanded the victims back, declaring that in future they would give no more. The whole district fell into disorder, and the opposition to the Government was organized under four leading chiefs. Chokra Bisaye came from Ungool; and attached all the people closely to himself and the chiefs, by promising that he would secure perfect freedom for the sacrifice in future. Thence the uproar spread into Goomsur, and a twelvemonth after to the Malias below the ghauts. Troops were therefore moved once more above the hills; proclamations were issued against the Boad chiefs and Chokra Bisaye; and the Agent felt himself compelled to ravage various tracts, with all their villages and depôts of grain. The conduct of military operations was committed to General Dyce, and after much loss on the part of the people, by the most conciliating, but firm proceedings of the Government, the rebellion was brought to a close. Such resistance on the part of the Khonds cannot be deemed unnatural. They had seen the firmness with which their English masters had for eight years adhered to their resolution of abolishing their beloved sacrifices. They had submitted in sullen silence, but had, year by year, given unequivocal proofs that they had not been convinced by the Agents' arguments, and still thought the sacrifices a desirable privilege. Boad, being more independent and having never felt the military power of the Government, naturally rose in rebellion on the first attempt to take victims on a large scale: and the chiefs openly avowed that they did so in order to thwart the designs of Government. While the extortions of the native officers must in some respects be regarded as the occasion of the outbreak, the love of the sacrifices was clearly its real cause. It ultimately proved a good: the people were compelled to feel that the Government had ample power to enforce its decrees, and that those decrees must be obeyed. It is right to add that the three guilty natives who had so abused their trust and misled their superior, were severely punished; and that Sám Bisaye, the Patriarch of Goomsur, whom by lies they had injured, was restored to his office and his home.

On the re-establishment of peace, Capt. Macpherson retired, and the Government placed the Khond Agency once more in the hands of Colonel Campbell, by whom its operations had been first conducted. Col. Campbell has retained it till the present time and has carried out its great objects to a most successful issue. His first visit was to the district of Boad, where, on several grounds, the re-possession of the surrendered victims was imperatively required. Col. Campbell made a thorough examination of the whole country; traversing districts, unvisited by Europeans, by the most difficult and circuitous routes; he thus laid a secure foundation for future operations, and destroyed any lingering hope among the chiefs that the Government were half-hearted in abolishing the sacrifice. The number of victims obtained was 235, of whom 120 had been taken from Capt. Macpherson. Next season, operations were commenced in Chinna Kimedy, and the subjected kindly but most firmly pressed upon the people: 206 victims were given up. In Boad none were sacrificed that year; and on the Agent re-visiting its chiefs, a hundred merias were given up to him. The total number of merias saved in 1848 and 1849 amounted to no less than 547: all of them from districts where the abolition had scarcely been begun. In his Report for the latter year, Col. Campbell has described so clearly his method of procedure, and the results which it produced, that we quote one or two of its most interesting passages, in order that he may speak for himself:

"From the very first, I openly and in the most plain and intelligible manner proclaimed the chief design of my appearance among them. Without any disguise or circumlocution, I told them that the Government had sent me for the sole and avowed purpose of putting an end for ever to the inhuman and barbarous murders yearly perpetrated by them, and if needful, of enforcing the cession of all the victims held in possession, and destined to die this cruel death. All their other ancient usages, I impressed upon them, would be strictly respected: the Government was anxious to befriend them, and willing to assist them. If any were suffering oppression, redress should be afforded, and justice meted out with an impartial hand; but this Meria sacrifice, this inhuman practice, must at once and for ever be laid aside.

"Daily and almost hourly were these wild mountaineers of Chinna Kimedy assembled in my Camp. I wearied both the Khonds and myself with every argument I could think of, to induce them to desist from a practice, cruel and guilty in the eyes of God and man. I very especially directed their attention to the fertile districts of Sarunguddah and Degi, where no human blood is shed to appease a sanguinary god. I recalled to their minds their own law of 'a life for a life,' and challenged them to gainsay, if they could, its justice, when applied to their own practice of slaying their fellow-creatures. I related at length how the Circar had traversed over Goomsur and Boad; had swept away every meria from those countries, and utterly abolished the revolting ceremony. I told them how their brethren in those neighbouring hills had most solemnly pledged themselves never again to sacrifice a human being, and how abundantly they had prospered in house and field since abstaining from the rite; but above all I emphatically declared, in terms most plain and intelligible, the firm and unalterable resolve of the Great Circar, at all risks to stop these atrocious murders. I did not for one moment profess to regard their abominable custom as a 'deplorable error,' but I made known in sufficiently expressive language, that the rite was an odious and an outrageous crime.

"From Chinna Kimedy I proceeded into the Boad Hills, where my Assistant Captain Macvicar had been travelling for some time: the results of his visits having already been communicated, no minute detail is necessary.

"The entire abolition of the rite of human sacrifice which so recently prevailed throughout the extensive Malias of Boad is a subject of sincere congratulation. Not one drop of blood has been shed this year on the altar of their barbarous superstition; nor was there manifested in any quarter the least disposition to break the pledge of abstinence which they had vowed last year. The whole of these hills have been traversed, and the same pleasing results exhibited in every quarter.

"In the Boad country we need in the first place to be most thankful to God, whose bountiful harvest, bestowed upon the Khonds, so powerfully and mercifully seconded our efforts: to His hand too we owe it that, during the year, the Khonds enjoyed immunity from all but the most ordinary sickness: and next we may ascribe much of our success to the felt and acknowledged power of the Government to enforce its will; that will having been openly and unreservedly, without the slightest compromise or hesitation, and in the most straight-forward manner, declared to the Khonds, wherever and whenever they were met by myself or my Assistant, and proclaimed universally throughout the country. There was no cautious inquisition as formerly recommended, but the glaring fact was dealt with as an enormity which the Government neither would nor could longer suffer to continue to exist. I mention this prominently, because the success which has attended our labours in

Boad and elsewhere, conclusively demonstrates the advantage of a firmer, bolder, and more determined line of policy, than was deemed prudent in the days of our earlier connection with these hills.

"When the present generation, and perhaps their children, shall have passed away: when, through the medium of schools, and other modes of civilization, such as roads, fairs, the introduction among them of better implements of labour, teaching them improved methods of clearing and irrigating the ground, &c. we shall have been able to change the current of their thoughts and feelings, and to direct them into a better channel, I shall have some hopes of their being as fully convinced in their hearts, of the utter folly, uselessness, and sinfulness of the meria sacrifice, as they now are of the impossibility of performing it save at a risk, which they most wisely prefer to avoid. They are not insensible either to the advantages which flow from the friendship of the Circar, and would not willingly forego them.

"We must therefore maintain the ground we have now won; the triumph in Boad has so far been complete; but care and cautious watchfulness must still be exercised. If then a vigilant supervision is kept up over Goomsur and Boad, we may most fairly and reasonably conclude, that the sacrifice of human victims is for ever at an end; but I have been most anxious that there should be no misunderstanding as to the real extent of our labours, or of the grounds upon which the suppression of the rite actually rests; hence I have continued my observations to a length which I hope will be forgiven.

"I would also respectfully observe that I have not alluded to the great precursor of civilization, the Gospel; not because I am insensible to its fitness for these wild races (who have no predilection for brahmins) but simply because it is not within the province of the Government of India, to introduce any Agency of the kind. I may however with propriety express the hope that, in due season, these poor savages will be visited by the teachers of a higher and purer wisdom than that of man."

Similar measures were adopted in Suradah and the districts where infanticide was practised: the folly and wickedness of the practice were pointed out, and the determination of the Government to punish offenders publicly announced. Colonel Campbell however, felt the great difficulty of meeting this peculiar evil. He says:

"Until then, we shall be enabled to establish village Schools, and introduce other wholesome measures for the moral elevation of this people; the best means of stemming the torrent appear to me to consist in maintaining a constant intercourse and paying occasional visits; always insisting on seeing the children and visiting with various marks of displeasure the Chiefs of those villages where the relative number of the sexes is so disproportionate as to leave no doubt of the destruction of the females; while on the other hand, the preservers of their infants will be specially rewarded, receiving such presents as will plainly evince the favour of Government.

"I am painfully aware how slender these appliances seem for the eradication of such a gigantic plague; but I have bestowed that attention which is due to the consideration of so deeply interesting a subject; and after long and anxious thought, I can devise no more hopeful remedies than those now suggested. Constant supervision and vigilance are at present, I judge, our only practical instruments."

The value of these operations, continued for five years, may be learned from the following striking fact laid before the Government in one of Colonel Campbell's last Reports. In the infanticide-districts of Suradah, containing seventy villages, with 2,150 families, Colonel Campbell in 1848 found *less than fifty* female children. In the beginning of 1853, in the same families, he found NINE HUNDRED GIRLS, under four years of age. What more striking proof can be offered of the complete success of the efforts made to preserve these children alive.

Perseverance in these firm but conciliatory measures has at length been crowned with the most gratifying success. Four years ago, the Malias of Goomsur, including the Bara and Athara Mutahs, Hodzoghoro and Chokapad; the Malias of Boad, and of Chinna Kimedy were almost entirely freed from the dreadful crime of human sacrifice. Constant watchfulness has kept them so: and new efforts have been pushed forward into Jeypore, Kalahundy, and the Khond districts near them, with the same gratifying result. Tribe after tribe has yielded obedience to the humane demands of the Government: victims have been surrendered; pledges given; and promises faithfully performed. And now that Nagpore is British territory, a few years more of the same zealous but conciliatory efforts may fulfil the hope that the meria sacrifice will be ENTIRELY abolished from the whole of Khondistan.

A careful review of the Agents' Reports exhibits the number of merias *actually saved,* since the first war in Goomsur, as nearly TWO THOUSAND. Of these a hundred were rescued by the efforts of Messrs. Bannerman and Ricketts: of Captains Hicks and Miller, and others. The Agency of Capt. Macpherson saved nearly 400: and Colonel Campbell, in his two periods of office, has rescued nearly 1500. Of these merias, Chinna Kimedy has surrendered 700; Boad, 400: and Goomsur, 500. From Boad none have been received since 1851: and from Goomsur, none since 1848.

An interesting question here arises: What has become of all these merias, thus saved from a bloody death? The larger number being grown up when rescued have been settled by Government, particularly at first, in the Maliás below the gháts among their own people. Land was given them and materials were supplied for farming. Many were already married; and were at once established in little farms, or settled together in villages. Others not so, were married, males to females. Of the large number saved during the last eight years, one fourth have been thus settled in comfort; a few have entered the service of private individuals: or been employed in the police. Of the females 247 have married suitably amongst other Khonds: 150 merias of both sexes have died: 80 have deserted: 170 have been restored to their friends: or have been adopted by others. Long since a few of them were placed in the missionary boarding schools at Cuttack; particularly those saved from the Boad Hills by Lieut. Hicks. Capt. Macpherson not only disapproved of missionaries visiting the Khond hills, and reproved one of his Assistants for maintaining friendly intercourse with them, but, with one exception, sent no children to their orphan schools. Colonel Campbell, however, has during the last few years sent more than 200 boys and girls to the schools at Berhampore, Cuttack and Balasore; where they are being trained up as christians. Many of these children I had the pleasure of seeing during my visit to Orissa in 1849. At Balasore, there were seventeen boys and twelve girls, from seventeen to fourteen years of age. They were all learning to read and write Oriya, in which they had made some progress; as their knowledge increases, Mr. Bachelor was hoping to give them instruction of a better kind. They were all active, and very anxious to be useful. It was a pleasant sight to see the happy faces of the girls, as they sat on the veranda floor writing the Oriya alphabet, or standing round Mrs. Bachelor singing Oriya hymns; or those of the boys, as they wandered about with their bows and arrows, in the use of which they are very expert. Woe to the stray paria dog or jackal, who found his way near their quarters! The schools at Cuttack contained about eighty of these children, most of them very young. On their first arrival, they met with children once like themselves, with whom they could communicate in the Khond tongue; through their means, they soon began Oriyá and were able to benefit by the religious and other instructions of the school. The girls sang several Oriya hymns very nicely when we visited them: and the boys sang some of their Khond songs, and danced some of their dances. They also described to us the mode of sacrifice, which several of them had seen. The children at Berhampore I did not see: but interesting notices of their progress are contained in the Reports of that station. Of course they were at first wild and uncultivated in the extreme, but after a few weeks grew tame and civilized. One of the elder girls named Ikedi, who is a member of the Church and herself a Khond, acted as interpreter for the girls, and devoted much of her time to their welfare. There were thirty boys and thirty girls in the Berhampore school. Several singular cases have occurred from time to time in which new comers have been recognised as the brothers or sisters of children already in the schools. Ikedi, the girl just mentioned, found her own brother. A lad named Philip, at the same time found his younger brother. Mr. Bailey says:

"On the day these children arrived, the Khond boys who had been with us some time ran with great glee to see them; and as they were placed in the front of my house in a line that their names might be called over, the name of Dasia was at length mentioned. Philip, one of the elder boys, immediately exclaimed with surprise, '*Dasia! Dasia!* why that is my little brother;' and he at once ran and fell upon his neck and embraced him. But I said, 'Philip, how do you know that he is your brother?' 'O,' he replied, 'I am sure Dasia is my brother: I remember his name, and the day on which he was sold; but now I see him again.' Many cases of a similar character have occurred before, in the reception of Meria children into these Asylums."

Of the children thus introduced into these excellent schools, many have profited greatly by their studies. Many have been settled in the christian villages; and have exhibited a character and life illustrating even the temporal benefits of religious and moral education which they enjoyed. And not a few both male and female have been truly converted, and have adorned the gospel of Christ their Saviour. Muster, one of the pious Khonds, was employed by Capt. Frye for assisting his studies in the Khond language.

It is a triumphant testimony to the Gospel, to see a humane and christian Government employing its officers, its influence and financial resources, to draw barbarous tribes from dreadful rites and crimes; and save the lives of helpless children devoted to sacrifice. It is a still further testimony to it, to see the Christian Church adopt these rescued ones, foster them, instruct them, and pray for them. It is a higher testimony still, to see the Lord of Glory himself look with compassion on these souls for which he died, changing them by his grace and fitting them for glory. To him be all the glory of all the good done among sinful men! Amen.

LECTURE SIXTH.

ON THE RELIGIOUS CLAIMS OF THE MADRAS PRESIDENCY.

In the previous lectures we have seen that the Presidency of Madras naturally divides itself into distinct districts, on its east and west sea coasts, with the high plateau of Mysore between them; how these districts are to a great extent occupied by different nations; and how the missions carried on among them fall into natural groups, determined by their geographical position and the different languages spoken therein. We have rapidly reviewed the TELUGU Missions on the upper coast of the Bay of Bengal, the CANARESE Missions in the district above the ghauts: and the GERMAN Missions in the provinces of Canara and Malabar. We then turned to the TAMUL Missions in Madras, Tanjore and Madura; briefly investigated their lengthened history, examined the decay of the early Tranquebar Mission and its offshoots, and traced out the causes of the strong CASTE prejudices which have prevailed so extensively in the Tamil churches. We next passed to the southern extremity of India, inhabited by the tribe of SHANARS, and considered the progress and results of missionary operations among them in Tinnevelly and Travancore. The last Protestant Mission examined, was that established among the ancient SYRIAN Churches of North Travancore; wherein we noticed the plan which was originally aimed at of reviving the Syrian body under their former regime, its failure, and the separation of the Church Missionary converts from that system, in order to form them into a branch of the Church of England. In contrast to these proceedings of evangelical churches, we surveyed the past and present efforts of the JESUIT missionaries, under the most extraordinary phases: and found that though their converts are declared to be 650,000 in number, they are not to be compared to the 100,000 Protestant natives of India in christian knowledge, education and religious character: that only in name have they become christian, while in the ordinary practices of life, they are as much heathen as before.

The Telugu and Mysore missions are comparatively limited; and their fruits appear only to be small: they each contain about 700 native christians: the German missions number 1400. The Tamil churches are much larger, the native christians amounting to 17,000. The Shánar converts number 52,000: those among the Syrian churches, 4000. The total number of native Protestant christians in the Presidency is above 76,000, of whom 10,600 are communicants. The missionaries in charge of these churches are 179 in number, with 405 catechists. About 30,000 boys are instructed in their schools: and 8,000 girls. These results looked at by themselves are truly gratifying, to all who can appreciate the grand difference between the prospects of a heathen soul and the soul of a true christian beyond the grave. They shew the present agencies and present position of the mission churches: and prove that the labours expended for their benefit have not been carried on in vain. We must add to them the converted souls that have passed into the heavens, of whose death, on many occasions, missionaries have spoken with hearty satisfaction. Nor is this all. We know that the object of all our missionary agencies is to bring men into the body of communicants, and to keep them there, worthily performing their duty to the Saviour so long as life lasts. But as time is required before these agencies accomplish their ends completely, we must remember, as part of our missionary results, all the *intermediate steps* that have been secured between the starting of the agency and the reaping of its fruits. We will look not only to the harvest reaped, to the harvest ripe: we will look also to the green standing corn, to the blade, to the ear, and even to the seed that lies hidden in the soil. We must look for results accomplished, not only to our church members, dead and living: but to the knowledge spread, the copies of the word distributed, to the schools where the young have been early impressed, to the diminished offerings to idols, to the decay of belief in idolatry, to the extensive conviction that its cause will fail, to the belief that christianity will conquer: to the diminution of dispute and argument against the gospel, and to the silence, sometimes the readiness, with which its truths are heard. If we do less, we do injustice.

But much as we seem to have accomplished, how much still remains. Contrast the scattered bands of christians with the dense masses of heathenism in which they live; the agencies employed, with the sphere to which they are applied; and we shall at once exclaim, what are these among so many! So great is the difference between the two parties, the one so swallows up and hides the other, that we cannot wonder at the objection which is sometimes brought against our statements; "Where *are* the converts—we never see or hear of them: nor do we expect we shall; look at the strength of bráhmanism, of idolatry and of caste; how can you ever set them aside and root them out of the country: what do these feeble Jews?" It is good therefore to look the difficulties of the work of the Lord fairly in the face, and see how much the church has yet to do before its labour is accomplished. The following considerations may help us to appreciate them.

EXTENT OF COUNTRY AND POPULATION.

The Presidency of Madras is of triangular shape; its greatest length from Cape Comorin to Goa is 530 miles, and its greatest breadth from Goa to Ganjam is nearly 790 miles. It contains therefore more than 200,000 square miles in all. It contains countries which for hundreds of years constituted independent kingdoms. That portion which is now in subjection to the Honorable East India Company is divided into twenty districts or provinces; and to these must be added the Mysore country: and the independent kingdoms of Travancore and Cochin. The total *Revenue* drawn annually from these extensive and fertile provinces amounts to nearly six millions of pounds sterling, which is shewn as follows:—

Revenue Co.'s Territory, 1851-2, ... Rs.	4,78,07,000
Ditto Travancore,..........................	41,58,000
Ditto Mysore, ...	70,00,000
Ditto Cochin, ...	4,86,000
Total,....	5,94,51,000

Besides the produce consumed where it is grown, the trade from one portion of the country to another is, even under its present disadvantages, most extensive. In spite of bad trunk roads, in spite of cross-roads ten times worse, the Government Engineer recently reported, that after careful consideration he had found that the annual traffic into and out of Madras on the western roads alone, amounted to 50,000 tons of goods, of the value of one million and a quarter sterling. Not less trade is carried on through the southern districts and those on the west coast. Indeed few branches of enquiry, give a higher idea of the value of these provinces of India than the consideration of the surplus produce which they export.

Look again at the immense POPULATION which this one division of our Indian empire contains:—

In the Company's Territory, ...	22,301,697
„ Mysore, ...	3,410,382
„ Travancore in 1836, ...	1,280,668
„ Cochin, ...	290,000
Total,....	27,282,747

These twenty-seven millions form a number about equal to that of all the inhabitants of the British Isles put together. Yet how different are their circumstances from those of our countrymen. They may have the means of sustaining life, but possess in general little beyond it. They are civilized to a considerable extent, but their knowledge of things beyond their own immediate sphere is very limited; and education, worth the name, is at the lowest ebb. Above all as following error in religion it becomes us to look at them with Christian eyes and to enquire what provision has been made for their full and faithful instruction in the way of truth. Of the whole number, twenty-four millions are Hindus: more than two millions are Muhammedans: the Catholics number 650,000: the Syrian Christians, 120,000: the Jews, 1600 at Cochin: while our native Protestant Christians amount only to 76,000.

Look again at the *different divisions* of the population, and you will see how little has been accomplished in the thorough spread of gospel truth among them. The TELUGU people below the ghauts are divided into seven districts; and amount to 6,650,000 people. Their territory, as we have seen contains nineteen missionaries and of the six millions and a half, 700 are Christians. Nor are matters improved by looking at the labours of the different Societies that have entered the country. The London Missionary Society, the first in the field, has taken up the districts of Vizagapatam and Cuddapah; but though they contain a population of 2,706,000 souls, the Society employs among them only *five* European missionaries. The Church Missionary Society has taken up Masulipatam with 520,000; and employs *four* missionaries. The American Baptist Society at Nellore sends *two* missionaries to 935,000: and the American Lutheran Mission, occupying the two districts of Rájmundry and Guntoor, has provided *five* missionaries for 1,580,000. We feel the destitution still more, when we look at the towns and villages which these districts contain. Vizagapatam contains 50,000 people; Vizianagaram, 28,000; Guntoor, 12,000; Masulipatam, 60,000; Ellore, 20,000. Masulipatam has a district of 4,510 square miles: and contains 1583 villages, with hamlets double that number. Near Masulipatam itself is the town of Godoor with 3000 people: Beizwarah contains 4000: more than fifty villages contain between 2000 and 4000 inhabitants each. Yet except the chief town itself, not one town or village of that large district contains even a missionary school. The district of Rájmundry again contains *twelve* towns, each numbering from 6000 to 12,000 inhabitants.

Passing onward to the MYSORE, the same appalling inequality is apparent. The Mysore proper contains 3,410,382, among whom are established only four or five missionary stations with *ten* European missionaries. If we add BELLARY and KURNOOL, on the same upper level of table-land, whose population are of the same tribe and speak the same language, Canarese, we add 1,503,789: and if we take in DHARWAR in the same country, we must add many thousand more, giving a total Canarese population amounting to more than *five millions* above the ghauts on the table-land. To these have hitherto been sent *twenty* missionaries who reside at ten stations. The total number of Canarese christians is 800. If we compare the Mysore with Scotland: how different does its supply of God's ministers appear. The Congregationalists in Scotland, with a hundred churches, are looked upon as a somewhat insignificant body, and yet they have three or four times the number of pastors which the Mysore has of missionaries. If we add the numerous ministers of the United Presbyterian Church; the eight hundred ministers of the Free Church; and those of the Establishment; we shall find more than *two thousand* ministers labouring among a population of two and a half millions, while for the *five millions* of the Mysore and Bellary there are no more than twenty. How can it be expected that, when marked religious progress is somewhat slow even in Scotland, it can possibly be rapid in our Indian provinces. Nor shall we improve matters by looking into the details. Scotland has large towns: but so has the Mysore: towns that may be considered numerous and well peopled, considering the poverty of the country. Bangalore in cantonments alone has 93,000 people; besides the thousands in and around the pettah: the town and talook of Mysore contain 88,000: Seringapatam, 12,000: Chittledroog has 14,000, without a missionary: the talooks of Toomkoor and Coonghul, with one missionary, 101,000. The Bellary district has four missionaries resident in the town of Bellary. That town is the head of the district; and numbers 37,126 inhabitants with a large military force. Were it situated in the more settled parts of the United States, it would probably have not less than forty ministers of the gospel. But besides Bellary the district contains *sixteen* other towns all of which have 4000 inhabitants or more. Thus Kumply has 7,000: Hospett, 8,000: Gooty, 4,400; Adoni, 19,000; Harponhully, 6,000; and so on. Many have been visited by missionaries, but in none of them have they made a permanent settlement. To these sixteen towns, with above 4,000 persons each, add the 12,000 villages which are spread over its surface of 12,000 square miles. Such instances might be endlessly multiplied.

The TAMIL country has been to some extent better supplied: but there are parts of it lamentably destitute. From Pulicat to Cape Comorin, the Tamil speaking population number 11,555,868 persons: they are divided into nine districts, some of which are very extensive and contain important towns. The total number of European and American missionaries resident among them is seventy-five: of whom sixteen are in Tinnevelly alone and seventeen in the province of Tanjore. I will not weary you with pointing out all the large and flourishing towns; and shewing the disproportion between the number of their teachers and the population to be taught. I will mention the case of one district alone, whose utter destitution you will at once perceive. NORTH ARCOT possesses a total population of 1,485,000. It includes in greater abundance than usual well peopled villages and towns. Thus Vellore contains 120,000: Arcot, 16,000: Wallajapett, 20,000: Raneepett, 18,000: Goriatum, 10,000: Amboor, 11,000: Arnee, 16,000: Tripatty, 9,000: and six others, each 4,000 or more; all carrying on good trade and in prosperous circumstances, yet among them all, there is but ONE missionary in the town of Arcot. If we enter the adjoining district of SALEM, we find one missionary among 942,000 people. In Coimbatoor, with 1,152,862 people, there are two missionaries resident in the chief town.

The province of TRAVANCORE is supplied in a similarly disproportionate manner. Out of its 1,280,000 the London Missionary Society has placed eight missionaries in eleven districts with 505,000 people;

and the Church Missionary Society eight missionaries in twenty-one districts with 775,000. Again we say: What are these among so many? In whatever way we take up the subject, whether we look at parts or at the whole, we cannot fail to realise a deep conviction that in South India the work of the Lord is but just begun. We may rejoice to know that 76,000 persons are called by the name of Christ and have the gospel regularly preached to them as their chosen authority in religion: or that more than 10,000 are so advanced in knowledge and character as to be admitted to the Communion of the Lord's Supper. But on the other hand we see but one hundred and eighty missionaries, European and native, in the whole population of twenty-seven millions: and find, scattered over the country, towns with fifty, thirty and twenty thousand inhabitants where none reside at all: while thousands upon thousands of villages have never been entered by missionaries to preach the gospel even *once* in the half century. The more fully therefore, we enter into detail, the deeper will our conviction grow, of the real spiritual destitution in which this great portion of our Indian empire lies.

Let us not forget another thing: the effect which such a state of things has upon a missionary's own mind: as he contrasts the feebleness of his own efforts with the vastness of the evils with which he contends. Mr. Fox has described it very clearly in one of his letters: "I am lost and bewildered in the multitude of my work. There lies before me the crowded population of this large town, Masulipatam, with 60,000 inhabitants: they are to be preached to, to have an impression made upon them. If I go to one part one day, and to another part another day, my time and labour are dissipated. If I keep myself to one portion, my labour is swallowed up in the great flood of heathenism. .. Again there are the villages in the suburbs: fine, populous villages. Again there are the numerous villages and still more numerous hamlets studding the country all round about. Where I am to begin, I know not. Then there ought to be schools, to be established, to be looked after, to be watched and taught. I cannot so much as begin them. And so, though I may be preaching continually to the adults, there is the rising generation growing up in their heathenism. ... Above all it is only a very limited portion of the day that I can be engaged in out-of-door work: the short periods before and after sunrise and sunset. Then comes the work of translation: tracts there are in some numbers: books are only yet by ones and twos. Who is sufficient to unite in himself these multifarious duties, for tens and hundreds of thousands?" Another extract from one of his letters illustrates the state of the people so situated. "I rode 250 miles in a straight line through a populous country, passing through villages every three or four miles, and seeing others in all directions; occasionally also coming to considerable towns: but in all that district there was not a single christian missionary, not one person from whom a heathen might hear the word of life. My road lay parallel to the sea coast, at no great distance from it, but I might have gone inland for 100, 200 or 300 miles and, except in one place, have found the whole land equally wanting in christian teachers. My district is nearly 100 miles each way, it is impossible that I can visit even the chief villages for two or three days each, during the six months in the year in which the weather allows me to be out." We have then the argument of *numbers* in an appeal to christian churches for greater sacrifices and more zealous efforts to instruct the people of Southern India.

THE STRENGTH OF SUPERSTITION.

But other arguments exist besides. The people of South India are idolaters equally with the Hindus among whom we dwell. They are in bondage equally with the people of Bengal: they have prejudged the question of changing their religion as firmly and as erroneously as have our neighbours. They have the same, if not stronger, obstacles in the way of accepting the gospel. Caste, which is so strong with the Hindus of North India, and produces so much open enmity to the gospel, is even stronger in South India than in Bengal. The existence of a large class of Párias, deemed outcast, has made all Hindus of caste the more watchful in keeping themselves from pollution. The bráhmans being fewer in number than with us, and the outcasts so numerous, the Sudras, who are of no rank here, are men of great respectability there. The varying degrees, in which different ranks may pollute a superior, are distinctly defined. The Párias may not sit in presence of the Sudras, and frequently have schools been temporarily broken up, because the missionary wished to teach both together. In Travancore the different classes cannot approach nearer than a fixed number of steps. One class, the Náyades, must never presume to enter a village even to purchase food: they must call out for some one, leave the money on a stone, and are left entirely at the mercy of his honesty, as to whether they will receive any thing in exchange. The lower classes are often severely beaten for infringing the prescribed rules. The extreme is reached in one poor set of people, so excessively low, so intensely degraded in public estimation, that they are never to be seen by the light of day. When so many Párias have become Christians, I need not stop to describe the estimation in which the whole body are held by the heathen: nor to exhibit the powerful obstacle which this high caste spirit places in the way of a candid acknowledgement of that truth which an unbiassed judgment must approve. The same cause has tended to promote great bigotry among all classes of Hindus, and to elevate the comparatively small caste of bráhmans into a class more powerful than with us. This is particularly the case in Travancore, in Madura and in Tanjore. Every bráhman in South India is a great personage, and I believe almost all live by their priestly office, instead of being driven like thousands in Bengal to support themselves by honest trade.

THE GREAT TEMPLE ESTABLISHMENTS.

ANOTHER cause of the great influence of Hinduism in Madras is seen in the wealthy *temple establishments*, by which numerous bráhmans are supported, and in which festivals are celebrated upon a grand scale. We have no temples in Bengal like the celebrated temples found throughout the Tamil districts of the Madras Presidency: and it may be interesting therefore to give some information respecting them. They are made somewhat in the following way. The actual shrine of the idol is usually a low, common-looking stone-building at the side of a broad, well-paved court. Near it will be found a large hall with a flat roof, supported in most cases by a thousand pillars; this hall has no walls on its outer sides, but is left entirely open. Sometimes the pillars are well carved, sometimes they are common slabs of stone. Near the great hall there is usually a tank, entirely faced with stone steps, and having a small temple of six or eight pillars, rising from a stone platform in the very centre of the water. The *court* in which the shrine, the hall and the tank are situated, has many smaller buildings about it, sometimes with massive figures of bulls; and is generally enclosed by high stone walls. In the entrance of these walls is built the most conspicuous portion of the whole establishment, viz. a tall heavy-looking TOWER, sometimes rising to the height of two hundred feet. These towers are shaped like a wedge, sloping off on the four sides, but wider than they are deep: their top is straight, and is ornamented with the representation of a flame of fire bursting upward. These towers are the most conspicuous objects in the temple; but are not particularly sacred. They are simply ornaments to the chief gateways. Sometimes a temple has several such towers.

Excellent specimens of these great temples are to be found in many parts of the Presidency. At Trichendoor and Tinnevelly in the south there are two very celebrated. At Madura, there is a very large one; at Conjeveram, near Madras, there are two; one to Siva, and the other to Vishnu. But the most celebrated of all are in the province of Tanjore, where Hinduism seems stronger than in any other part of India, except Travancore. The province is full of temples. Within a small range of territory, there are no less than seven pagodas of great note; distinguished among the natives by the name of THE SEVEN. They are the pagodas of Chillumbrum; Combaconum; Trivalur; Manárgoody; Tanjore; Avriar and Seringham. All have the sacred shrine; the hall with a thousand pillars; the sacred tank; and several immense towers. Nothing strikes a stranger in connection with Hinduism in Tanjore so much, as the number and the height of these pagoda towers. Numerous bráhmans are attached to each; and the fat of the land is in their possession. The total revenue of the Tanjore temples, as far as they were or are connected with Government, amounts to £31,780 a year. This income was once entirely derived from land: but since the Government resumed several of the large estates, the bráhmans receive the net proceeds in money, without the trouble of collecting them. In point of finish and beauty of structure, the temple in the Fort of TANJORE is the finest in all South India. It stands in a large, well-kept court, paved with stone: the tower is built like a pyramid, the four sides of the base being equal: and it is 220 feet in perpendicular height. It is covered with the usual figures, and is coloured red and green in different parts of the cornices and mouldings. The top of the tower is a copper dome. The shrine stands close to the tower so that the two form one building, a thing quite unusual. Behind it on the east side is the GREAT BULL, an immense figure formed from a single block of black marble and well carved. It is perhaps the most celebrated idol in South India. Numerous smaller temples and cars crowd the pettah of Tanjore; on these 10,000 Rs. a month are spent by the Rajah; who receives a large pension, and inside the fort is independent.

But the most celebrated of all the South India temples is that of SERINGHAM: it is distinguished by its great wealth and the immense space over which it is spread. A few miles above Trichinopoly the river Cavery divides into two branches, leaving a broad tract between them; after running on for twelve miles, the two used to unite again and thence go onward to the sea; they thus inclosed an island called Seringham. (It is an island no longer; as the Government by their celebrated anicut have prevented the Cavery rejoining its northern branch, the Coleroon; and have led it away in a thousand channels to water the province of Tanjore). Towards the north end of this island stands the temple. In the shrine itself there is nothing remarkable: it is low and dirty. Nor do its pillared halls deserve much praise; they are dirty in the extreme and (like all the temples of South India) full of bats, with not a few monkeys. But there is this peculiarity. The Court in which the shrine stands is walled off: so that strangers cannot approach it. The great hall stands on one side of a second court outside the former: each court being nearly square. A third court stands all round and outside the second: each of its four entrances having an immense tower over the gateway. A fourth court follows, with similar towers, enclosing the third; a fifth, then a sixth, surround them: each growing larger and larger till the outside is reached. The gateways all stand in a line, and also the towers: at intervals on an average of 350 feet. The outside walls thus become 1400 yards, or nearly a mile long. It would take nearly an hour to walk round them. The number of towers altogether amounts to fourteen large and several smaller ones. The chief tower of entrance, the Roy Kobram, is unfinished: it contains several stones, each thirty feet long and five feet thick. The four outer courts are like streets, and contain numerous dwelling-houses and bazars. One street of bráhmans on the east side looks particularly clean and neat. More than a 1000 bráhman-families reside in these courts, containing 5000 people: together with five thousand others of good caste connected with the temple and its services.

This temple possesses a great number of valuable gifts, which are freely shown to English visitors who wish to inspect them. The most valuable of them are ornaments, such as natives wear, consisting of jewels of various kinds, as rubies, emeralds, diamonds and pearls, set in gold. They include bracelets, armlets and anklets; ornaments for the forehead and breast; chains for the arms, neck and waist; a gold palankeen, worth Rs. 20,000; an umbrella of gold and velvet, ornamented with figures made of seed pearls. Amongst them are six pieces, made on one pattern, which form the outer casing of a figure about two feet high: they include a breastplate; a backplate; legs, back and front: feet, hands, and a crown of the shape of a bottle. When put together, these six pieces form a hollow figure, two feet high: wanting a head. Each piece is made of pure gold; and is profusely set with diamonds, emeralds and rubies. Their total value is Rs. 22,750. Again there are portions, incomplete, of the casing of a figure, fifteen feet high. They include a gold tiara, two feet high: flat earrings, a foot long: two gold hands, differing, about a foot and a half long: two gold feet, two feet long: two immense armlets; anklets with bells: and bracelets of gold balls, strung together according to the present fashion among English ladies. The whole of these jewels are of gold, somewhat thin; their total value is Rs. 24,000. Besides these, I saw a gold ghurra or pitcher, worth Rs. 13,000: a water-pot, worth Rs. 2000; a gold vessel used by Rajas and smokers, 7000: a milk cup, 2500: two spoons and a plate, 6000: several other water-pots, 3600. The silver articles also are exceedingly numerous and of very great value in all. The total value of these jewels amounts to no less than twenty lakhs of rupees or £200,000. The annual income from lands, of this single temple, as paid by the Government, is Rs. 43,000: the offerings must be all superadded: and it will then be seen how large that income is in all. The whole property is in charge of native superintendents, and it is said that, of late years, glass is rapidly being substituted for precious stones.

Such facts exhibit in a broad light, the power which Hinduism still exercises over the minds of its votaries. Rich Rajahs, widows, landholders, and merchants present these offerings: and the poor flock in thousands to the annual festivals. The temple of Seringham is but one of many; all of which have their particular attractions at particular times. Add these considerations respecting the temples, the caste-spirit and bráhminical power, to those already offered concerning the immense population still unblest with the gospel: and you will comprehend not only the wide extent of the field opened, but the obstacles which exist to the reception of the gospel which is preached.

ENCOURAGEMENTS.

Yet the Church of Christ has no reason whatever to despair of success in the work which it has undertaken. Large as the field is, it has begun admirably to occupy it. Most important positions have been made good: fruits have already been reaped. Much knowledge of Christ has been spread abroad: much opposition to the truth has been silenced. The heathen have been compelled to feel that there is reason on the side of

Christianity; that its doctrines are hard to be rejected: and that its missionaries are clever, obstinate men, who will not get angry in discussion, and who will not be put down. The temples, great as they once were, are all falling into decay. Marks of neglect are profusely stamped upon every one of them: the bats in countless numbers already possess them. In all South India, the only temple I saw kept really clean and in good repair, was the temple in the fort of Tanjore, where a wealthy Hindu Rajah rules. There is a legend among the natives in Tanjore, that the great Bull behind that temple was once very small; else, say they, how could it have got between the pillars where it now lies; but it went on growing larger and larger till it attained its present immense size. When the infidel Company came, it ceased growing. There is a world of truth in this legend after all. Since the days when common sense came into the land: when foreigners began to expose idolatry; to speak against caste; to spread the Bible; to instruct the young; and argue with the defenders of this ancient system fearlessly, the Bull of Hinduism has ceased to grow. Its influence has begun to decrease, and although it may still appear vast and powerful, and may now and then put forth spasmodic efforts, its inward strength is fast going to decay. These things are parts in the great process of the country's renovation: and much as we rejoice over actual converts, we may rejoice too over the diminution of obstacles by which converts are kept back. If we have not yet built up much, we have pulled a great deal down; and have made extensive preparations for pulling down and building up a vast deal more. "Experience hath produced the hope" of ultimate perfect success: while the promise of God stands perfectly sure: The idols he shall utterly abolish: to Jesus every knee shall bow. Unappalled then by difficulties, the church must go in and possess the land. Its agents must preach much to the old, must instruct the young; must spread the inspired word that is like fire, and able like a hammer to break the rock in pieces. Thus will the great harvest of South India be prepared, while we pray, in obedience to our Lord's command, that he will send forth more labourers to reap the harvest.

CHRISTIAN UNION.

Let us consider the call which these facts make to all christians to labour in the field of missions with thorough unity of affection and of purpose. Can any one body of christians fully instruct a field so vast, as that which we have contemplated? Can any one supply money and men and labour sufficient for the full cultivation of these well-peopled domains? No: and hence we find in the Madras Presidency no less than ten different Societies engaged: and in all India, twenty-two. Again, we may ask, has any one of these dealt fairly by the limited districts which they have appropriated as a sphere of labour. Not one has done so: what need then that all should look, not to their own things, but to the things of others: that Ephraim should not envy Judah: and Judah not vex Ephraim. That there is a great deal of cordial co-operation among these various divisions of the missionary army, must be acknowledged with gratitude and pleasure. Looking at the case on a wider scale we may ask, is it not a remarkable fact that in modern days, evangelical christians are brought so very near to each other in point of doctrine. In respect to the depravity of our nature, the uselessness of meritorious works; the perfect propitiation of the cross of Christ; the sanctifying influences of the spirit; and the necessity of a holy life for converted men; how wonderfully all these bodies of christians are now agreed; although in former days they discussed and fought these questions with each other, and set each other down as high and low, latitudinarian and bigoted, with considerable rancour, bitterness and scorn. But why has the Master taught us better. Is not our present union both an effect of common efforts in his service, and an incentive to greater self-sacrifice and greater union still? We constantly hear that the Bible alone is the Religion of Protestants; and we have heard it so often that we are accustomed to receive it as fact. *But is it true?* Is there one body of christians, that can honestly declare that the saying is perfectly true of us, in respect both to our doctrine, our practice and our system of government. I wish it were true of us all. The more it is so, the more shall we be ready to relinquish human devices and human systems and human plans, as authoritative; in order to give expression to christian love in joining heartily in the Lord's work with all who trust his name. If however any adhere to their own systems as superior to all others, let them prove the fact, by being more self-sacrificing, more liberal, more zealous, more holy, more humble than their neighbours. The object of all systems of government is to maintain a pure fellowship and supply pure ordinances. The Lord grant that his people may increase in real unity everywhere, and join together with one heart, as his living army to war against the kingdom of darkness.

The work of the church is sure to be successful. Full as South India is of idolatry; mighty as are its temples; numerous as are their idols and their idol votaries; the land belongs to Christ. All souls are His. He is Supreme King. At the appointed time He will take his power and reign. Every province shall submit; every tribe, of every language, to Him shall bow the knee. No locality, no people shall be excepted. Even the town of Tanjore, the stronghold of Hinduism, shall yield itself unreservedly to the King of kings. Its numerous cars shall become fuel to the fire; its idols perish; and their shrines pass for ever away. The tower of its great pagoda shall become the vestibule of a Church of Christ. Its numerous people, renewed in the spirit of their mind, shall gather within its walls as Christian worshippers. They shall yield without reserve to his authority; shall lay their gifts upon his altar: and rejoice in his eternal joy. All hearts shall be full of obedience; all hearts shall enjoy his peace. And the name of the city from that day shall be JEHOVAH SHAMMAH: "The LORD is there."